Dedication

I have to thank my dog Reilly for being the catalyst, a teacher, and my muse on my journey of personal transformation. As with all good journeys, there has been a lot of luck involved, along with some good planning and hard work. I have gained enough self-awareness and gratitude to realize when I have landed in a good spot and to luxuriate in my blessings. Reilly, you have been a tremendous blessing in my life. I owe you a lifetime of long runs and "hunting" trips for everything you have taught me. Thanks, to the most balanced pack member a pack leader could ask for.

Table of Contents

INTRODUCTION

A growl instantly moved me from pack member to pack leader with my dog. Unfortunately, it was a bit more complicated for me to learn how to be a pack leader to the humans in my life. But without the lessons I learned from my dog, Reilly, I might never have transformed myself from a submissive, insecure, physically abused woman into the assertive "alpha" personality I am today.

How did I learn to claim my place in the human pack and stand up to those who wanted to dominate and control me? While I might have come to these insights on my own, it's extremely unlikely. At the time that my second marriage was coming undone, I had the fabulous good fortune to adopt a smart, balanced dog by the name of Reilly. While it seems improbable, the spark for my life-changing insights was a German Shorthaired Pointer with a good Irish name.

My experiences living with and training Reilly taught me not just about dog behavior, but also about human behavior in ways that no self-help or psychology book ever had. What I would learn from her and because of her would rip blinders off my eyes that had blocked awareness of my behavior for more than 40 years. Reilly provided the code that unlocked my insight into why I had two failed marriages to alcoholic men, one an abuser; a meandering and unfulfilling career path; and distant relationships with family and friends.

Quite simply, Reilly's lessons taught me how to assert myself and become a stronger person. Then I discovered that in the same way I had become a pack leader to my dog, I needed to become a pack leader with people. Once I learned that lesson, I also realized Reilly's lessons gave me the keys to understanding the behavior of other people as well.

Now, several years later, I have read extensively on human behavior and I have earned a master's degree in clinical psychology. I have

1

a fulfilling career, have great friends, and I am happy and healthy. And I enjoy living with a terrific, well-behaved dog as well.

I began to realize that if I could claw my way out of an abusive marriage and learn how to break a lifetime of unhealthy behavior patterns, maybe I had some wisdom that would be helpful to others, especially overly submissive people who habitually get into relationships with controlling, dominating people.

Once I made the connection that pack leader behavior isn't just "for the dogs," I realized Reilly had been teaching me many lessons all along. Trust me: Even if you have never owned a dog, these lessons from Reilly will help you finally understand human behavior. Once you make the connections between animal and human social behavior, you will see why the Pack Leader Psychology paradigm works so well – in both dogs and humans.

You will gain skills to take control of your life, learning how to:

- instantly spot those who want to dominate, manipulate or abuse you before you let them into your life
- become less manipulative of others
- strengthen your relationships
- be happier and more emotionally balanced and
- raise emotionally healthy children – the next generation of pack leaders.

The Teacher Appears

When I adopted Reilly she was eight months old, the last of a litter of puppies that had been raised entirely in an outdoor kennel. She lived with her mother, father, and grandmother, along with other littermates until they had gradually gotten sold off.

Reilly may have known how to behave in a dog pack, but she did not know very much about the human world. At first, she didn't know how to navigate stairs and she tried to walk through glass doors and windows. She had never worn a leash or collar and fought those. Obeying human commands to "come, sit, stay" was a totally new experience for this headstrong girl.

Training was also difficult because Reilly had eight months of pent-up puppy energy – which, if you know German Shorthaired Pointers, is a heckofa lot of energy. In the first few weeks if I didn't have two hands firmly on her collar she broke away and tore off to go hunting in the woods behind my house. She snuck off and pilfered the neighbor's trashcans routinely, running back home proudly with her finds of pizza crusts and pork chop bones. She killed any critter she could grab a hold of. I was at my wits' end during those early days. I needed more discipline with her.

The symbolism is quite obvious and ironic to me now: At the same time, I also needed to exert more discipline over my husband, Ray. I had no skills or knowledge to manage a wild puppy or a jealous, controlling husband. I didn't realize both were dominating me in unhealthy ways and, with my submissive behavior, I was ignorantly allowing them to manipulate me. I felt angry and powerless, not realizing I held the keys to asserting myself with both dog and husband using just some simple behavior and attitude changes.

So I set about training Reilly, not realizing that what I learned would eventually help me train myself and allow me to take control of my life.

Being a writer and researcher, I headed to the library for a book on dog training. My previous dog, a Vizsla named Kiva, had been an obedience class superstar, so I wasn't too worried. Kiva had known hundreds of words and was a field-trained bird dog. He ran off leash at my side for miles and would turn or stop on command. He walked calmly through crowds and was friendly to everyone. While I guessed that Reilly would be more difficult to train, I was hopeful because I had experience successfully training a hunting dog.

I was fortunate enough (one of many episodes of good mojo on my journey) to discover a dog-training book that introduced me to the concept of the "alpha" or dominant position in the pack. Not all dog trainers believe in this concept. Most focus only on using traditional word commands.

Like many people, I had heard the term "alpha dog" and believed I understood what it meant: the leader of the pack, the boss. But it turns out I had only a vague, intellectual understanding. I had never viewed dog training as a way of communicating in dog language. I had trained dogs with a human perspective only.

Right away, I did a few things the book recommended, such as:

1. Don't look at your dog or talk to her when you first come home. Ignore the dog if it jumps up on you or demands your attention. After five minutes, call the dog to you. This is a sign that the pack leader controls contact by the lower members of the pack.
2. Put the dog food bowl on the kitchen counter when you fill it and eat a cracker or other food first before giving the food to the dog. By eating first, you established dominance. The pack leader eats first and controls access to the food.

These two small tricks seemed to work very well. Reilly's behavior was improving daily, but I had much more to learn as she became an obedient pack member and at the same time showed me how to become a pack leader.

Those early days with Reilly and the coincidental borrowing of a library book would plant seeds that would become full-blown theories of human behavior and radically alter my life and worldview.

Becoming a Pack Leader

A year or so later I stopped channel surfing one night to watch a dog training show. In one of life's happy accidents, I happened upon a TV show called "Dog Whisperer" starring Cesar Millan. As I watched the show, I realized I had been behaving as a pack leader to Reilly, even though I didn't know the term. I learned a few more techniques to use on Reilly, and I saw Cesar really did "train people and rehabilitate dogs." Cesar is, of course, more of a people trainer than a dog trainer. He makes people into pack leaders and that instantly changes their dog's behavior. Dogs behave poorly because they lack leadership. They crave the discipline and structure that a balanced pack leader provides.

Then on one show Cesar used the term "red zone" to describe how a dog acts when it is in attack mode. With heart-stopping awareness, I instantly made a connection: This was exactly how my ex-husband, Ray, had behaved when he was attacking me. Of course! Just as that dog was doing, Ray had reacted with a fight instinct because he felt threatened. And just as that dog was misreading the threat from that tiny poodle, Ray had misread the threat from me. I hadn't been cheating on him or abandoning him or rejecting him, however that is what he believed.

Parallels Between Dog and Human Behavior

As I applied this new Pack Leader Psychology paradigm to the human world, I suddenly realized all those anxious, misbehaving dogs I saw on Cesar's show were just like anxious, misbehaving people I knew:

- When I saw a dog go into a "red zone," attacking with a ferocious, unstoppable intensity, I recognized my second husband in a violent, abusive rage.
- When I saw a meek dog cower and show its belly without provocation, I saw myself fearfully submitting to husbands, family, bosses, and even strangers.

- When I saw an aggressive dog growl and intimidate, I observed that it was actually insecure and fearful – just like my first husband.
- When I saw a dog cling nervously to an owner's side or act frightened of loud noises or obsess over a toy, I made a link to the many anxious, fearful people who suffer from depression, anxiety disorders, phobias, obsessions, and compulsions.
- When I saw a dog avoid eye contact and keep to itself, I saw shy humans who shut themselves off from others as a protective measure.
- When I saw a timid dog unexpectedly lash out, I saw a friend who is quite nice and passive most of the time, but who also sees threats in nearly everything around him, from an innocent personal question to government conspiracies, then attacks with paranoid comments.

It certainly seemed as if the instability and anxiety expressed by many dogs had a parallel in humans. These parallels were so uncanny they had to be based on some primal, indisputable facts – and they are.

First, it seemed natural to ask: "If, as Cesar Millan says, a lack of pack leadership makes an anxious, unbalanced dog, why wouldn't the same be true in human relationships? Were humans acting in unstable ways that might be addressed with a pack leader approach?" As I had experienced personally, when a person acts with more calm assertiveness, others also become calmer, more secure, and less fearful. Clearly, a lack of pack leaders in the human world might be causing the development of so many of the anxieties and misbehaviors seen today.

As I continued to dig deeper, I saw other parallels between dog and human packs. Based on their innate personality, dogs seem to prefer certain modes of behavior: dominance or submission. When they are threatened or perceive they are threatened, they react with fight, flight, or avoidance. However, mentally unhealthy dogs often overreact to threats. This is what causes a fearful dog to bite unexpectedly or causes a shy dog to cower at the sound of a ringing telephone. If humans were as unbalanced as modern dogs, I wondered if these primal comparisons explained a complete range of human emotional and behavioral issues. I recognized my submissive nature and my ex-husband's obvious dominant personality and saw how unbalanced and unhealthy those patterns were for both of us. I looked around and saw the same patterns in so many relationships.

Explaining the Why of Behavior

These observations lead me to develop a new paradigm for human psychology that explained and categorized behavior in a simple, yet powerful, way. Suddenly, the value of becoming a pack leader to my dog had larger implications: The Pack Leader Psychology paradigm not only helped me become emotionally stronger, but explained why people behave the way they do. I observed that when people felt threatened they responded with fight, flight, or avoidance according to a favored personality style: dominance, submission, or avoidance.

So I dug even deeper: Why did people feel so threatened? Was this normal, natural behavior? The lion was no longer at the door of the cave, threatening us physically, as it did our ancient ancestors. But why were so many people anxious and fearful? Did earlier societies have so many bullies? Was it healthy to act as submissively as people do today? Is it adaptive to feel so paranoid, obsessed, or depressed? Is it human nature to have so many mental illnesses?

When studying most tribal societies, anthropologists find extremely low levels of mental illness. When I looked at my happy, calm, balanced dog, and saw how much more contented I was after I gave up my overly submissive behavior and became a pack leader, I knew the answer was obvious. Dogs quickly relinquish their unbalanced behaviors once a balanced pack leader shows them how to behave. Even dogs know that anxiety, fear, submission, and aggression are not normal, healthy behaviors.

Once I saw these powerful connections, I unexpectedly felt the urge to write a book about what I had learned. I wanted to help others – especially those who had been dominated by abusive partners. But I hesitated. I had no psychology training at that point. I didn't have an advanced degree and had only read a few dozen self-help books.

I worried that my theories were an oversimplification of human behavior. Or could it be that a simple, primal paradigm was actually more explanatory than the complex, inaccessible explanations offered by the psychology profession? Despite the fact that the social and emotional concepts underlying the Pack Leader Psychology theory are right in front of everyone's eyes, had we gotten so far removed from our primal roots that we couldn't see how elemental fears were shaping our behaviors, personalities, and interactions with others? When I looked at how I had ignored my intuition over the years, I had to guess this deficit in instinctive insight could have hindered others from reaching these conclusions as well.

Soon I realized that my lack of advanced training in psychology might actually be an asset. Perhaps it takes someone from outside the forest to see the trees, to make connections that experts may not recognize. I wasn't bogged down in researching some tiny detail of human behavior or providing daily therapy to patients. I could look at the big picture in a way that a trained psychologist might not be able to.

I have, however, since earned a master's degree in clinical psychology. During my studies I learned about the hundreds of psychological "disorders" the profession has labeled. By using the indisputable primal behaviors of fight, flight, avoidance, submission, and dominance, I could simplify these disorders into just three key categories.

The Pack Leader Psychology paradigm explains so much about human behavior:

- why some people are aggressive, dominant controllers and others are submissive, pleasing accommodators, and others avoid and withdraw
- why we unwittingly attract certain types of people into our lives
- why most relationships today are unhealthy and turn into fights for control
- why so many people suffer from low self-acceptance
- why low self-acceptance causes fear of criticism, which leads to fight-or-flight fear responses
- why some people overreact to imagined emotional threats by becoming anxious, depressed, phobic, aggressive, or obsessive-compulsive
- why children learn to be self-critical due to the way their parents raised them

More important, my new paradigm allowed me to predict behavior. The psychology profession, with its jumble of jargon and labels, has never developed a system to predict human behavior. While no one can guarantee exactly what someone will do, I now had a system to easily identify the type of person I was dealing with within minutes of meeting and predict broadly how he or she would behave. That ability alone makes the Pack Leader Psychology paradigm a powerful tool to help you recognize the type of person you are dealing with and plan appropriate responses.

It also explained the underlying causes of my own behavior, which was vitally important for me. After two marriages to men I had totally misjudged, I did not want to repeat another unhealthy relationship. I had also gone through unfortunate career choices, poor relationships with my family, and a lack of close friends. Breaking the cycles – plural – was paramount to me if I wanted to live a happy, fulfilling life.

Living As a Pack Leader

What helped confirm my theories was watching what happened when I began to more consciously practice pack leader behavior with the humans in my life. It changed the behavior of those around me, just as it changes dog behavior. People were responding to me differently when I was calm and assertive, compared with when I was insecure and needy. I observed I had spent years acting submissively to people in an attempt to gain affection, yet this behavior had led them to lose respect for me. I began to hear people describe me as strong, confident, self-assured, dignified, calm. Oh, and I treated myself more respectfully, too, all of which automatically fed the cycle of making me happier and more self-assured, and those around me more relaxed.

People also began to look to me for leadership in situations at work and in my personal life. I found people liked to be around relaxed energy and liked it when it was clear who was the pack leader. This new personal strength not only made me a better person, but also helped me attract more emotionally healthy people into my life.

Keep reading to discover how you, too, can benefit from what Reilly taught me about how to assert myself and become a pack leader. Her common-sense lessons form a very easily understood framework that you can quickly and effectively apply not only to yourself, but also to other people in your life to help you understand and predict their behavior completely and simply.

Here are the fascinating lessons Reilly taught me that gave me a dramatically new perspective on life, relationships, and human behavior. Each chapter of the book starts with information from the animal world that is then translated into a lesson for the human world. Each chapter head and subhead is a phrase that succinctly communicates a valuable tip Reilly taught me.

The book is divided into four main sections. In Section One I'll explain the characteristics of a pack leader and the power of the pack.

In Section Two I will describe what is happening in today's society that causes so many people to allow fear and anxiety to take over and make them abandon healthy, balanced behavior. We'll consider why humans have such a difficult time with their social relationships and social hierarchies, and how this affects our interpersonal relationships. I'll discuss parenting and disciplining traditions that I believe may lead to a number of emotional and behavioral problems and certainly cause a lack of pack leader behavior. Section Two will also help you understand what issues you may need to overcome to become a pack leader.

In Section Three, you'll learn how to spot people who do not behave as pack leaders.

In Section Four Reilly offers up 7 Lessons On How to Be a Pack Leader. You'll discover how you can successfully integrate these behaviors into your life, helping you lead a more fulfilling and emotionally healthy life. Perhaps you will be able to learn a simpler, more natural, more powerful, and more authentic way to behave, as animals in the wild do.

Note: I have included examples of human behavior in this book. Except for the names of my family, I have changed the names of the people in these examples to ensure privacy. I recognize that exposing and discussing these examples may make some readers uncomfortable. If you find yourself feeling offended by the examples cited, I would encourage you to consider several things. My goal in including these examples is to educate others, not to shame or criticize. I hope that my honest, direct writing style helps teach a lesson – that honesty is not something to be feared. (For more, see Lesson 3: Be Honest!) If you experience discomfort with the directness of this book, perhaps this may give you reason to pause and consider that reaction. It may be your first lesson on the road to self-awareness and becoming a pack leader. Good luck!

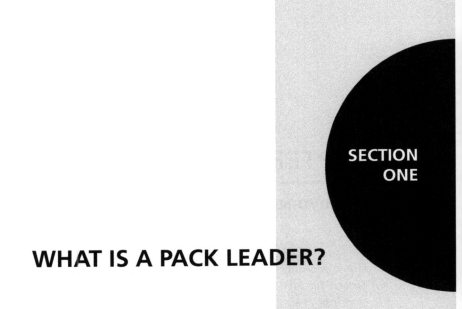

WHAT IS A PACK LEADER?

CHAPTER 1

Anyone Can Become a Pack Leader

When training Reilly in the first weeks after I adopted her, one episode was pivotal for both of us. That first book I read about dog training said the owner might even want to growl at the dog to show dominance. At first, of course, this seemed crazy, so I didn't think much more about the idea. One day Reilly picked up a shoe, a common habit of hers in those early days. She would nab shoes and drag them all over the house. Fortunately, she never chewed any, because she is very soft-mouthed, as most good hunting dogs are. However, it is irritating to find your best pumps slobbery and wedged under the couch.

I caught Reilly in the act one time and bent down to take the shoe away. I don't know why it popped into my head, but without a thought or a second's hesitation – purely instinctive – I grabbed her by the throat, put my face right next to hers and growled. I growled in such a natural, primal way even I was surprised. Reilly certainly was, too! I stared directly into her eyes and didn't back away. Unlike in the past, I didn't reach for the shoe and try to pull it away. I just focused on communicating with her in a way I hoped she would understand. With that growl I told Reilly the shoe was mine. My energy and intention were clear, yet no words were spoken.

Reilly is a very strong-willed dog, but she instantly dropped the shoe. I could see in her eyes a switch had flipped. Her entire demeanor changed. It's as if her body said: "OK, you're the boss now. Whatever you say goes!" It was a decisive turning point in our relationship. I had moved into the top dog position by acting like a dog. While to that point she had been very quickly learning human household rules, her learning curve skyrocketed as she now looked to me to be the pack leader (although I didn't know the phrase at that point). Oh, and Reilly never touched another shoe again. Ever. She also never touches anything of mine – I had clearly established that rule. I can even leave her alone in the car with bags of groceries, including meat, and she doesn't go near the food.

I, too, changed after this episode. It may sound corny, but I felt a shift. This incident was so primal in nature, both in my instinctive growl and in Reilly's reaction, that I felt a rush of energy immediately after. A sense of power surged in me, making me finally understand the phrase "giddy with power." At the same time, I was also very calm. And it felt amazingly good – totally different from any other sensation I'd experienced in my life. Although I had behaved in a very odd way (from a human perspective), it had felt very natural and right. I had acted very "aggressively" according to my understanding of traditional dog training (and certainly to my mode of behaving at the time), but the reaction was very positive. Reilly had been completely accepting of this unusual behavior and had instantly treated me different. Was I asserting myself in a way that was the natural order of things?

As I caught my breath after the incident, I had a chance to think it through. I first realized the growl was perfect – I sounded just like a dog. How did I do that? I had never growled before in my life. I hadn't given it one millisecond of thought. Of course this was exactly why I produced such a perfect growl: It wasn't practiced or premeditated. It came from a primal place inside me that just reacted, purely and with instinct only, not with deliberate intellectual intervention. I just let out how I was feeling at that instant. With one growl I communicated: "Reilly, this shoe is mine. Your behavior is inappropriate and you have to behave differently NOW." So much simpler and more direct than all those words...that a dog wouldn't understand anyway.

After the growling incident, I was sold on the dominance theory of dog training. (It wasn't until later that I would understand how it applied to human training as well.) I continued to learn from Reilly and practice my pack leader behavior. With Kiva I had used traditional obedience training and he knew word commands, such as sit, stay, stand, and heel. This episode with Reilly, however, reinforced that dog training isn't about teaching commands, but about assuming the pack leader position. Your intention and energy will guide the dog almost intuitively after that. Now if I need to give Reilly a command, I don't use a lot of words. I communicate with a short, guttural "hey" that sounds more like "eye." I've only taught Reilly a few commands for specific behaviors, but she usually understands exactly what I want with the "hey" command to get her attention and perhaps a glance or hand signal. Over the years I have witnessed many examples of how Reilly seems to know automatically what I want without me shouting commands. When I moved into a new house, she instinctively stayed in the yard without an electric fence or any training. I must admit, however, I struggled for several years to teach Reilly to heel. Her insatiable prey instinct made heeling a challenge, despite my best efforts on our daily runs and walks.

It still amazes me that if I hadn't reacted instinctively and growled at Reilly that day, I might not have experienced the subsequent insights. With one incident I turned an important corner. I was starting to understand that we don't need words to communicate with animals. I was accessing my instinctive side and discovering the power that was available – that I had never used before with dogs or humans.

A Balanced Pack Leader Is Essential to the Pack

Most of us have heard the term "alpha" as the name of the two leaders – one male and one female – of the wolf pack. Wildlife biologist David Mech coined this term in 1970, although he now says that it is not an accurate description and that the term places too much emphasis on the idea that a wolf pack has a very dominant leader or leaders. He now prefers to use the terms "breeding male" and "breeding female" to emphasize that the two most high-ranking pack members are generally the only members allowed to reproduce in smaller packs. Some researchers believe that by limiting who can breed the pack avoids overpopulating its territory and over-reaching its food supply.

What is the role of the leader in a wolf pack? Quite simply: To provide structure to the pack that will help ensure its survival.

Being a pack leader is a big responsibility, not some honorary title or prize-fight belt given to the meanest wolf in the pack. Pack leaders, while they are ultimately concerned about their own individual survival, are also concerned about the survival of the pack.

Because the pack leader's role is to ensure the survival of the pack in general, and not individual members, the strongest members of the pack get special privileges. Pack leader power generally is used to determine who eats first and how much. The pack leader eats first off a kill, then she allows the strongest members to eat next. Weaker members get the scraps. Seems cruel to us, but if the goal is to keep the pack as a whole strong, this is what must be done. If every pack member gets less than they need to survive, all will starve. Better to have a few members well fed and able to hunt, than have the whole pack weak and incapacitated. (An added benefit: Those who didn't get enough to eat are very motivated to head off for the next hunt!)

In a wild wolf pack being a pack leader is a huge job. Securing food and safety for the pack is his or her responsibility every minute of every day. These are life-and-death issues to the wolf pack. Being a pack leader is a sobering role, not one for power-hungry egomaniacs. As a result, pack leaders must be balanced – a balance of all types of energy and emotion. They must be strong, but caring; fearless, but thoughtful; calm, but decisive and assertive. They are emotionally stable, not easily excited or scared.

A wolf pack is not a rigid, force-based dominance hierarchy, but rather a collection of individuals working together where one or two individuals happen to be looked to as leaders. The alpha wolves are not leaders in the human sense of the term. They do not give orders; rather, they simply have the most social freedom in choosing where to go, what to do, and when to do it. The rest of the pack usually follows.

Biologists studying wolves in the wild have found pack leaders are not necessarily the physically strongest or biggest wolves, although in much of the animal world the largest, most aggressive male is very often the most visible group leader. Females play leadership roles, but in a way that is less noticeable to human observers. In many types of primates the female leaders are much less obvious, because they govern mostly by encouraging friendships and promoting harmony.

In many animals, high-ranking status is based mostly on confidence or strength of character. Like a respected elder, the leader inspires the pack by setting an example, rather than ruling with fear and intimidation.

A dog that is a balanced pack leader:

- *projects calm and deliberate energy in all situations*
- *uses this calm confidence, rather than physical dominance or aggression, to show he or she is the leader*
- *may be the strongest physical member of the pack but rarely uses force to discipline pack members*
- *is adaptable and not anxious in new situations or when meeting new people or animals*
- *approaches other dogs and humans in a calm, respectful manner*
- *is expert at reading other dogs' energy, anxiety, and status*
- *is attentive to the needs of the pack, but not a doting nanny*
- *motivates and inspires the pack by example*

When pack leader techniques are used to train a dog, the dog quickly and eagerly accepts the owner as pack leader. That's because most dogs do not want to be the alpha dog and are not cut out for it. They gladly relinquish the responsibility to someone more capable of the role.

Growl if You Have to, But Be the Pack Leader

It was just a few months after the growling episode with Reilly that I kicked Ray out of the house and filed for divorce.

Of course I can't claim that this incident inspired my decision, but the timing of it is now symbolic to me. Was that growl the first step on my road to becoming a pack leader? Was this lesson in primal reaction the trigger I needed to prod me into pushing back against Ray's aggression? Was this my first taste of self-respect and assertiveness?

The incident certainly taught me I hadn't been a pack leader with my first dog, Kiva. Although Kiva was well behaved and obedience trained, in the last year of his life he had occasionally snapped at people. I had put it off to senility or that he was in pain. However, as I learned more about dog behavior I realized those explanations did not hold water.

I was forced to admit that Kiva's bad behavior was due to the fact that I was not the pack leader in the relationship. Kiva was behaving as a pack leader would by snapping at people as a way of disciplining his pack. I had treated Kiva as a person, had spoiled him, and had abdicated my responsibility. I had unwittingly, yet with the best of intentions, become subservient to a dog.

It is quite clear to most dog trainers that people generally do not behave as pack leaders to their dogs. Many are overly eager to be friends, but in the process of submitting to their dogs lose their respect.

As this lesson from Reilly (and the flashback lesson from Kiva) was sinking in, I began to realize I had not only been a doormat to my first dog, but also to all the people in my life. It wasn't until later I would consciously recognize the parallels between animal and human behavior and would develop theories that are the core of this book. I now firmly believe in the power of assertive pack leadership with the humans in our lives.

As I spent more time with Reilly I learned more about what it meant to be a pack leader and the specific attributes pack leaders have.

Just as an animal pack leader, a human pack leader:

- does not rely on others for approval or acceptance
- accepts accountability for his or her behavior
- is assertive, not overly aggressive, avoidant, or submissive
- exhibits gentle strength, not force and dominance
- communicates honestly and promptly and is not afraid of conflict
- leads, but does not try to control others
- is calm, serene, and brave, not anxious or fearful
- lives in the moment
- respects himself or herself and others
- "claims the space" by setting rules and boundaries
- doesn't needlessly excite the pack
- rewards good behavior

- doesn't manipulate with emotions
- is observant
- trusts his or her instincts
- gets along with others
- is resilient and adaptable
- owns his or her own feelings
- is accepting and empathic, but does not tolerate misbehavior
- is nurturing and compassionate
- is competent and efficient
- tolerates change and ambiguity
- is spontaneous and enjoys unpredictability and creativity
- has confidence in her skills, perceptions, and evaluations
- is expressive, vulnerable, flexible, and willing to take risks in relationships
- is fair and even-handed
- is independent, autonomous, and self-motivated to seek fulfillment
- is down-to-earth and has realistic perceptions
- is optimistic
- competes on merit, not by diminishing others
- works for the common good, not just personal gain
- has the compassion to lead with morality and generosity
- has the courage to lead with dignity and integrity
- has the wisdom to lead with humility

In the past, I probably would have looked at that list and thought I had some of those characteristics. However, I lacked the most important one: the first on the list. I relied almost entirely on others for approval or acceptance. I was extremely externally focused for my self-worth. While the sum of those listed character traits is necessary to be a pack leader, without a strong sense of internal self-acceptance, the other traits will be impossible to achieve. Previously, I had not understood what it meant to have true self-acceptance and probably would have thought that I was self-accepting. It is only in hindsight and improved self-awareness that I am able to recognize that I spent far too much time and energy focused on the opinions and needs of others, and that focus was actually all about me. I did so mainly to get something back – approval.

Balanced people have a strong sense of self. They are self-aware, but not self-absorbed. They are not narcissistic nor do they feel they are special, which, unfortunately, has come to be the definition of someone with "high self-esteem," a phrase I avoid using. Self-awareness means a balanced sense of humility and confidence, not arrogance.

Just as with animals, a human pack leader must behave in a predictable, dependable way that leads others to believe they can trust her and rely on her. This brings confidence and security to the pack. Behaving authentically is the surest way to become trustworthy.

Now you know what defines a pack leader. I'm sure this description seems very straightforward and commendable. Who wouldn't want to be a pack leader? Yet if pack leader skills are so essential and natural to dogs and other social animals, and helpful for humans as well, why are there so few pack leaders in modern human society? Why aren't more people behaving in a balanced, emotionally healthy way? If wolf packs in the wild don't have mentally unstable members, why are large numbers of people so emotionally unhealthy today? What is causing so many in the world today to be anxious, unhappy, aggressive, narcissistic, paranoid, violent, depressed, obsessed, phobic, and any number of other behaviors? Wild animals from elephants to crows seem to manage their relationships and groups without mental illness, domestic violence, child abuse, substance abuse, poverty, crime, and war, but we humans, who have largely forgotten how to be emotionally balanced, seem to have great difficulty getting along with others.

....

Being a pack leader isn't a glamour role, all about the power and glory. It's not about having everyone like you. Not at all. Don't try to "become" a pack leader so you can control others into following or obeying you. If you have thoughts of learning how to be a pack leader just so you can manipulate others or be in the spotlight, you've failed the first test of being a pack leader. If you're thinking of ways to use pack leader skills to take advantage of others, this thought in itself proves you are NOT a pack leader. Using power for your own advantage is the exact opposite of a pack leader skill.

In a wolf pack, the pack leader is in many ways serving at the mercy of the pack. Well-socialized dogs and wolves do not tolerate unbalanced energy. The pack would never allow an unbalanced, controlling wolf to be pack leader. Unfortunately, in modern human society, we've allowed many individuals to rise to power over us, individually and as groups, who are unbalanced – not true pack leaders.

....

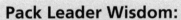

Pack Leader Wisdom:
A pack leader is self-aware, self-accepting,
and accountable for his or her actions.

WHERE HAVE ALL THE
PACK LEADERS GONE?

CHAPTER 2

We All Need a Pack

After I growled at Reilly she willingly accepted her role as part of my pack. I provide calm, clear leadership, so she is not forced to take on the role of pack leader.

Reilly clearly wants to be part of a pack and wants to be near me whenever she can be, which caused problems one day. I was writing at home when a neighbor knocked on my door. He and I often walked our dogs together. I was on deadline, so he took Reilly for a walk along with his dog. They headed toward a nearby woods where we often let the dogs off the leash to run. About 10 minutes after they left I heard something scratching at the back door. When I went to check and found Reilly alone, with my neighbor nowhere in sight, I immediately guessed what had happened. Once she was off the leash, she had bolted for home where I was. As much as she loves hunting, her need to be near her pack was even stronger.

I had seen this behavior before with Reilly. When she is running off leash and loses track of where I am, she becomes worried. She will stop and look for me. If she can't spot me right away, she starts casting around, often turning and running back the way she came, deducing that I might be back there. She likes to stay within eyesight of me at all times.

While Reilly is quite independent and not clingy or needy, her instinct to be part of a pack is very clear.

Reilly knows that just as a lone wolf can't bring down an elk, hunting as a pack is more powerful than hunting alone.

Hunt As a Pack

As I learned from Reilly about the power of the pack, I could see the urge to belong is very strong in dogs. At the same time, I was getting divorced from Ray and began seeing a therapist in Chicago. She confirmed I was too accommodating to Ray. Surprisingly, it was the first time I learned about control and accommodation as major elements of human behavior. Because I was married to an abusive and controlling man, it struck a primal chord that I had been much too eager to be loved by my husband. Further reading about social psychology and primatology made me aware of man's need to belong to a group. I began to recognize that my overly accommodating nature was due at some level to an elemental urge to be accepted.

This desire to belong, get along, and cooperate is deeply engrained in human behavior through the evolutionary process. Because of the benefits, evolution has encouraged the tendency among many types of animals to join a tribe, herd, or troop. Many of our human social pacts are engrained codes that encourage us to fit in and group together. In fact, an ancient saying notes the human need for community: "One man is no man."

Most human societies, until the last few centuries, were organized to value the group over the individual. Just as in a wolf pack, individual needs were subsumed to those of the tribe or clan. While this might have taken away some individual power, the tradeoff was worth it. We gained protection, sex, companionship, hunting partners, babysitters for our children, and a steady supply of food. Social groups bring many benefits to animals and humans, but one of the biggest emotional benefits may be a perception of safety so that group members can relax – the feeling that someone "has your back."

The need to feel part of a tribe is so strong that it can lead to positive behaviors, such as altruism. The extreme example may be soldiers who take huge personal risks so as not to let down their band of brothers and to defend their countrymen. Many research studies have looked at pro-social behavior and confirmed that people generally, given the opportunity, try to get along. Despite our image of predatory animals as selfish, many species share prey, a clear sign of cooperation, even in wild animals. All members of the wolf pack help raise pups, even though they are not allowed to breed. They babysit when the parents are out hunting and will return to the den and regurgitate food for their young pack mates. Wildlife researchers have observed wolf hunts where only a few members have been actively involved in the kill, yet the carcass is shared among all pack members. Evolution has rewarded those species that can hunt together, protect and care for each other, and share resources.

Don't Bite Me and I Won't Bite You: Trust Is the Glue of Relationships

Reilly's confidence and curiosity make her upbeat and inquisitive about everything life brings her way. She runs fearlessly through the woods at top speed and is unafraid of loud noises or new situations that would make an anxious dog very nervous. She travels with me to crowded art fairs and through automatic car washes. This shows that Reilly has no anxieties or insecurities that manifest as misbehaviors. And she is this way precisely because she trusts and respects me, knowing I will care for her, feed her, and not lead her into danger.

That trust also goes in the other direction. When clipping Reilly's toenails I can get near her face, knowing she won't bite me. I can take food, bones, and dead animals away from her without fear she will attack me.

Trust is established mainly because as a pack leader I behave in a predictable, calm manner. The few times that I have gotten angry with Reilly, I am quick to notice her reaction and it stops me in my tracks. She is clearly shocked when I yell at her. She cowers and becomes tentative and skittish – not at all her normal confident attitude. She suddenly can't predict my behavior and trust me to be calm and dependable. Not surprisingly, her anxiety goes up.

Trust has broad social implications and deep roots. Evolution has given a head start to groups of animals that can trust each other and cooperate. A lone wolf can't bring down a moose, but a pack hunting together can. Underlying those skills is a very important emotion: trust. With trust you can cooperate; with cooperation you gain a survival advantage.

To cooperate, social groups need "reciprocal altruism." We know this as, "You scratch my back, I'll scratch yours." The emotion of trust is essential for reciprocity or trading, a key component in the primal game of, "I'll share my fish today, if you'll share yours tomorrow."

The social contract of reciprocity, however, is broken by cheating and unpredictability. If the person doesn't share his trout tomorrow, you're going hungry. Now no longer just an emotional game, but one of survival, this is why we punish cheaters so ferociously.

Trust is just one of the social emotions needed to facilitate moral behavior of the group. You have to understand and predict another's behavior before you can trust him.

Altruism and caring require that we sense distress in others and respond to it. In fact, all social animals use emotions to read others, develop concern and express caring for others. Researchers now know that many animals exhibit pro-social behaviors, such as sympathy, embarrassment, caring, and attachments.

Enforcing fairness requires that we can identify cheaters – those who don't return the favor and share their fish – and punish them. Hierarchies and the social cues that define them bring powerful benefits to pack members, one of which is to organize the pack and reduce conflict. By establishing accepted and predictable behaviors, the pack develops a shorthand for emotional security. You learn exactly on whom you can trust and depend. The hunters can go hunting knowing that the gatherers are gathering. People develop finely tuned skills at detecting: "Should I collaborate and cooperate with this person? Or will he deceive me and steal from me?" Elaborate social rituals become habit and give us automatic insight that helps us easily answer: "Friend or foe?"

It's plain to see why distrust triggers such strong emotions even in the modern world when it may involve an event that is not life threatening, such as a spouse cheating or a lie about whether those pants make you look fat.

Small Is Better

One theory, called the Social Brain Hypothesis, contends that humans are smart because we live in complex social groups and need to keep track of what is going on in our group. We need to determine, "Who is the leader, who can we rely on to join us in fighting off the rival clan, and who will help care for my child?"

Successful cooperation, however, relies on having certain rules that result in predictable behavior among pack members. To develop mutual trust, we need to live with a small, stable group of people who behave predictably following known social cues.

Research has proved that despite a powerful social brain, we can only manage information about a limited number of people. Researcher Robin Dunbar, who has studied the social networks of humans and other primates, has concluded that we feel most comfortable in a core social group of 12 people. A group of about 150 people is the maximum number that we can manage socially. Numerous studies show that cooperation and altruism start to fade in large groups.

Researchers have found that people have an innate need to cooperate and be altruistic, but if you barely know the people you live next to or work with or sit in a church pew with, you are much less likely to care about them. We need small groups and frequent contact to make the social reciprocity system work, something we lack with our large cities and mobile societies. If you never expect to see someone again, you may feel guilt-free cutting him off in traffic. In a small group, however, members can understand and trust the other members, give and receive honest feedback, and have the ability to shun and reprimand law breakers.

Research about when people cheat shows that the power of social shunning decreases in larger groups or when the participants didn't expect to have to deal with someone again in the future. Makes complete sense to me: If you think you can get away with cheating, you will. But if you think you'll run into that person again, you might think twice about screwing him over.

Psychologists have used game theory to show that most people learn to cooperate in the long run. While they may lose points in the short term, they learn that cooperating rewards them – and their opponent – with more points eventually.

A common saying applied to life in a small town is, "Everyone knows your business." While that intrusiveness may seem annoying or even threatening to some, it is an example of the social pressures that help keep people in line. When you live in a small town someone will notice your odd or criminal behavior and will call you out on it. This is a good thing. The saying, "It takes a village to raise a child," speaks to the same concept.

Sadly, the pro-social behavior that worked so well to propel the human species to its success seems to be less valued, and, in fact, seems to be a detriment to our success in the modern, dog-eat-dog world. "Every man for himself" behavior seems to be much more helpful today.

I strongly believe that we all must discipline each other for society to work well. We all must, essentially, growl or nip when a child or adult is behaving outside the bounds of normal, accepted behavior.

However, another innate behavior may get in our way. Evolutionary psychologists are learning that an accommodating, trusting nature is a more normal and healthy part of human behavior than distrusting dominance. Yet our avoidance of conflict, with its roots in our primal fear of rejection, trips us up. As a society we have become "socially correct" – we have come to believe we can't criticize others even about egregious and unacceptable behavior. We think, "I'll just let him slide this one time." We also hope that someone else will do the hard work of confronting that miscreant.

Many misbehavers hone their misbehavior over years because they are not chastised for it and also are rewarded by their success: "People are intimidated by me, so they don't say anything, and I get what I want. Perfect!" Consequently, they keep repeating their emotional manipulation or abuse or deception.

Unfortunately, statistics on mental illness and criminality show that there has been an increase in the number of people with behavioral problems over the past several generations. (Although the increase in mental illness can also be attributed to the much broader scope of definitions of conditions by the psychiatry profession.)

I have to believe the growth of behavioral problems is due to the fact that our anonymous social culture is no longer disciplining people. It is easy to get away with cheating, manipulating, social loafing, abuse, criminality, and non-altruistic behavior because we don't have the small clans and powerful leaders who know the importance of keeping misbehavior in check. Some folks have learned they can take advantage of the natural human tendency to be trusting, helpful, and altruistic, and no one dissuades them from this view.

Because of our mobility, these types of people can easily take their deceit down the road and scam the next victim. They can disappear into a large group and avoid retribution for their behavior. Unlike in a small town or tribe, it's easy to fly under the radar when you live in a big city. Retribution may never be enforced.

When I divorced Ray I wished there was a tattoo I could stamp on his forehead to warn other women to stay away from him. Yet I knew there was nothing I could do – he would likely find a new victim, charm her, then abuse her. I felt frustrated that no one was going to discipline him to get him to stop his behavior. I now realize that rather than slinking off in embarrassment, I should have told everyone he knew about what he had done. I had a fantasy about taking out ads in the local newspaper – that might have slowed him down a bit. But at that time I was more worried about my physical safety, proving, of course, that Ray's intimidation was successful. If I had shouted about his behavior from the rooftops, he would have been very hesitant to stalk me and beat me up in the future, because everyone would have known he was the most likely suspect.

The problem is we have lost the strong leaders who keep the overly dominant in check. Very few are willing to threaten the thugs, glare at the manipulators, or intimidate the bullies.

Balance Trust with Discipline

Trust and believability are assessed at instinctive levels, bypassing our intellect. One of the first things all babies learn is a fear of strangers – they learn whom to trust. Throughout our lives we rely on the unspoken language of trust, balancing the need to trust others with our distrust of those who might hurt us or deceive us.

But trust and reciprocity must be managed through discipline, assertiveness, honesty, and even anger. Our built-in sense of civility must be allowed to flourish, because it informs us who is helpful, fair, and shares their fish.

But what happens when a person fails to develop a healthy, balanced emotional repertoire that includes assertiveness and honesty?

As I came out of my second marriage to a very angry man, I wondered about that tendency. It seemed as if some people could not be trusted. Many also cannot trust others. Ray seemed to sense treachery where there was none. I had given him no reason to doubt me or question my loyalty, and he had a great life, with me working two jobs, paying all the bills, and doing all the housework. Despite my outpouring of love and caring, he clearly felt I might betray him and take advantage of him. And, clearly, he gave me no reason to trust him, however I continued to do so far too long.

With a look around at the large numbers of divorces and dysfunctional relationships, it would appear as if much of the population is losing the ability to read the trustworthiness of others. As I'll discuss at length in future chapters, one type of person quickly and proactively attacks even when there is no threat or harm being sent their way. Another type of person responds with passivity and overly trusting naïveté.

I believe that humans have not stayed in balance between the range running from accepting altruism to unfounded anger. The result is an increase in the number of people on each end of that emotional spectrum. We seem to have too many emotionally unstable people who choose to dominate and take advantage of others through intimidation, as well as those who behave submissively and over-rely on niceness to get along with others.

Trust is such a deep, primal emotion that when we lose our ability to trust our sense of trust, our distrust and suspicion trigger a primal response. It is natural to feel fearful and on guard when you believe you can't trust someone or if your emotional sensors for trust are not well developed.

I believe that one source of this inability to trust is an inability to recognize and believe our own emotions and instincts. Lacking empathy for their own needs and wants, many people then fail to develop empathy for the needs of others. For some people, this deficit in emotional intelligence also can make it difficult to respond to the emotions of others – including the emotion of trust.

On the extreme end of the untrusting and untrustworthy are those psychologists call by various names: sociopaths, psychopaths, or those with antisocial personality disorder. These people are unable to empathically respond to others with compassion, are not sympathetic toward others' feelings, are cold and detached, and repeatedly harm and manipulate others.

As you'll learn in future chapters, when some people feel threat-ened their "fear" response is engaged. Clearly, a sociopath is reacting with the "fight" response – unconcerned about the other's emotions, only concerned that he survive what he perceives as threatening, untrustworthy behavior from someone else. Seen from a social psy-chology standpoint, these people have been trained not to fully partic-ipate in the social and moral standards of the tribe. They are predators gone wrong, preying on their own tribe.

Sociopaths are an extreme example of what I believe is occurring currently in society. Without clear pack roles, we never establish pre-dictable behavior. Without this, there is no trust. Without trust, our fear sensors are repeatedly triggered and anxiety results. We are, in essence, constantly on alert: "Friend or foe?"

We used to have a primal need to draw circles of trust around our-selves to ensure our physical survival, but now we still rely on trust to ensure our mental health.

Beware of the Need for Belonging "Gone Bad"

Conformity, agreement, and compliance are innate in humans, because hunting, fighting off predators, and caring for young are much easier as a community. Reciprocity also feeds and drives our need to fit in. Our reputation is important if we want to be part of the tribe. Most of us don't want to be seen as cheaters and therefore ostracized, so we cooperate and are generous with others to boost our reputation. We conform, agree, and don't make waves. We not only share tonight's antelope, but this cooperation ensures that we can hang out with the group around the fire tonight and be safe. We social creatures have an inborn urge to cooperate, if only so we don't get kicked out of the tribe.

This urge for social integration is so powerful it drives much of individual human behavior even today, when we don't need to band together to fight off a lion or the neighboring tribe. It's a natural desire for all people to avoid feeling helpless and cast out.

The "longing for belonging" can, however, lead to less-than-admirable behaviors.

Because this urge is so elemental to us, the threat of social discon-nection can trigger an automatic fear response. Our primal brain senses our survival is at stake and responds. Some researchers even use the phrase "social death" to describe the phenomenon – an indication of the power of exclusion.

Feelings of isolation are toxic emotionally and even physically. Neuroscientists now know that the same part of the brain that evaluates physical pain, the anterior cingulate cortex, is also used to judge the emotional pain of social rejection.

Conversely, the feeling of inclusion is physically healthy, bringing lower heart rates, improved sleep, and reduced stress hormones, according to numerous medical studies. Other research shows that married people have lower rates of illness and live longer. Feeling alone and excluded triggers feelings of fear, anger, and anxiety that result in physical symptoms, such as high blood pressure and heart disease.

However, unbalanced people take the fear of being cast out to an extreme. It shows up in the nearly insatiable need for acceptance and the approval of others. While this need has its roots in a primal drive for survival, it has become a cause of most of our modern psychological and behavioral problems. People labeled by psychologists with many different diagnoses, including paranoid and depressed, are often hyper-alert to being emotionally victimized or rejected by others.

In the past, I was eager to get along with others, but I took my submissiveness too far, subsuming my needs in the service of getting others to like me and accept me. In taking the primal need for cooperation to an unhealthy level, I cooperated with everyone – even those who wanted to harm me.

I will discuss in later chapters much more about how a fear of rejection from the pack can overpower us and cause us to act irrationally, leading to a fear of criticism and a desire to avoid conflict and please others.

The need to feel part of the group is such a fundamental, primal driver of human behavior that we need to recognize how pervasively it drives individual behaviors. The fear of being cast out affects everything from relationships to career choices to how we raise our children.

Pack Leader Wisdom:
We all need a pack.
But beware of an excessive "longing for belonging."

CHAPTER 3

A Healthy Pack Needs a Hierarchy

All healthy wolf packs establish a hierarchical ranking of status. This hierarchy is very valuable because it neutralizes aggression, reduces conflict, and promotes social order. Acceptance of social rank is a way to deter constant fighting and encourage pro-social behavior and cooperation, and it is widely accepted to be an evolutionary benefit to wolves and other social creatures.

Evolution has given social animals a strong, intuitive understanding of pack hierarchy and how it is expressed. Pack instinct is a very strong motivator for social creatures. They crave a stable and organized pack and enjoy rules and structure. Predictable behavior and trust result when each member knows his exact status in the pack structure.

Most wolf packs are, in fact, very trusting of each other. There is actually very little aggression or challenge to the pack leaders. Dominance contests are rare, perhaps because most wild packs are mainly made up of family members. In 13 summers observing a wolf pack in Canada, wildlife biologist David Mech saw no overt fights for leadership. Pack members do not question a pack leader's power on a daily basis. It may occasionally be challenged by a rival seeking to gain the pack leader position, and that challenge can end in a fight.

However, when a group of unrelated wolves or domestic dogs is suddenly placed together, the more dominant members will aggressively challenge each other for primacy. They naturally know they must determine who is dominant. Wild primates, such as chimpanzees, seem to have a much more fluid hierarchy and fights for dominance occur more regularly.

In dogs, once rank order is established in a pack it is usually maintained, not through violence or force, but through nonviolent communication. Dog and wolf behavior may seem difficult for humans to understand because of our reliance on words. But to pack members it is very clear. If you want to understand dogs, you must be alert to very subtle signs most people are not trained to notice. Dogs, of course, don't use words humans can hear – these physical signs are their words.

31

Wolves and dogs use an elaborate system of body language, eye contact, ritualized fighting, and posturing to let each other know their rank. These displays are the only thing needed to maintain social stability. When confronted by another animal, a naturally dominant pack leader will quite quickly and effortlessly establish her more superior rank with some specific behaviors. Physical control is rarely used. For example, dominant wolves will freely look other animals directly in the eye; this declares and reinforces their superior rank. Subordinate animals will look away and act with deference.

A balanced dog approaches other dogs with its body in a neutral position. Its head is up and alert, but it is not belligerent. Its tail is not too high, but not between its legs and submissive. Ears are held relaxed, not perked up and not pulled back in fear. Eyes are alert, but relaxed.

The intensity change from a calm, neutral dog to one behaving aggressively is noticeable physically and through its energy. A dog in an aggressive posture will have her chest out, head high, eyes will be intensely focused on the prey or target. The tail will be held high and will probably be wagging slowly.

How wolves and dogs greet each other is very important and gives many clues as to status. A lower-ranking dog knows it greets a higher-ranking pack member carefully. A pack member does not make eye contact with a pack leader or superior dog. It keeps its tail low, its head low and ears down. It is restrained, not energetic. It slowly works its way close to the superior dog, and usually does not come face to face. Instead it will head for the hindquarters, to do that ever-popular sniff that embarrasses us humans so much.

Contrast this with the way most poorly socialized pet dogs behave. They greet each other and humans in ways interpreted as aggressive and dominant by more-balanced dogs.

- *They bound right up without hesitation.*
- *Their head, tail, and ears are held high.*
- *They immediately begin to sniff the face.*
- *They bark or vocalize. Socialized dogs rarely bark except in warning or as a sign of aggression.*
- *They jump up, especially when greeting humans. A pack member would never jump on a superior pack member.*
- *They look right at the other dog – a clear sign of a challenge. A pack leader does not allow pack members to make eye contact unless she permits it.*

It is very rare to find a balanced pack member among American pet dogs because they have been so poorly socialized in dog behavior. The biggest lesson dogs fail to learn is the importance of pack hierarchy and how status is expressed. Because of this, they live with elevated anxiety as they are forced to establish and re-establish their pack ranking with each dog and person they meet.

A Subordinate Dog Is Balanced

However important the role of pack leader is, the ability to behave in a subordinate manner is just as important. The pack would not be stable if all members fought constantly for dominance. In a balanced, healthy pack, subordination is necessary in a hierarchy because it encourages cooperation and reduces conflict, a fundamental behavior in stable social organizations. Subordinate pack members help promote friendly relations and bind the pack together. In balanced packs of wolves, members recognize their role as followers and gladly accept that role.

Keep in mind: Subordinate wolves agree to be subordinate for the good of the pack. Even a subordinate wolf can be a 120-pound killing machine that could clearly injure any other pack member if it wanted to. So a higher-ranking pack member relies more on the conditional cooperation of the rest of the pack than on any physical control over subordinates. In other words, while people may consider a pack leader as a dictator, a wolf pack is really more of a democracy. The pack must agree on a leader.

Subordinate Does Not Equal Submissive

I would like to make a clarification for all of you who can't get rid of your "human paradigm." There is a difference between subordinate and submissive. Well-socialized dogs and wolves know that being subordinate is not a weakness. Being subordinate is a good thing in the dog world and a good thing for your dog to learn in your family pack. A subordinate dog knows her place in the pack and obeys pack rules. It doesn't mean she is frightened, insecure, or anxious. She doesn't quiver, hide, show her belly, or cower. Those are signs of extreme submission driven by fear. A dog with a capable pack leader is happily subordinate, content in her role, and does not exhibit misbehaviors based on anxiety. Reilly is subordinate to me, but doesn't view herself as weak, and no one else would either.

Unfortunately, humans have come to believe that subordinate means weak – cowering in the corner. This is actually what I would term submissive.

Early animal researchers (mostly men!) focused on the easily observed, brute force displays of dominance by the male – the tree-shaking threats of an ape, for example, or the head-butting of bull elk. More-recent researchers now recognize that most animal groups spend far more time developing alliances, promoting harmony, smoothing over fights, cuddling, doing favors, persuading, compromising, cooperating, and sharing resources. Primate researchers have found that females are less likely to use physical strength to establish dominance in the hierarchy, relying more on respect from followers, rather than intimidation. Being nice counts in establishing power in the animal world, apparently, probably far more than we may like to admit. Western human culture favors the aggressive, dominant role of the individual, rather than the power to be found in a supportive, trusting team.

While packs need leaders, a single-minded focus on the "alpha" persona is a mistake. I believe we need more people to show a range of pack characteristics in order to have a more balanced society and more emotionally balanced individuals. Reilly is subordinate to me and obeys me, but she is hardly meek and timid. It takes self-assurance and a strong self-identity to surrender power to a larger cause – the pack.

Stable Packs Feel Safe

Change happens slowly in the wolf world. Each animal knows exactly where he or she stands in the pack order. The ranking of the pack stays the same, unless a pack member dies or perhaps a lone male wanders into the territory. The pack can assess him to decide if he is subordinate and they want to admit him. Perhaps the lone male is strong enough and dominant enough that he will immediately challenge the pack leader to a fight.

If new puppies are born, at first the pack cares for them, but the pups don't have an identity or rank in the eyes of the rest of the pack until about one year old. As the months go by and the pups grow, perhaps following behind on a hunt, the rest of the pack slowly assesses each new pack member. During this growth and learning phase, and as the pups are near adult size, the pups and entire pack have come to an understanding as to the ranking of these pups in the existing pack.

The wolf pack and its hierarchy do not change very often or very drastically, which is a safe, healthy, predictable situation.

Predictability is Healthy

Humans a few hundred years ago and beyond probably lived largely according to these same rules for social hierarchy. Imagine living in a small village anywhere in the world several generations ago. Your social world changed about as often as the wolf pack. New babies would be born. Maybe a stranger would ride into town a few times a year. Some hunters would go off to kill a buffalo and some of those young men might die in the attempt. Older people and the sick would occasionally and predictably die. But those were the only changes to your village structure during your entire life. You knew where you stood in relation to others at all times. You never had to question whether you had more power than the village chief. You never wondered when you would become a warrior, because a ritual was held and you were now a man.

Most important, you felt safe – at least safe from other human threats. You knew that you could depend on the behavior of those in your tribe or clan. You could rely on a predictable tribal structure and you only had one tribe to keep track of.

Now called collectivist cultures, ancient tribes, villages, and clans conferred the same benefits of any pack or social system:

1. People lived in one group for most of their lives, bringing stability, trust, and lower stress.
2. The support of the tribe was predictable. Group members would be there for you if you played by the tribe's rules. Someone would "have your back."
3. You knew your rank in the tribe and it rarely changed.
4. Every member of the tribe behaved authentically and predictably. You didn't have to constantly worry about how a person would behave.
5. You could be the authentic energy and role you were destined to be. You didn't have to be a leader if you didn't want to be. If you were a subordinate follower, that was OK.
6. A small tribe could discipline and control the behavior of its members.
7. You knew exactly who the leader was and could look to her for guidance and security.

Sadly, the stability and predictability that occur in an animal pack are now missing from much of modern human society. In the animal world, a social group offers many benefits to its members that humans are now forfeiting by not grouping together.

Humans Have Too Many Packs

With our mobile Western society, we uproot ourselves from our hometowns, the churches where we were baptized, and our neighborhoods with a frequency that is psychologically destabilizing. Nearly every sociological and psychological measure shows our stress levels are much higher than they were a few hundred years ago. Many blame it on the faster pace of life and technology, but when did all the problems start in most societies? When populations started to grow to the point where people moved out of small towns into large cities. Mobility tore the stable family and village structure out of society. How much of our stress is caused by the fact that we don't have dependable, predictable social structures throughout our lives?

In addition, I have come to believe that most of us have too many packs. Look at our lives: We have our immediate family, extended families, maybe even stepfamilies and step-grandparents. We have several circles of friends: our poker buddies, our bird watching group, the knitting circle, a volunteer committee, and the congregation at the mosque. Add in work: You may be a boss of one group of people, but you may also have a boss, who has a boss, on up the line.

This huge number of packs must be downright confusing at a very primal level.

I was fortunate that I lived in one house until I was 17 and went off to college. But the stability stopped after that. I can't even count the number of times I moved in and out of dorms and houses in college, and then back and forth to home during summers. I spent a few months in Chicago when I was 19. Just counting from when I was 22, I moved 16 times before the age of 46, living in four states. I have watched my address book totally change over the years as one set of friends and colleagues and neighbors got left behind and a new set was installed. While I enjoyed living in new places, this sort of upheaval left me without that strong, stable base that comes from having a friend your whole life or knowing your rabbi well enough to ask for advice.

I am lucky in that my parents didn't get divorced. Think about the many changes that may happen to other children: parents divorcing and dating multiple people and perhaps remarrying. Then maybe stepbrothers and stepsisters are added to a new family. Grandma and grandpa and extended families live thousands of miles away. Kids may move homes and schools several times in their life.

Most of us at age 18 move away to college or to a job and essentially start all over – establishing our own packs. With each move, new job, and marriage, we rebuild sets of friends and re-establish social structures.

In addition, more and more of us live alone and don't even have the support of nearby family. My father lives about an hour away, but I only see him two or three times a year because he is so busy and travels so much. My brother lives in Massachusetts and my sister lives in California. How many of us today can say we know on whom we can depend for support? How many of us who are single and live far from our families, really have a sense that if we got sick we'd be able to depend on someone to take care of us? With no one to rely on, we don't feel that anyone has our back. Being adrift from a pack gives many a deep sense of insecurity that can't even be identified or labeled.

While it is impossible to parse out the exact causes of long life, it would be interesting to study the social structures of those who live over age 100. It might show most of these centenarians come from small towns and villages, lived most of their life in one spot, and lived with a consistent group of people. Imagine Ivan, a 95-year-old living up in the Urals in a village of 20 people. Ivan knows everyone and has known his fellow villagers for decades. He knows that Yuri from next door is not a threat. He can predict how Yuri will behave every day. Ivan knows where he ranks in the village and knows after decades of living with those villagers he can depend on each of them for support.

Compare that to the stress of walking down a big-city street. It is a low-grade assault on our most primal fight-or-flight instincts. Because of thousands of years of evolutionary honing, we are on edge, attuned to each person walking toward us: "Is she a threat? Or him, or him, or them?" We don't even realize this, but our primal side is alert to an attack or a dominance move. Even though we logically know that no one is likely to jump us or confront us on Main Street or Fifth Avenue, our ancient recollection of being prey is telling us to beware nearly every minute of every day. That is stressful.

It is my contention that the reason we don't make eye contact with every person we pass on a busy sidewalk or in a crowded subway car is because it is just too much information. It is an overload on our fight-or-flight decision making to have to size up each stranger who strolls by. So we shut down our receptors, avoid their gaze, and just pretend they don't exist. In fact, I heard an interview with a writer who described how he refused to wear eyeglasses, despite the fact that he was quite nearsighted. He admitted that this was a way to avoid making eye contact with other people, an innovative solution to this issue.

Society is also actively teaching children to fear strangers. Schools and parents legitimately educate children on "stranger danger" to avoid child kidnapping and molestation. In 2007 a group of 270 child psychologists and therapists from around the world wrote a letter theorizing that boys and girls being taught that every stranger is a threat and the related parental anxiety and overprotection may be behind an explosion in children's diagnosable mental health problems.

If people believe they can't trust anyone, does this lead to increased psychopathology? While a reasonable fear of an unknown "foe" used to be healthy for physical survival, what happens when so many people in society feel nearly everyone is a "foe" and they have no "friend," no core tribe of people to trust? What happens to the human brain and body when a person is on alert 24/7? I believe we are witnessing that scenario in much of today's world.

What is the result of all this upheaval? Constant, low-grade anxiety. I believe the lack of a stable pack structure in our lives is causing most of us to experience low-grade stress, which leads to behavioral issues and an array of social ills.

I have to wonder if most people are feeling chronically lonely and fearful in part because of this sense of being uprooted and unsupported, of feeling emotionally alone and unsure, of feeling threatened by the unpredictable behavior of those with whom they interact.

Importantly, as a result of this insecurity, any perception of being rejected by the very limited tribe they do have may be especially hurtful. You'll learn more about this important concept later in the book.

Packs Provide Discipline

As we've learned, reciprocity greases the wheels of a communal society. However, if you are only and always out for yourself you become the lone wolf, lacking the support of a pack, but also lacking the guidance and discipline of that pack. For humans, one of the important skills we learn from others is an understanding of the social emotions: empathy, love, caring, and cooperation. If our packs dwindle down, if we live alone, and if the people we deal with are also unschooled in these social emotions, how will we learn them?

We need strong, balanced pack leaders to coach others on the appropriate language of social interactions. Wild animals understand that every member must get along and that the pack should correct non-reciprocal behavior. Why don't people follow these same simple rules?

In the current scenario, sadly, everyone loses. Let's say someone has an irritating and odd tic. This behavior isn't horrible, not bad enough to criticize, you say, yet you distance yourself from this person. Everyone else does the same. When no one explains how this behavior affects others, the irritating person keeps on acting in his wacky way. What happens? He doesn't have friends, he doesn't succeed at work because his boss thinks he's a goof, he can't find a woman to date, and he becomes lonely and even odder. So we step even further away in disgust and embarrassment. But everyone is the poorer for this lack of communication. At the extreme, some misbehavior may become criminal, and as a society we pay the price with violence, prisons, and social disruption.

Consider, instead, what would happen if you knew you had to spend a winter in a small cave or igloo with the person with the odd behavior. What would you do? You'd have to speak up! You'd say that the odd behavior bugs you, and perhaps everyone in the cave would agree. The other person would learn not to act so oddly and everyone would be improved.

I also think this concept could be applied to modern marriages. If only the wife points out that the husband's behavior is wrong, he can easily dismiss her and refuse to change. When the entire tribe says he is an abusive jerk, maybe he'll be more likely to get the message and alter his behavior. Is our high divorce rate the result of single-family homes, a lack of close extended families, social isolation, and a reluctance to speak up, coupled with a reluctance to admit fault and change?

These examples point out the paradox of the longing for belonging. We want to get along with others, so we often fear direct communication and the possibility of conflict. Evolution has taught us to avoid rocking the boat. However, avoiding confrontation is not the solution for long-term balance and harmony in a social group. Someone must resist the power hungry, the abusive, the food grabbers, and the social misfits, or everyone suffers. With no pack leaders to step up and correct misbehavior, I believe society will continue to face a rapid escalation of inappropriate, even criminal, behaviors.

Juggling Pack Roles Is Stressful

Because we have so many packs, we also have a constantly shifting pack role that is confusing and stressful to us. For example, at home with your children your role should be unquestioned pack leader. Go visit your parents and you may feel more comfortable reverting to a subordinate role with them. You are equals with your poker buddies, but then at work have to step up to be boss – but not too dominant because your boss might be threatened. Or you may be a boss at work, but come home to a bossy, dominant wife. You may run a volunteer committee, but then have decisions overruled by an executive board.

I believe we are not built evolutionarily to change our ranking in the pack every few minutes. Could it be that part of the stress of modern life may be because we have too many packs and roles to manage? We are forced to ask constantly: "How do I stand in relationship to this new employee, my new mother-in-law, or my new neighbor? How do

I modulate my behavior and words to keep peace?" Our social brain is built for this very task, but I believe we are asking too much of its capabilities.

Because modern humans no longer establish a single social hierarchy and stick with it, we must constantly establish or re-establish our role in a pack because no role has been defined for us. Rather than behaving in an authentic, balanced manner, we may look for ways to control others to bring the sense of stability we crave. We are also forced to be on guard against the unstable behavior and power plays of our family, friends, neighbors, and co-workers.

According to the Pack Leader Psychology paradigm, many of the problems in human interactions are due to ongoing manipulative games played in a battle for dominance. Worrying every day about the unpredictable behavior of the people in your pack is stressful. Add in the fact that you may meet dozens of new people and cross the path of perhaps hundreds of strangers every day and this brings an additional level of stress.

Sadly, many of us have even had to be on guard in our love relationships. When our most intimate partnerships are based on domination and control, not on mutual trust and respect, it may be that every minute of our lives feels like a stressful fight for survival.

Human Behavior Isn't Predictable

Some of us also grew up not learning and understanding the value of social intelligence. I, for one, was raised not to question the motives of others and was not taught to be vigilant for others taking advantage of me. I failed to listen to my intuitive sensors when meeting new people.

When dogs meet, they check each other out. Some of the exploration can happen a block away. Dogs sense another dog's ranking and energy from quite a distance. Then, if they get closer, they watch for body language. They are especially alert for signs of aggression or an unbalanced dog. Smart dogs know: Don't get too close to a dog that might bite. (Why didn't I learn this lesson before my second marriage?)

If they get close enough, dogs smell each other. They dance around a bit, confirm who is dominant and who is subordinate, and it's over. Once dogs know their place in the pack, their behavior is predictable. "I won't bite you and you won't bite me. You eat first, I eat second."

Packs are fearful or anxious around unbalanced dogs – dogs that project the wrong energy. You can only be top dog if you really are top dog. Pretending doesn't work. Dogs sense fake.

But the human world isn't so simple. Because social hierarchies are no longer recognized, some people don't clearly communicate their pack status. In fact, many people are busy covering up authentic energy. They may adopt false roles and exude false energy, making it hard for others to read and predict behavior. They don't want others to see their inherent insecurities, so put on false fronts of bravado. Or they feel others will be threatened by their natural leadership style, so they soften their edges and become overly submissive and nice. This makes it difficult to read a person's authentic nature, especially if you have limited and unexercised skills at this task.

Having a large number of packs also may force us to act in ways that are not our real nature. A natural pack follower may become a fake pack leader with her children or on a project at work. A natural pack leader may be coerced into being submissive to a spouse or an unstable boss, creating additional stress.

A balanced dog feels competent and capable, so trust and vulnerability are part of his life. He is honest and upfront about who he is. He doesn't try to hide his true nature or mask his intentions. That's because a well-socialized dog knows that the pack just wants to figure out where this new guy will fit into the pack order. When balanced dogs meet, there isn't any hidden agenda, such as, "How can we take advantage of this new dog?" Even if one dog is subordinate to another, once the pack order is established, the discussion is over. They do not continue establishing control over him or thinking of ways to manipulate him at every turn.

Yes, people size each other up when we meet. As dogs do, we check out a new person's energy – are they calm, balanced, not a threat? That is why first impressions are so important. But because we are not behaving authentically, it is difficult to assess each new person we meet and deal with.

Lone Wolves Are More Fearful

Although humans innately value belonging, togetherness, and interdependence, Western society is now structured to value individualism and independence, and to devalue group inclusion.

We are increasingly isolated lone wolves. A record number of households are now single people. If you do have a family, you usually live in a single-family household, separated from your extended family.

The downside of our culture's strong push for each of us to "go it alone" is that we are alone – either physically or emotionally or both.

American society is increasingly a culture where people live alone, play alone, and generally avoid each other's company. We are also emotionally alone – we feel alone – because we have been socialized not to ask for help from others, not to pitch in, and not to join in. Social change and increased mobility are also weakening the stability of the family and community that gives us self-identification, security, and support.

I believe some of the problems in modern society stem from the fact that people are now deeply conflicted by these divergent needs. We attempt to portray strength and forbearance, even if it results in feeling lonely and scared. Because we then lack social supports of strong packs and pack leaders, this makes our normally social selves very scared. Because we feel weak and vulnerable, we react with fear, perhaps triggering one of the primal responses of fight, flight, or avoidance.

Clearly some people choose to push away from others in an avoidant style of behavior. These anxious types fear the emotional entanglement of relationships or the possible embarrassment of social situations and elect to avoid them. Severe cases are, of course, the hermits, hoarders, and loners living by themselves. But I also wonder if guys like my ex-husband Ray back away from emotional attachments with a large group of people because of their insecurities. Ray wanted to feel attached, but focused on one person. He picked the weakest, most submissive person he could find and defined me as his pack. Because of that very limited attachment, any minor, perceived criticism by me was a rejection by his entire social group. If I said, "You forgot to pick up milk at the store," this innocent comment felt like a survival-threatening blow to his inclusion in his pack of two.

A balanced person can permit herself to have a diverse group of close confidants because she knows her boundaries with each person and can manage those interactions with varying levels of intimacy and involvement. An insecure person puts all his emotional eggs in one basket and overreacts when that basket threatens to overturn.

A balanced pack member is not threatened, but rather, strengthened, by having a pack to support her. In fact, belonging to a larger group lowers stress and, as a result, improves physical health. Social support has been associated with dramatically lower death rates in several different populations and with reduced stress hormone levels.

Where Are the Pack Leaders?

Because we no longer live in structured tribes with a strong leader, many of the benefits of social hierarchy have disappeared from our culture. I have to wonder whether we not only miss having a pack, but a pack leader. Let's face it, most people need a pack leader. When we don't understand our rank in the pack or don't have a firm pack leader and we are forced into this role, some folks are likely to become uncertain, insecure, and fearful.

We now generally live in small single-family units, which forces more of us to become pack leaders. But are so many of us meant to be pack leaders? Even if we had more social training in pack leader skills, is this scenario forcing too many followers into a role they are not eager to embrace, which then leads these people to become fearful, false pack leaders? Has this lead to an increase in the number of insecure, anxious people with symptoms we now label as mental illness? The misbehaviors of an unstable dog forced to become pack leader are remarkably similar to the behaviors of most unstable humans I meet. I can't help but wonder what would happen if we went back to a system with balanced, mature leaders heading up larger clans.

This unhealthy system and the inherent insecurities some people carry with them may cause some people to learn inappropriate behaviors that appear to be those of a pack leader yet are not: bullying, bossing, controlling, manipulating. Clearly, this type of behavior is not good for marriages, relationships, or raising children. A good leader recognizes the value of supporters and followers and treats them respectfully.

Packs of wolves seem to know that the leader is just another role, no more valuable than anyone else's role. However, they show respect because they know being pack leader is a difficult job and because they know that respectful, subordinate behavior makes the pack work better. There can only be one coach on a team.

Unfortunately, in much of the world we are now raised to believe that if we are anything but "top dog" we are losers. Either you're a champion or a loser. Being a pack follower is absolutely an admission of weakness in our society. We are taught that we must always be angling for the top spot. Society doesn't value supporting roles as much as it does the MVPs, CEOs, flamboyant gangstas, red carpet celebs, and glamorous pop stars. This is evidence that the idea of cooperative pack structure and roles is increasingly a lost concept, which is unfortunate, because it means we've forgotten our understanding of how to relate fairly and cooperatively with each other.

True champions hit sacrifice fly balls or make assists, rather than hit only home runs or make only showboat slamdunks. Society and civilization absolutely need followers. We can't all and shouldn't all be leaders. Our cultural set point needs to revert to the more primal, tribal idea that we submit to the leader for the good of the tribe, not because we are sissies. We agree to go along. And others in the tribe don't label our subordinate behavior as giving in or take advantage of us for doing so.

According to Pack Leader Psychology theory, it is healthier to admit that not everyone is a pack leader and that it is OK to be a pack member. Many of us would breathe a sign of relief, just as dogs do when an owner takes over as pack leader.

At a deeper level, does our culture's push for us to exemplify strength, independence, and a "wild West" attitude go against our instinctive need for a community? Are these mixed messages causing us a deep-rooted confusion? We are encouraged to make our own way, strike out on our own, and cut the apron strings, but deep inside our tribal instincts are telling us to team up, join a group, and work together. Our society seems to encourage and foster aggression, rather than work to reduce it as the social structure of other animals does.

Fear Causes a Loss of Human Kindness

Just as fear drives so much individual human behavior, I believe that an overreaction to primal fear is adversely affecting society. As a result, we're losing our ability to confront tyranny – both individual and group, which reduces the value of pack structure in promoting a healthy social environment for humans.

Research by cognitive psychologists shows that when a person is frightened, the ability to behave altruistically goes down. When research participants were given a public speaking task and told to walk across a campus to give that speech, they largely failed to stop to help someone in trouble. Their fear response to the public speaking task lead them to abandon their natural "good Samaritan" behaviors of altruism. It is easy to see that if we are unbalanced, fearful, and in fight-or-flight mode much of the time, our ability to reach out and care for others is going to diminish. How much of our current culture's hate politics, conspiracy theories, prejudice, road rage, and "I've-got-mine-screw-you" greediness is driven by primal fear?

I believe that the recent vast increase in personal insecurity and fear of criticism has significant implications for society, politics, charities, and even international relations. Our fear of "the other" is natural and primal. But when our individual insecurities begin to escalate, this social fear becomes magnified, leading to paranoia, radical politics, hate groups, and mob mentality.

Value and Teach Pack Skills

Very few of us learn the characteristics of a balanced pack leader. Just as most dog owners don't step up to become pack leader with their pets, most humans don't learn how to be strong, balanced, assertive leaders with people. I believe that our modern societies have stopped teaching us how to be calm, well-intentioned leaders and well-balanced tribe members.

We seem to be in denial about the natural existence of social hierarchies. Power and dominance are almost never mentioned in psychology textbooks or widely taught psychology theories, but this behavior underlies all human relationships.

I believe this is because dominance has become aligned with those people who use it in service of an unbalanced, manipulative character flaw. In the animal world, dominance is not accompanied by hostility, shame, or abuse. It is just a fact.

We no longer value social hierarchies and many of us don't learn how to play according to the pack rules. Some people do not have a clear understanding of the social cues that communicate that social status, a key element to a smoothly operating social hierarchy. If you growl at me and I don't understand what that means, we'll have a hard time getting along and a very hard time hunting together. A known social hierarchy with a clear pack leader is the first step toward emotional and behavioral health.

Pack Leader Wisdom:
Unstable, unpredictable or nonexistent packs cause fear.

CHAPTER 4

Puppies Learn From the Pack

When I adopted Reilly she was eight months old. Her mother, father, and other adult dogs were living in an outdoor kennel along with Reilly's littermates. She was the last puppy to be sold.

This situation seemed, at first, quite unfortunate. As humans we think, "Gee, she was raised outside without a proper home." Later, I realized this situation was actually a normal pack setting for a dog. Because of Reilly's eight months with her birth pack, she learned healthy dog socialization without the confusing messages of a human owner. I believe this is the reason she is so balanced and why she so easily accepted me as her pack leader. She knew exactly how to be a subordinate pack member once I assumed the pack leader role. She knew how to behave just fine around dogs; I was the one who needed to be trained how to behave around her!

Compare Reilly's situation with how most puppies are raised. They are given to new homes at seven or eight weeks old. This is like shoving a toddler out into the world and saying: "You've learned everything you need. You don't need any more help from your parents. Behave as an adult." As a result of my experiences with Reilly I firmly believe all puppies should be kept with their littermates, as well as a pack of other adult dogs, for much longer. Two months is much too short a time for puppies to learn how to behave. Unfortunately, most breeders don't want the hassle of keeping a litter of rambunctious puppies for months. The food and vet bills are high. And owners also want the joy of having a cute puppy around. So it is unlikely this current system will change, even though it produces unbalanced, unsocialized puppies that are difficult to train.

It makes complete sense that puppies need a complete, strong, balanced pack to instruct them on the proper ways to behave as a dog. A healthy pack in nature would never kick a puppy out at seven weeks old.

Reilly had the good fortune to be born into a pack that instructed her on how to behave as a dog in a pack. She wasn't forced to learn how to be a dog from a human pack that didn't know a thing about how dogs behave.

Pack Leaders Make the Best Parents

NOTE: For those who think this chapter is just for parents… don't stop reading. While this chapter will also help those of you in the midst of being parents, it is intended as a broader illustration of how most of us were raised and how that affects us today. Learning how your parents' childrearing tactics influenced you will help you understand your current behaviors. Chapter Five has corollary lessons in how discipline or the lack of it is used in parenting and throughout life in interpersonal relationships. I tend to use examples from child/parent relationships in the next two chapters, however these lessons apply to nearly all human relationships. You can substitute spouse, friend, or partner for references to child or parent.

It is a simplification, but this is powerful fact: How your parents raised and disciplined you directly affects your internal thoughts of self-acceptance, and those thoughts then influence your behaviors and personality throughout life.

Obviously there have been thousands of books written about parenting and discipline, many with excellent advice. While I certainly do not intend this chapter be the definitive source of parenting information, I do intend to look at parenting from the paradigm of pack leadership and delve into how it influences human behavior. Just as Cesar Millan's training is much more elemental than the typical "sit, stay, heel" obedience class, I hope my parenting advice helps parents and others make a fundamental change in their behavior. Once a parent is a pack leader, the details of how to parent will fall into place. For example, once I was pack leader, I didn't have to teach Reilly specifically not to chew on shoes, furniture, socks, or each object she might come across. She knew that if it was mine, she wasn't to touch it. A parent also should have to spend less time explaining that a child should make his bed or clear the table, because once a parent is accepted as leader, the debates should diminish.

For those who are not parents, keep in mind that these same lessons work in the adult relationships in your life. If I had made it clear from the beginning that I would not tolerate abuse or excessive drinking, my marriages would have been much less dysfunctional.

Fearful Parents, Fearful Children

Unfortunately for the typical modern baby, she is born to two parents with a lot on their minds. They are insecure about their capabilities in general and they may not feel too confident in their parenting abilities. They live alone, so they may not have aunts, grandparents, or friends to turn to for everyday child-rearing advice or day-to-day support. Parents are now parents 24/7 with little relief. Financial worries are a constant concern because they are totally responsible for their own support. And emotionally they have many lingering doubts about themselves and their marriage. They try to compensate by rushing around and doing everything they can for the baby once she is born. They jiggle her constantly, nervously watch her every movement, gasp if she hiccups too loudly, and run to the doctor for every sneeze. The parents were never around babies when they were growing up, so have no clue how to manage this new life they have been entrusted with. Mom feels as if she may have post-partum depression. Baby senses all this anxiety and tension and she begins to worry: "Why are these adults so nervous? Where are my pack leaders?"

Research in neuroscience confirms that our brains have a primal ability to sense fear in those around us. It is a key survival skill and an ability that helps us get along socially. So it's no surprise that infants and children would use this skill in reading the emotions of their parents, especially since the emotional stability of parents is so important to a child's survival. Children are very adept at sensing energy levels in a situation, especially in their birth family, that most crucial pack of their lives.

Sadly, many parents are emotionally insecure and wrapped up in their own self-preservation, busy overreacting to imagined threats, and defending their self-worth. These parents are going to be too self-absorbed to notice a child's fears, concerns, facial expressions, and body language. A child will be able to intuitively discern that a parent is not attuned to his needs, and this will trigger a child's concern and even fear: "Who will protect me if my parents do not seem to be worried about me?" Even parents, as in our scenario, who are doing all the "right" things for a baby in terms of feeding and physical care, can be sending signals to the child that they are not attentive emotionally.

A pioneering researcher in child attachment theory, Donald Winnicott, described two types of parents. The "good enough" parent sets aside his or her need for emotional support and guides the child toward becoming authentic based on the child's needs, not the parent's needs. The "not-good-enough" parent relates anxiously with the child because the parent feels insecure, fearful, and craves emotional support. When parents react to the child primarily out of their emotional needs, the child will fail to recognize her own needs, and may fail to develop an authentic way of being. The child will conform to the parent's expectations, live in a conformist manner, and develop a false sense of self. In the Pack Leader Psychology paradigm, the lack of parental attunement is felt by the child as social rejection by their birth " pack."

Sometimes self-centered behavior is apparent in merely the language people use. During a meeting with an adult substance abuser and her extended family I heard several of the family members describe how the abuser's behavior had been harmful to the abuser. For example, "You have lost your job and your children have been taken from you." However, when the addict's mother's turn came, the language changed. Every phrase was about how her life had been affected by the substance abuser: "I have been hurt by your addiction, my life has been destroyed." This was a clear signal that this parent was not truly concerned about the child's needs. Not surprisingly, this attention-seeking parent made a showboat suicide attempt immediately after the adult daughter went into a rehab facility. This mother's focus was on her own emotional neediness for attention and affiliation, rather than her daughter's. Clearly a pack leader would behave with more selflessness.

Intuitively, it seems quite obvious that signs of anxiety in parents cause anxiety in kids. If a child is surrounded by an unstable pack, without a strong pack leader, it could lead the child to develop low-level fear.

Imagine a family where the mother and father are fighting for dominance. This power struggle makes a child feel he has to be on guard, worried about his own security. He may wonder: "Who will win this fight? Who is the real pack leader? If my parents are preoccupied with fighting each other, will they be able to keep me safe?"

Or consider a family where the parent is drunk or high or just irresponsible and unable to care for the child. When a child grows up watching parents wrestle for control over each other or wrestle with lack of control over substance abuse or anger, this primes the child to have her senses on alert at all times. It establishes a baseline of anxiety with which she faces the world. She may never learn to trust anyone – or herself – because she lacked the feeling of a secure, safe, stable tribe as a child.

Inconsistent parenting can have the same effect. Kids need reliable rules. When parenting is chaotic and unreliable, children are stressed because there are no patterns to follow, giving them the sense that they don't know the rules of the pack.

Then add in the fact that with today's social structure a child may be raised in a single-family home, often without the benefit of an extended family nearby. To a child, this means that if mom or dad isn't emotionally available, no one else is. The resulting feelings of abandonment and aloneness run directly counter to the primal need for belonging and security we all are born with.

I am glad that I was not raised in a family where the parents bickered, constantly fighting each other for control and dominance. I had a sensation as a child that my parents weren't engaged in a power struggle. Parents must learn to unite as a team of pack leaders, develop inner calmness, and project this calm over the family.

Pack Leader Wisdom:
Parents must become pack leaders.

CHAPTER 5

Discipline Keeps the Pack Balanced

One of the fundamental paradigm shifts you must undergo to become a pack leader is the understanding that your dog wants and needs rules, boundaries, and limitations. These guidelines help keep her balanced and, as a result, keep the pack balanced. Without expectations of how to behave and who is in charge, a dog will become anxious and misbehaved. More than love and spoiling, a dog wants structure.

Although how you teach that structure is important. And teach is the key word.

As I was working on this chapter, I took a break to go running, then I played fetch with Reilly as we often do after a run. She is usually very good about dropping the tennis ball into my hands, but lately had wanted to chew on it for a few seconds before releasing. I usually don't have to give her a command to "drop," but I had noticed that now I was giving the command and my voice was sounding irritated. I wanted to grab the ball and pull it from her mouth. If you do this with a dog, however, it will trigger an instinct to protect her "food," so she will instinctively bite and pull away.

Instead, I thought, "Be calm." Instead of immediately giving her the command to drop, I just held my hand out patiently and waited for her to drop her toy. When she didn't drop it, I just waited some more. I relaxed, exhaled, and softened my eyes. I didn't say anything. She looked up at me and I looked her in the eyes. She held my gaze, made one more half-hearted chew, then dropped the ball and looked away submissively. With the next fetch, I did the same, but paused again and added a very calm, deliberate "drop." I immediately realized the difference between my previous commands and this one. This one wasn't a command as much as it was an instruction. The tone was as if I were reminding Reilly of what to do. This is the same tone you'd use to show a preschooler how to tie her shoes or button her shirt: patient and instructional, rather than anxious and punishing. I shouldn't have been surprised when Reilly responded immediately. She stopped her chewing habit on each retrieve and dropped the ball immediately into my hand. Here was another lesson from Reilly: Dogs clearly respond better to an instructional tone, intent, and energy.

This lesson was driven home one day when I did lose my calm and yell at Reilly. I was shocked into stopping when she cringed and cowered, something she had never done before. I immediately realized that my anger frightened her. Yet I didn't want to frighten, but teach. Too many people misinterpret this cowering of a dog as guilt. Instead, the dog is merely trying to appease a threatening human. If you trigger the fight response by yelling, you will only get an instinctive, fearful reaction, not the thoughtful one you had hoped for.

Balanced dogs don't overreact to a situation with an emotional response. As I've seen with Reilly, a balanced dog disciplines another dog matter-of-factly and without drama. It's a bark or a nip and then they're done with that discussion. (Don't look to the average pet dog for this type of behavior, as you're unlikely to find it. They are more likely to behave anxiously, overreacting with aggression or submission.)

Discipline must also be pre-emptive. Reilly's biggest problem is that she becomes too focused on hunting. You can see the switch flip and she will start stalking an animal with intensity. Once her brain has "left the building" she's not focused on heeling or listening to me.

My job as a trainer is to prevent her from getting into this hyper-alert situation and keep her mind on me and walking on the leash. If I don't do that then I must snap her out of her focus so that she can actually learn, work, and obey. If I let her get too wound up it is much more difficult to get her refocused.

What helps keep me calm is that when Reilly does something I don't like I remind myself that dogs rarely misbehave out of willfulness. They don't chew on the couch to make us angry – so we shouldn't become angry. Humans tend to see dog misbehavior as disobedience, as if the dog consciously chooses not to obey us. Sadly, most people are unbalanced enough to be threatened by this perceived disobedience, as if the dog is not respecting the owner's rank. Dogs misbehave for a variety of reasons, but it's not usually a willful disrespect of power. (Remember that dogs want leadership.)

It's amazing what Reilly learns even when I am not consciously teaching, which just proves that discipline is about guiding, not punishing. When I run with Reilly I often go to a place where she can safely run off the leash. She gets more exercise and I can run without the worry of a dog at my side. We occasionally run on a golf course at a local university. When a maintenance vehicle does appear on the road, I call Reilly back to my side. When the truck passes, she is allowed to run free again. I never consciously taught Reilly this by teaching her a "car" command. This situation also only happens once every few months, so even if I had taught it, it is not a skill she practices regularly. But she learned it anyway. We were running one winter morning and the snow banks at the side of the road were eight feet high. As I rounded a corner, a truck appeared suddenly. Reilly was ahead of me and the truck was approaching fast. Before I could act, Reilly saw the truck, turned on a dime, and headed back toward me. Once again, Reilly showed me the truth: Just consistently demonstrate to a dog the behavior you want and she will respond.

Intriguingly, Reilly has translated this lesson to bikes as well. She turns and comes trotting back when she sees a bike approaching.

Once you accept the Pack Leader Psychology paradigm, you recognize that teaching obedience to a dog doesn't begin with sit, stay, and heel. It begins with the dog respecting you as the pack leader. Once that is accomplished, commands are easy to teach. Without respect, however, commands like "come" are impossible to teach. When a dog is off leash, that is the true test of your authority. You have no leash to enforce your will. The dog comes to you only because she wants to and only because you are the pack leader.

Discipline is Guidance, Not Punishment

Discipline is essential when training a dog and also when dealing with human relationships, from family to work to friends. The need for discipline is everywhere in our lives and is a key element to becoming a pack leader. Unfortunately, I believe many of us have developed a very non-pack leader concept of what discipline involves and this is leading to dysfunctional relationships of all kinds, including poorly raised children who become poorly behaved adults. The need for proper discipline certainly applies to all human relationships, so keep reading even if you are not responsible for disciplining children.

The story of Reilly and the truck illustrates a distinction I believe is very important: the difference between discipline and punishment. In the Western world, our definition of discipline has been corrupted and has taken on the meaning of punishment. These are two separate concepts and it is an important distinction.

In dictionaries, discipline is defined as: "Training that is expected to produce a specified character or pattern of behavior, especially that which is expected to produce moral or mental improvement."

I like the use of the words "training," "expected" and "pattern of behavior." You can't produce a pattern of behavior in the future by following a dog or a child around and waiting to punish every little infraction. You must instruct them on the correct behavior, then expect that they will learn the lesson and repeat the pattern on their own.

The point of this semantic exercise is to define discipline as guidance in how to behave. Discipline is not punishment. In the dog world, when a puppy gets playing too roughly with an adult dog, the adult dog will be patient up to a point, but will nip or growl as if to explain,

"You've taken it too far." The dog doesn't respond just to punish the puppy or to hurt it; it does so to communicate the boundaries of behavior the pack expects.

Establish Rules First

Reilly is the second hunting dog I've owned. I have found that an electronic training collar is helpful when training off leash, as it enforces a command such as "come" when the dog is far away. The collar also has a buzzer function. Once Reilly learned that she got a bit of a nudge if she didn't come when called the first time, this beep is all that is usually needed.

The big caveat with training with an electronic collar is that the dog must know what you mean when you yell, "come." You must have trained this command on a leash or rope first. The dog will learn absolutely nothing from getting the shock if she doesn't know the command first. All she will think is, "I got 'poked' by something and I don't know why." She will become skittish and nervous from being shocked for no reason and you will still not have a dog that comes when you call.

This scenario shows another important rule about discipline. With pets and people, you must educate them on the behavior you expect before you give a command and expect it to be obeyed. You must also model the behavior, guide them as they are learning, and react when they knowingly disobey. Discipline is about explaining what you expect so people can perform accordingly. If we never explain what we expect, then we can't be disappointed when others treat us poorly or misbehave. Discipline as guidance teaches.

I am convinced that this rule translates perfectly to many human relationships. I spent many years resentful of an alcoholic husband, but I never once said, "Your drinking so much is disrespectful to me, it is unsafe and unhealthy, and our relationship would improve if you stopped." I never explained how I felt and established a boundary. I expected him to be a mind reader and respond accordingly. No surprise when he didn't. In hindsight, I realize that the divorce was a type of punishment, although without any previously set guidelines of behavior.

Obviously, parents must explain and set the rules. When a child is a certain age, explain how you expect a clean bedroom: "The clothes must be put away, the bed made, the toys in the toy box, the books on the desk." And explain why: "Clothes don't get wrinkled when they are hung up and you can wear them again. You won't trip on your toys and your books won't get ruined." Then kids will know why they should clean their rooms.

Remember, if you are "shocking" your child with commands for no reason, he is not learning anything. Without establishing the rules and boundaries first, discipline can't become guidance, but is just punishment. And when you punish for no reason, the child only learns that you are unreasonable. What smart child will follow an unreasonable pack leader? What child would respect a pack leader who doesn't offer respect in return?

Punishment Is Felt as an Attack

When I discipline Reilly I make a concerted effort to be physically and emotionally serene. I give commands in a monotone, but with strong authority and intention. I try to send out peaceful, calm energy, rather than anxious energy. If I find myself escalating to anxiety because she isn't obeying, the results are never good. What does my anger and anxiety teach her? That I am fearful and insecure and that she should be afraid of me. Not much learning is going on in that situation – at least not about the lesson I intended to teach her.

When you beat a dog in irrational anger, he is not going to think at all – he'll run away, cower, bark, or bite you – the normal fear responses.

It's not any different with humans. What happens when you use emotionally reactive punishment? When you are yelling, angry, or irritable, a person senses that you are attacking him. What happens when someone feels attacked? Stress triggers the primal fight-or-flight response. When the sympathetic nervous system is aroused, the thoughtful brain shuts down. Not much thinking will go on. When you punish in anger, a person will react to your fear with his own fear.

These lessons from parents are especially powerful because a vulnerable child is at its caregivers' mercy for emotional support and physical survival. Comments parents make can feel, at some level, very destabilizing. So when a child feels threatened by judgment – "You should be embarrassed" – he quite naturally will respond with fear. Repeated training teaches children that when they feel emotionally threatened in any way they should respond with fear, a very unhealthy response that may also be repeated for a lifetime.

When attacked, children may either push back at you, starting a power struggle, or lash in at themselves in self-blame. These defensive reactions appear to be a way to gather strength and survive what the child perceives as an onslaught of criticism and blame.

Do you really want to have your child feel you are attacking him? He's not going to learn the lesson you think you are teaching. Instead, you reinforce that when he feels threatened he should respond in an unbalanced mode – attack back irrationally or submit passively or go blank with fear. He is going to learn that you are unfair, unstable, and unpredictable. Instead of teaching a child the correct way to behave, you've modeled for him an unhealthy method of behaving that he may repeat for the rest of his life.

One of my friends was recalling how frustrated she was with her son's arguing and rationalizing. She recounted a situation where she was punishing him and he started pointing his finger at her and arguing back. She told him to stop back-talking immediately or he would lose a month of video game privileges – his favorite activity. But he didn't stop; he kept on yelling and arguing. My friend raised the punishment to two months of no video games, but her son would not back down.

With her anger, my friend had clearly triggered her son's "fight" response. He later admitted that he felt he "couldn't" stop, despite the threatened consequences, a self-aware assessment for a pre-teenager. And he was right. He hadn't developed the emotional maturity – and some people never do – to back away from a fight. He believed his only response was to fight back. He felt pressured by what he perceived to be an attack by his mother and he had difficulty backing down.

Be Calm to Get a Calm Reaction

The most obvious reason not to discipline with anger is that it models calm behavior. Think of it this way: If your goal is to teach your child to behave calmly, will yelling, screaming, and threatening him teach this? Just as a dog grows more anxious when you yell, "no, no, no," a child will sense your anxiety and grow more anxious himself. He certainly won't learn much at that point.

Your lack of emotional reactivity shows that you, as the parent, choose how you respond and proves you can't be manipulated by your child's emotional demands and behaviors.

An angry, frustrated response clues the child (or your spouse or partner) in that he has power over you, that he can control and manipulate you. Every time you react with emotions, a child discovers he can provoke an emotional response in others. And what a confusing message the child learns from a parent's emotionally laden discipline. He learns that he is shameful, but also powerful. He learns that emotions can be used to dominate, manipulate, and control.

These lessons, culled from millions of daily interactions with parents, shape a child's interactions with people for the remainder of his life. Children learn their behaviors have the power to make people anxious and upset. They intuit that what they do and say causes other people to react. Different personality types draw different conclusions from this information, as you'll learn later in this book.

Untether Shame and Discipline

After I applied the Pack Leader Psychology paradigm to people, I examined my parents and their parenting skills. They certainly did many things correctly, mostly related to teaching us to be book smart. My siblings and I got an abundance of music lessons and church camps and museum vacations. Yet if they did all these "good" things as parents, why is it I grew up to feel so dumb, so worthless, so much a hapless pawn of other people's control? I knew I wasn't alone in these feelings, yet why do so many people in society today have such feelings of low self-esteem? I could not accept that this was the result of an upbringing by emotionally balanced parents. A balanced dog living in a balanced pack does not feel worthless. Reilly is a proud, strong dog with no insecurities. I began to wonder how we could raise more children with those same pack leader characteristics.

It seems that for a variety of reasons, including social, cultural, and religious messages, most people in Western society today are raised with messages of shame. Our parents almost certainly played a large role in planting the seeds of self-shame. I came to understand that the way that so many parents discipline fosters feelings of low self-worth and high self-blame in their children.

I was raised in the 1960s when a certain style of parenting was popular. "You should be ashamed of yourself," was a common statement and underlying theme in my childhood despite the fact that I was tremendously well behaved. How could I not feel rejected by my parents – and by myself – by these statements? Obviously, it very directly communicated that I should feel unworthy and shameful.

Of course, I now recognize that this shame-based style of parenting could be considered a manipulative and controlling way of managing children. My parents played on my natural desire to please and seek approval by withholding their love and affection as a way to ensure my compliance. As I discovered later, this pattern played out in many relationships in my life, with a more dominant person using my own need for approval to keep me submissive. I sent signals that I was eager for belonging and could be manipulated to achieve that goal, then did all the work myself, cowering and groveling. While it may seem harsh to make the comparison, I now recognize the parallels between a parent who intimidates with covert control and an abuser who intimidates with overt violence.

When my parents reacted with expressions of disappointment and shame to my natural outbursts and misbehaviors I learned that other people held the key to my self-worth.

This demand for perfection meant I learned at an early age I was defined by my parents and other adults. I believe telling children to be humiliated and embarrassed teaches them that others hold a powerful axe over their emotional head: Others can judge you, find you lacking, and reject you. And if others wield what seems like such a powerful axe, we quickly learn that if we can manage other people and keep the axe of criticism from dropping, we can manage our sense of self-worth along with the possibility of a rejection by others. We may learn to use unhealthy behaviors to reduce our fears, then repeat these behaviors for a lifetime, reinforcing habits with each repetition.

If, instead, my parents' goal had been to teach me that a certain behavior was morally, socially, or ethically wrong, then the discipline would not have been freighted with such emotional baggage. The discipline would have been about the fact that I did something wrong, not that I was shameful.

As humans, we tend to escalate many conversations to the "punishment" or "command" level. We associate discipline with negative emotions, believing that punishment should be used to provoke fear. Discipline ought to be used to express that the behavior was not appropriate, not that the person was "bad."

Contrast this with how I train Reilly. I often use no words, relying instead on a look, a quick hand gesture or even just calmly ignoring her. At most I give a calm, "no." In contrast, an unbalanced dog owner might scream, "bad dog!" This is shame-filled, anxiety-filled punishment, not educational guidance.

Unfortunately, most people discipline both dogs and children with emotions – usually fear, anxiety, frustration, anger, humiliation, disappointment, and shame. Especially shame.

What lessons do children learn when their parents are emotionally reactive during discipline? They learn powerful lessons about self-worth, manipulation, lack of self-compassion, and lack of compassion for others. If parents react with shame, we learn we are shameful. If parents react with disappointment, we learn we can disappoint others. If parents react with judgment, we learn others have the power to judge us and reject us.

This points out the problems with another common message my parents used: "What would the neighbors think?" I was raised to behave in ways my parents felt were acceptable to their friends, neighbors, and the country club members. It was drilled into my head that my behavior reflected on my parents' reputation.

Avoiding the emotion of embarrassment in front of their peers seemed to be the primary concern for my parents. I began to wonder if shame-based discipline stems from the fact that most parents are themselves insecure, unbalanced, and look to others for approval. So as we continue down this road we can see that if parents are preoccupied with their own emotional needs and fears, perhaps lashing out at the child in their disciplining efforts, the child may learn merely to conform as a way of gaining the parents' approval, love, and security. What gets lost in the equation is the child's self-approval, self-love, and self-respect.

Conformity Leads to Loss of Authenticity

Beyond the use of shame in discipline, conformity and the loss of authenticity begin early and are taught with the best of intentions. Well-meaning parents can take a spontaneous, curious, vulnerable child and quash much primal authenticity in some fairly benign-appearing ways.

Imagine a typical scenario: A child falls, is hurt slightly, and begins to cry. How do parents usually respond? Often with pat phrases and clichés that are intended to reassure the child, such as, "You're not hurt that bad. You'll be fine."

However, from another viewpoint, these phrases are very dismissive of the child's felt experience.

Contrast that with a response in which the parent attempts to accurately reflect the child's experience. With an older child, you can ask: "How do you feel?" With a younger child: "Did that hurt? Did it scare you when you fell?" Note that these are questions, not statements. They recognize the pain but also address a deeper, primal sensation: fear. That is really what the child is crying about – he is frightened by the fall. Reflective listening attempts to help the child understand, feel, and manage his own experience, rather than insert the parent's interpretation and disallow the child's feelings.

Another way parents inadvertently engage in dismissive behavior is as a way to "build self-esteem." For example, say your daughter says the painting she created isn't very good. You disagree, pointing out its qualities. This may seem as if you are building up your child's self-esteem.

But what you are actually doing is ignoring your daughter's thoughts and feelings. You are denying her opinion, demeaning her authentic voice, and destroying her faith in her own opinions and emotions.

A better response is to ask questions or reflect the child's feelings and responses back to her. For example, "Sounds like you aren't satisfied with the painting. What would you change about it?" Then allow the child to elaborate and ask further questions. This encourages her to come in closer touch with her feelings and her ability to express them, experience them, and learn from them. Disagreeing with her, while it may seem supportive, is damaging in the long run.

When adults don't honor a child's feelings, or correctly interpret facial expressions or body language, the child may fail to learn about her inner self. Even with infants researchers have found that the best parents mirror the baby's emotions first before they reassure. If the mother only comforts, the child may not learn to connect his experiences and emotions. When parents fail to recognize a child's true concerns and fears, the child learns to dismiss those feelings as unworthy. And if a person ignores her feelings – that most intrinsic essence of our personhood – as unimportant, what is left of the self?

The cascade of harmful lessons continues. The child tempers her authenticity in an effort to be acceptable to the parents' expectations. Out of fear, she loses the ability to communicate honestly and directly. Because she doesn't feel heard and valued, she feels misunderstood and ignored, devalued and underappreciated. It is not difficult to see how low self-worth and lack of self-awareness might arise.

And on it goes: If a child is unable to identify his emotions, he may also learn it is unacceptable to express them. If he isn't allowed to be a little upset, when he becomes anxious he may resort to an extreme response: get violent, throw a tantrum, scream. Or he may deny all emotions, withdraw, or become depressed.

Teaching kids to ignore their own emotions may also teach them to ignore the emotions of others. Social learning suffers, as these children fail to consider social nuances that are key to getting along with others, such as how to join a play group, how to respond to social cues, how to sense the reaction of others to your behavior, and how to interpret social feedback.

A child who lacks social intelligence may lack the ability to correctly perceive emotional threats, a deficit that has major implications throughout adulthood. Many inappropriate behaviors arise because a person mistakenly interprets behaviors as threatening or demeaning.

A lack of empathy between parent and child teaches that others know best and that they know you better than you know yourself, leading to feelings of powerlessness, inadequacy, and a loss of self-identity. When older, a child may then submit to the control and dominance of others, leading to dependent and weak relationships. He may learn to feel safe only when other people are controlling him and informing him of the "correct" opinion. Other personality types may learn to push back against this control, resent it and manage it with manipulation, dominance, or withdrawal.

Many parents also feel directly threatened by the uniqueness and individuality of their children. They try to force children to conform to their views, to fit their mold. Consequently, kids learn harmful lessons, including a lack of authenticity. Children discover they are accepted only when they do what adults expect of them. When children experience what is called conditional positive regard, they learn to abandon their true feelings and intuitions. They learn that only certain parts of them are OK, such as the part that earns good grades or wins the softball game or is quiet and polite. The parts that are silly or creative or unathletic or emotional are not as good.

These parental messages that dismiss a child's authentic self may also teach that everyone must share the same viewpoint. The child may fail to develop feelings of empathy or understanding that others have different ideas, emotions, and needs. This sense that others should be exactly like us may lead to big trouble in relationships. We may expect that our partner or friend should understand us completely, believe as we do, and act as we do. If he or she acts independently, it feels like a rejection of our very self, a criticism of our views and being – and hence a primal threat. You can see how these lessons in self-shame from parents set a fundamental worldview in motion in children affecting them and their relationships and behaviors for a lifetime.

I also am intrigued that these ideas all connect back to the concept of pack hierarchy. If we feel shameful and inadequate, we intuitively know we are weaker in our pack rank. If we are weak, we certainly can't be pack leaders or even well-balanced subordinate members. If we are then forced to act as pack leaders, perhaps because our parents are abdicating the role, we believe we aren't up to the job and anxiety results.

I'm sure that parents who discipline with shame and punishment are afraid that the child will never learn to behave. Perhaps they envision a 25-year-old throwing tantrums (and some do!). This fear drives their urgent attempts to permanently and instantly correct a child, which is, of course, an impossibility.

It may help to remain calm if you remind yourself that a tantrum thrower's actions do not reflect on you.

Parents must remain in control of their emotions and must not be reactive to a child. We must strip our human disciplining rituals of shame and humiliation. Discipline should only communicate that the child's behavior is wrong – a fact – not that you are humiliated, disappointed, ashamed, or embarrassed by his actions.

If you find yourself disciplining with anger and frustration, ask yourself if it is mostly because you are embarrassed by your child's actions. Think of a time your child acted out in the grocery store or at the family reunion – what was your main concern? Was it teaching your child how to act calmly and appropriately? Or were you more concerned with what other people thought about you as a parent? If your goal was to teach calm behavior, were you modeling that same behavior? Or were you exhibiting anxious anger and frustration? Also, did you assume the child was misbehaving out of disrespect and feel threatened by this?

I heard a story about a 10-year-old boy who had a tantrum, ran into his room, and violently shook his bunk bed. He did not hurt anyone or lash out at anyone, just went to his room and expressed his emotions in a very strong way. His grandfather yelled at him to stop, getting very angry, and saying the child was disrespecting him. However, a step back into the mode of an observant, calm pack leader would have illuminated the following about the situation. The family was in the midst of a very chaotic move at Christmas time. His divorced mother had recently gotten pregnant with a fourth child then hurriedly married the child's father, her second husband. She then quickly got divorced right after the baby was born. In a variety of ways, the mother was not a balanced pack leader. Compassion would have permitted a new perspective. The child was not acting out just to make people mad. He was frightened. Things were chaotic in his young life and he didn't know what to think or feel. He felt as if no one strong was in charge and that fact is upsetting to a child. He was likely feeling fear, but had learned only to express that fear as anger.

What would have calmed the situation and child more, an adult's anger or empathy? Parents or not, we could all remind ourselves regularly that adding anxiety to a situation like this rarely helps. Perhaps responding with understanding and reflective listening are better choices with upset children.

Reflective listening also teaches a child to recognize and process emotions he is feeling. However, our traditional reward and punishment method of parenting implies that a child is naturally unruly and disobedient and requires training to be otherwise. So we teach the child to listen, not to his internal cues, but to his parents who "always know best." Like it or not, we set our children up to grow dependent on someone else to tell them what they are feeling and whether or not they are acceptable.

I know that many people will immediately think, "But we have to judge children and make them ashamed of their behavior or they won't learn." But do we? Sure, social conformity is generally a good thing in all social animals. We need what sociologists call social shunning to help teach appropriate behaviors: No killing, no stealing, be respectful, be charitable to others, etc. However, parents would do well to remember that we are all born with very strong desire for group acceptance that drives us to behave in socially acceptable ways and get along with others.

Research clearly shows that infants of just a few months old will react with concern and may even start to cry when they hear another baby's cries of distress. Toddlers will share toys and will express caring for the pain expressed by others. Reciprocal behavior is innate in humans and other animals.

I didn't have to teach Reilly to want to be with her pack and please her pack leader, and I don't believe we need to teach children this desire either. We certainly must teach children the proper behaviors we expect as a society, but we don't need to teach them the desire to belong. They will be sufficiently shamed when they learn that what they did was inappropriate. Children don't need additional helpings of humiliation as encouragement to fit in.

I now strongly believe that this use of shame-laden discipline is the root of much of human anxiety. This one parenting technique may be causing much of the insecurity now rampant among the last few generations.

Discipline Immediately and Honestly

Anyone who has successfully trained a dog knows that you must react instantly when you see your dog start to consider misbehaving. The microsecond that the dog's attention wanders off to that poodle across the street, you have to correct him or the opportunity is missed. You have to stop misbehavior as it happens, not later.

As I learned, honest communication is best if it is done immediately after an event. Just as a dog does not wait 20 minutes to nip a puppy for misbehaving, we become stronger pack members and pack leaders when we respond quickly, rather than allowing the situation to linger and worsen.

When disciplining, a prompt response does not mean it can't be calm and instructional. If the situation has escalated to anger and punishment, then no learning is going to happen. Of course, when people become angry or frustrated, this is when they may snap back, offering irrational punishment, rather than helpful guidance. You'd be best to wait until later when you can be calm.

Perhaps parents should be the ones taking the timeouts.

Get Them to Think

Every teacher knows the best way to teach a child something is to get her to think out the answer for herself. When I was a child my parents wouldn't just tell me an answer, such as how to spell a word. I was told, "If you want to remember how to spell a word, look it up." And they were right. The act of getting the dictionary and looking up the word made me remember the spelling better than if someone had gift wrapped it and given it to me. That learning process isn't "thoughtfull." The correct spelling never is imprinted in the mind, because it went right from the ears to the pencil.

This same lesson works for dogs, children, and the troublesome people in your life. If you want to teach them your rules, you have to make them think for themselves. Explaining why they should do something engages their brain and helps them learn.

When I was teaching Reilly new behaviors, I could at times imagine the gears turning in her head. For example, when I taught Reilly to not charge the door, I could reconstruct the thinking process going on in her head. "Ah, she is standing in front of the door as if she owns it. She doesn't want me near the door when she is in the door. She is the boss and I don't want to offend the top dog. So I shouldn't go near the door." By allowing Reilly to choose her behavior, I was forcing her to think, and this helped her learn.

But what do most people do when their dog is charging the door? They grab the dog's collar and drag her back. When you drag the dog back by the collar, she hasn't been forced to think at all. In fact, her attention is even more firmly focused on getting at the door. The dog isn't learning anything new, but merely repeating the same behavior it was doing with even more force.

Kids Question Rules, Not Authority

Just as puppies play roughly until they are growled at, children will test rules and boundaries. It is a natural part of how they learn. Parents must expect this and react calmly. Parents should recognize that when a child pushes the limits, he is testing merely those limits.

What happens, though, when an insecure parent is at the helm? I believe the parent interprets testing of the rules as a challenge to her fundamental authority. The parent misperceives the situation, viewing the testing as a personal threat or criticism and an attempt to usurp power.

What is likely to happen? The hammer comes down with proclamations such as, "Because I said so," and "Just do as I say." These responses are exactly like a dog snapping and snarling because he is afraid. That's right. Afraid. Is it possible your angry, emotional reactions are signs that you are anxious because you feel you are being attacked as a parent? You may believe your children are somehow threatening you, so you fight back. Would a secure, balanced pack leader feel threatened by a puppy?

A fearful overreaction by a parent does not improve the learning aspect of discipline. What do kids learn when parents say, "Go clean your room...because I said so"? Not much about why they should clean their room.

Significantly, they do learn a very powerful, instinctive lesson that the parent is operating from an insecure, fearful position. "Because I said so," is a response based on your fear – fear that the child is testing you and you are not up to the challenge. Kids learn that when they question you it is scary for you, that you feel they are questioning your authority. Your fearful response does not provide guidance on correct behavior, it is only "barking" for no reason.

Do you think your overreaction cements your position as pack leader? Do you think they will stop questioning you when you respond with a fear-based command? Just the opposite, especially as they reach the teenage years and they are searching for their route to independence. They will have had years of learning you have a weakness they can exploit.

Good discipline is respectful. "Just do as I say," doesn't earn you respect and it does not respect the thoughtfulness of your child.

A pack leader will remain calm at all times, even when a child is testing limits. Certainly children should obey you just because you are the parent, but if a parent does not first act respectfully and earn respect, the child will correctly interpret this response as unbalanced. Kids are generally much more intuitive than adults and are observing your behavior very closely. They will much more quickly sense the fear at the root of irrational and inconsistent punishment, compared to calm, instructional discipline.

Getting angry also teaches that you have no self-control. Ideally, parents manage their own anger, showing the child by example how to behave, but also disciplining the child for his inappropriate behavior. On the other hand, being passive and letting the child throw a tantrum without a response is also not showing parental pack leadership.

Think again about the dog world. The adult dog knows that the overly playful puppy just doesn't know how far it can go. When it barrels into the adult too hard, the pup will get nipped to show this behavior is too rough. The adult dog knows that the puppy isn't trying to muscle in on the adult's rank in the pack. The adult dog reacts calmly, but assertively, and doesn't overreact in an expression of fear and anxiety.

Sadly, there are cases where dogs are not well socialized to pack rules and don't understand how to correctly discipline puppies. I heard a story about someone with a new puppy who went visit a friend and took the puppy along. During the visit, the puppy was playing with an adult dog when quite suddenly the dog killed the puppy. Everyone was shocked and didn't know what to think. I'm sure what happened is the puppy got playing a bit roughly and the poorly socialized, insecure adult dog mistook this action as a fundamental threat to its power. The puppy was just playing, but because the older dog had never learned how to discipline puppies it overreacted with fatal consequences.

I think one reason that parents get angry and frustrated is because discipline problems seem to come out of nowhere. But do they really? Can you do a better job of expecting problems and even setting up situations that reduce the possibility for misbehavior?

A good dog trainer knows that a key aid in remaining consistent and in control is by blocking unwanted behavior before it happens. Just as a dog owner needs to snap a dog out of his fixation on another dog before an attack occurs, parents need to recognize and forestall bad behavior.

Say, for example, your 11-year-old son has been at his friend's house and they've been gaming and wrestling and being boys for hours. When he comes home, do you think he will be calm? Or do you think he will be amped up and not thinking clearly? Can you imagine he might not be in the right frame of mind to deal respectfully with others? Certainly. This is when pre-emptive parenting works.

Be observant of when your child is too energized, too anxious, too tired, and likely to disobey. Set up rules to deal with the situation before it escalates. Enforce a few minutes of quiet time with no TV or games. Until a dog is calm, he can't comprehend discipline and he isn't allowed to continue with an activity. Same rule for children.

While it is easy to slip into punishment mode, if you sense yourself escalating toward anger or frustration, pause, breathe, and remember your child is looking to you for calm leadership, not anxious reactions. Tell yourself you are likely angry because you feel the child is questioning your authority. Remind yourself it is just a test of the rules, not your fundamental position as parent. Take a breath and remember that by showing your frustration and anger, you are showing your inner insecurity. This is not the sign of a balanced pack leader. The fact is, parenting and pack leading are 24/7/365 jobs.

Be Persistent – Over and Over Again

When I first got Reilly she had never worn a collar or been on a leash. The first time I put them on her she threw a fit. She spun around, wriggled, backed up, and tried like heck to get out of her collar and get away. This temper tantrum was the natural response of an animal being "broken," as horse trainers call it. She was not used to being controlled by a leash or a human. The tantrum was a wild animal's fearful response to the unknown: "I don't like the feel of this leash and I don't know what will happen." But most dogs will calm down fairly quickly if you persist calmly. They will realize it doesn't hurt and their fear will subside. It usually takes just a minute or two before the dog wears herself out and learns she can't win. You must be patient and finish what you started. If the dog wins, she learns she can win!

Dogs throw temper tantrums, just as humans do, and both do it for the same reason – out of fear and as an attempt to control the person trying to discipline them. If you back down and let the dog triumph, he knows he has dominated you. With dogs, children, and the adult tantrum-throwers in your life, you must not back down. This is a time to practice your best calm, assertive, patient responses. You'll be surprised at how soon someone will calm down once he realizes you won't give in. Responding with anger and frustration to someone else's anger and frustration means you've lost the battle.

Ray learned many times that I would not insist on him behaving correctly and would give in. So he kept throwing tantrums and misbehaving. When I didn't enforce consequences, I taught him that he could succeed in manipulating me with his anger and fits.

Kids learn the same lesson. They will fight back, especially if they are not used to having a pack leader give direction. They may get loud and overreact. Now is not the time to back down. Firmness and resolve are your only possible responses at this point, because if the child gets you to recant, he has discovered your weakness. He has learned how to manipulate you and, consequently, lost respect for you.

Be the pack leader. You are the adult; your patience can outlast a child's, can't it?

Famed horse trainer Monty Roberts says, "If you act like you've only got fifteen minutes, it'll take all day. Act like you've got all day and it'll only take fifteen minutes." This is exactly true with dogs and people. However, most dog owners are rushed and stressed. When the dog starts to misbehave they yell repeatedly, chase the dog, get anxious and tense. This just makes the dog misbehave even more. When a dog gets excited, you, as pack leader, must do the exact opposite and become extremely calm and deliberate.

Just as I wait at the back door with Reilly until she calms down before I let her outside, parents need to learn that pausing calmly and waiting is a good educational tool. Unfortunately, most parents are rushed, stressed, and just want the child to obey right away. You wouldn't beat a dog that didn't learn a command in the first lesson. Be patient when your child is learning, too.

Discipline Is Consistent

Discipline requires consistency. Again, think of discipline as a learning process. What if your child's schoolteacher said one day that 2+2=4, then the next day said that 2+2=6, then 2+2=43. Your child would never really learn the correct answer. Same for behavior rules. If one day it is OK for your son to punch his sister, then don't expect him to restrain from punching her the next day. By not disciplining him you taught him just as valuable a lesson as you will for the next day's reprimand.

And, yes, many of us have seen this come true in spades with dog training. If you let your dog on the couch one time, it is amazing how easily it remembers that incident and expects to get on the couch afterward.

Rules must be applied consistently, fairly, and forthrightly. Arbitrary rules are purely manipulation. I wonder, also, if an inconsistent application of discipline teaches children some very fundamental lifelong lessons. What do kids learn when a parent fails to enforce a command consistently? They learn, of course, they can disregard the parent's commands. This lesson may seem unimportant when it involves not riding the tricycle over the cat's tail or getting into the bathtub before bed. But what about later in life? If children learn, deep down, their mother or father is not an assertive pack leader and this pattern continues over years, they absorb a very scary lesson – that they can't rely on their parent to be secure shelter for the safety they crave. They think, "If my mother can't make me take a bath, is she strong enough to protect me from the dangers that are out there in the world?" And, "If my mother doesn't care enough to be consistent, does she care about me?"

Could this inconsistency in discipline be one of the roots of the "fear of abandonment" that so many people experience throughout their life? Does it lead to children who feel unwanted and unprotected in a primal way that is very damaging to their emotional health? And, as we've all witnessed many times, this type of failure to discipline promptly and consistently often leads to the expected: Yelling, anger, and frustration – energy that signals a fearful, unbalanced parent, not a pack leader. That energy tells the child that the parent knows she doesn't have control of the situation. This is a frightening admission to a child. A pack leader would remain calm and in control of her emotions and the situation, no matter what the child did.

A key part of calm consistency is realizing that the pack leader's job is never done. Your children are watching you every second. This is what is difficult about parenting – not the diapers or the spit-up or the endless carpooling. It is the 24/7/365 mindfulness that is required of parents. Always remember that your child is hanging on your every action and word, not only learning how to behave, but watching intently and intuitively for any small sign that you are not a competent, selfless leader in charge of every situation. Your child desperately wants you to be in charge. He needs the security of knowing you can take care of him every minute of the day.

No matter what your natural personality style, you owe it to your children to behave as a pack leader around them. Those who don't have children have an option of choosing to become a pack leader or not. Parents don't have that choice.

But don't despair if you haven't been consistent in the past. Kids want stable pack leadership so much that they will "live in the moment" and will quickly forget your past mistakes.

Discipline Is Not Control

Reilly taught me that discipline is not control. Trying to physically restrain a dog or control its behavior is nearly impossible, especially with a large dog. Even a medium-sized dog can easily overpower most humans within seconds if it wants to. Being a good pack leader to a dog isn't about being more powerful physically. A dog is much more consistently obedient when it is choosing to behave, rather than being coerced or bribed or controlled. The same should be true of being a parent to a child or in an adult relationship.

It is easy to think that disciplining a young child is about controlling unwanted behavior. You don't want him standing up in the grocery cart, so you push him down in the seat. However, this sort of physical or direct control should be limited to emergencies. After a certain age, a child can understand that you want her to sit down in the cart.

Giving an instruction to a dog should be a matter of fact; it's not an argument or a debate. It's not a dominating demand or a submissive request. It's not controlling or needy.

If discipline is about teaching and guiding, the best way to teach is to let the child learn for herself. Pushing her down in the grocery cart doesn't help the child learn. If she chooses to sit down and you praise her for that behavior, she will learn to make that choice, rather than always have her parent make the choice for her. As a parent, you show her the limit: Children do not stand up in a grocery cart. She then chooses how to respond.

The larger issue here is that pack leaders earn respect not by dominating and controlling. Actually, the pack grants authority to those who have the confidence to lead, not control others. Reciprocal, healthy, positive relationships do not involve control.

Earning Respect Takes Time

It takes time, commitment, and self-control to discipline your child this way. But the stakes are high. If you don't discipline calmly and consistently, the child learns he cannot trust you. Without trust, there is no respect, and both are essential elements of healthy relationships of all kinds.

Remember that children don't really want to usurp your role as pack leader. They don't want to weaken your authority. In fact, research has shown that kids want to trust and respect their parents – just as all of us social humans feel safer when we can trust those around us. The good news is that developing a trusting relationship will make your job as a parent much easier.

If we don't make this fundamental change in how we raise our children, future generations will grow up as they are growing up now – to be constantly anxious and scanning their interactions with others for possible criticism, or seeking to please or dominate others to gain judgment-free acceptance, or avoiding and downplaying their emotions and needs. None of these behaviors or personalities is what we want for our children.

However, if we educate and guide, rather than punish and shame, we accomplish better results with dogs and humans.

Discipline Is Respectful to You and to Those around You

One goal I had when writing this book was to attempt to educate people about the damage caused by unbalanced behavior. As I was writing, I realized that the best way to break the cycle was to educate parents about how to become balanced pack leaders so that they would be more likely to raise balanced children. Unstable, controlling parents raise emotionally insecure and needy children who become adults and repeat those same behavior patterns with their children. Each generation of children we raise who are shamed and feel the need to seek affection in submissive or aggressive ways leads to marriages based on power struggles and to parenting skills based on unhealthy domination and punishment. Parents have a responsibility not only to themselves, but also to their spouses or partners and to their children to do the best they can to become pack leaders, so they can provide calm, assertive guidance to their families.

A pack leader is selfless when it comes to the emotional and physical needs of loved ones.

Pack Leader Wisdom:
Do not discipline with shame.
Discipline is guidance, not punishment.
Discipline with respect.

· ·

The Pack Leader Psychology paradigm offers a framework to help people simply and easily understand human behavior with the hope of turning the tide toward improved social harmony. I realize the Pack Leader Psychology paradigm is completely new and untested, but it is anchored in simple, evolutionary logic that has worked in the animal world for millions of years. Why question nature? These concepts of the importance of the pack, social hierarchy, and the need for a pack leader are the foundation for a much more detailed paradigm that explains a wide range of human behaviors.

Now that you've learned about the parallels between the animal and human worlds and how we have diverged in unhealthy ways from the primal traditions of social groups, we'll move on to learning how to spot individuals who exhibit behaviors that are a result of these unhealthy social patterns.

· · · · · · · · · · · · · · · · ·

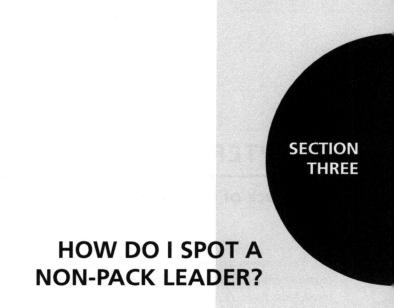

HOW DO I SPOT A
NON-PACK LEADER?

CHAPTER 6

Lack of Leadership Causes Fear

Reilly seems to have no fear. She runs full speed through the woods, launches herself into lakes, clambers over rock piles, and dives headfirst into woodchuck holes. It is a joy to watch her live her life with no hesitation in her thoughts or actions. Anyone who saw Reilly hunting would say unequivocally that she is brave.

However, fear is one of the most primal emotions in all animals because it is fundamental to survival. Without fear, an animal would quickly become lunch for another animal. In social animals, we have also evolved with a strong ability to sense fear and uncertainty in others. If you can react quickly to a signal of fear, you have a better chance of surviving. Think of yourself as part of a herd of zebra on the African savannah. If another zebra spooks, you'd be well advised to heed the warning immediately and react quickly. That warning could mean a lion is stalking through the grass. Your ability to stay with the herd will help you avoid the lion's bite. I see herds of whitetail deer nearly every morning. If the tail goes up on one deer or one stomps its hoof, the rest pay attention. When a beaver thumps its tail on the water and dives, the others also head underwater.

All animals – including humans – have common, primal reactions when they feel threatened. An animal will usually react in a certain order of behaviors when a threat is detected:

1. *Freeze or Avoidance: It will stop moving, on guard for noises and movement that might signal a threat. This freezing is a survival advantage in the wild, because predators are less likely to detect immobile prey.*
2. *Flight: If the threat becomes real, the animal is next likely to flee.*
3. *Fight: The animal defends itself physically if needed.*
4. *Fright: Recent research has shown all mammals also experience tonic immobility or a severe "fright" after they have been attacked. This*

may enhance survival because a predator may loosen its grip if it thinks its prey is dead, giving the victim a chance to escape. Predators have an instinctive urge to attack something moving, so the fright state may lull the predator into switching off the attack mode. This is usually called "playing possum."

Think about what happens when a wild animal is confronted or cornered: If possible it may choose to act weak and nonthreatening or try to run away. When forced, a dog may bark a warning and may eventually perform a bluff charge. The fight response occurs throughout the animal world mainly in life-or-death situations. Animals know that fighting is the last option to choose because it is the most likely to cause injury.

Unbalanced Dogs Become Fearful

A balanced dog can choose which response to make from its primal arsenal, alternating between aggression, flight, or avoidance and will only use these reactions when truly threatened. However, an unbalanced dog will react with fight, flight, or avoidance in inappropriate situations. She might react at an inappropriate level or far sooner than a secure dog would.

But what causes an unbalanced dog? I believe most domestic dog misbe-haviors are the result of an animal that feels alone and without a pack. The dog feels she has no one to trust because her owners aren't behaving properly according to accepted pack rules. Quite simply, the owners don't understand the proper hierarchy. The dog may be forced into the role of pack leader because her human owners have abdicated the role. Dogs know someone must step up to the job of pack leader; this job cannot be left vacant. So a dog will reluctantly assume the role, despite the fact this dog may not be a natural pack leader. In this new human pack, she is trying her darndest to lead these clueless humans who don't know how to play by the (dog world) rules.

Aggression Is an Unhealthy Fight Response

Animal shelters are full of problem dogs that are chronically aggressive with other dogs and people. These dogs may be up for adoption because they do not know the proper way to project strength, so they substitute bully behavior. In contrast, a dog that cowers in the corner may be emotionally unhealthy, but is unlikely to cause the owner to send her to the animal shelter or to a dog trainer.

The good news is that even dogs bred and trained to fight other dogs prefer to return to a balanced mode when they can. Pit bulls rescued from NFL player and convicted dog fighter Michael Vick's kennel were rehabbed so that they played with other dogs. Even fighting dogs don't want to stay in fight mode if they don't have to. They know that fear responses are meant to be used only in survival situations, not as a daily mode of behaving.

Unfortunately, in America we have a much more positive attitude about the word "fight" than the other three words. Our culture places a high value on winners and fighters. We think any other response is a sign of weakness, and weakness is a negative behavior. Just the opposite is true in the animal world. I've seen this play out myself with wild animals. Where I live Reilly will occasionally find and chase a coyote. Interestingly, the coyote have never tried to fight her, despite the fact they could do serious damage to her. They run away every time. They know even if they "win" a fight with another animal, they risk getting injured, which in the wild may be a death sentence. It is the better part of valor to tuck tail and run – and live another day.

Submission Is an Unhealthy Flight Response

The flight response shows up in dogs that are scared of many normal situations, are unsure and anxious around strangers, and are timid in new situations. Some dogs are even afraid of things like the click of an oven being turned on. Flight-oriented dogs tend to cower and hide, and are overly anxious and submissive. Fears can trigger an irrational phobia of a situation or thing, or a compulsion about an object. In an extreme example, Cesar Millan trained one Rhodesian ridgeback who chewed on rocks until his mouth bled.

My first dog was a Vizsla and so when Cesar's TV show featured this breed I made sure to watch. The dog on the show was extremely timid, startled by every noise and movement, ready to flee at all times. It was the most overly submissive and flight-oriented dog I had ever seen. The good news is that Cesar quickly gave the dog confidence so that it could live a normal life.

The diagnosis for nearly all poorly behaved dogs is fairly simple. These dogs need their owners to take over as pack leader to alleviate their insecurities and fears. In addition, if aggression is directed at other dogs, the dog needs to be socialized as to the correct way to behave.

A balanced and properly socialized dog will behave appropriately in whatever situation you place it. Reilly is not afraid of noises or people, isn't worried about a car ride, and isn't afraid of the vet, because she trusts me to take care of her and because she doesn't have a wagonload of anxieties and phobias due to living in a pack without a leader.

It is remarkable to watch this change happen with dogs. The minute a strong pack leader arrives, the dog visibly calms down and is quite content to abdicate her role as reluctant pack leader, and give up her anxious, unbalanced behavior.

Sadly, most humans today do not understand this very primal fact and allow their pets to dominate. Because they don't understand dog language and behavior, owners let their pets challenge and usurp their supremacy as pack leader.

Dogs do not want to live in an unbalanced state – it is mentally draining. They are unhappy and anxious in their unfamiliar role as pack leader and quickly revert to a more calm, balanced state when they are allowed to.

A Pack Leader Does Not Under-react or Overreact; She Just Reacts

As I was learning more about animal behavior, I began to make many connections between the dog and human worlds. I had many "a-ha" moments while watching Cesar's TV show. One eye-opener came when Cesar described a dog as "in the red zone." This is his phrase for a dog that feels threatened and has flipped into attack mode. The dog becomes so focused it is nearly impossible to snap him out of it. Picture a dog lunging, barking, snapping, eyes lasered in on the target like a killer. Picture a dog wanting to fight to the death.

When I saw this I had an insight: Humans also go into the red zone. I had experienced being the "prey" in a red zone attack many times. My ex-husband Ray went into a red zone every time he flew into a rage and became violent. Anyone who has been a victim of domestic violence probably knows a red zone attack is different from a normal argument. Someone in a red zone rage cannot be snapped out of it easily. No matter what rational, logical arguments you make, he keeps attacking. If you ignore and avoid him, he keeps attacking. If you try to leave the scene, he keeps attacking. If you try to placate him and calm him and talk sweetly to him, he keeps attacking. Attacks can be merely emotionally threatening and demeaning or they can involve violence. A red zone attack is an extremely frightening thing to experience, as I can attest. You feel totally helpless, because every response you try is unsuccessful and you can fear for your health or life if the physical violence continues or escalates. The switch has been flipped to "attack" and there seems to be nothing you can do to switch it off. I can now clearly see that this is the fight response gone extreme, gone red zone. (Of course, at the time I didn't realize I had another response other than submission: I could stand up for myself and behave more assertively. More on that later!)

Since Walter Cannon identified "fight-or-flight" behaviors in humans in 1929 we've recognized that people have the same primal response to fear as other animals do. When our senses detect a threat, the signals go to a part of the brain called the amygdala that handles emotional processing. The amygdala sends signals to the hypothalamus, which signals the adrenal glands to release hormones such as epinephrine or adrenaline.

The body instantly responds with physical symptoms, such as increased blood flow, faster heart rate and breathing, and sweating, all preparing the body to quickly flee, fight, or freeze. This process happens at a bio-chemical level so that we are not aware of it, yet is so powerful it allows us to jump instantly out of the way of a runaway car.

These hormonal responses also heighten the emotions. When you feel threatened, your emotions will be on high alert and your emotions can be easily hijacked. If you've ever been in a car accident, you know the sensation of your heart pounding and palms getting clammy after-ward. You may have been quick to anger – did you want to yell at the other driver even if the accident was your fault? Conversely, you may have felt shaky and tearful. You may not have realized you were at the mercy of a primal survival reaction at that moment.

Of course, in modern society we now use our fear response to react almost entirely to emotional threats, rather than physical threats. We tend to respond to imagined danger, rather than real danger. And that imagined danger tends to center on our relationships with others, espe-cially if we feel we are at risk for social exclusion. When we feel victim-ized, rejected, or shamed, this can trigger the fight-or-flight response. How many arguments escalate unnecessarily because people become overwhelmed by their fear response – fighting back when no fight is necessary?

When the fear response is triggered regularly over an extended period of time, these emotions can change physiology throughout the body because we do not get the physical release we used to have when running away from a predator.

Fearful Humans Become Dominators, Submissives, and Avoiders

After my second divorce I read many self-help books and took psy-chology classes. I also spent quite a bit of time observing the behavior of people around me and rethinking my previous relationships. At first I hoped to develop a system that would allow me to spot controlling dominators before they took power over me. I also wanted to root out my accommodating behaviors and stop sending unwanted signals to potential controllers.

I saw control and accommodation caused many problems in relation-ships. I asked myself questions. Why had I chosen to behave in such a pas-sive way? Why were people like Ray so violent and controlling? How had I attracted him into my life? And because I like to think about the big pic-ture: Why did people do this to others? What could be causing so many people to behave in such unhealthy ways? Did humans always have this many problems relating to each other? Was this the natural state of human relationships?

Then one day while running with Reilly, I experienced a flash of insight. I realized that I was just like a dog rolling over and showing her belly to anyone who walked up. I was exhibiting my weaknesses without question to everyone, even unstable, controlling men like Ray who clearly did not have my best interests at heart. I was too trusting and naïve. The word "accommodating" suddenly seemed far too insubstantial for how I was behaving. I was submissive. Much too submissive. I actually cowered like the lowest omega dog in the pack that is happy to receive some scraps from the carcass, pleased that that the pack doesn't beat it up or chase it away.

The terms used in the animal world became much more meaningful to me. I had observed that while dominant and subordinate roles are natural states in dog packs, some domesticated dogs don't behave in well-adjusted ways. When a dog doesn't have a balanced pack leader and feels fearful, it will adopt one of three main behavior modes: overly dominant, overly submissive or overly avoidant.

I immediately made the connection that people, almost universally, behaved in similarly unhealthy and unbalanced ways. Once I recognized this distinction, I could look around at the difficult people in my life and see that they often fell very clearly into one of these three categories. I named people with these behavior patterns quite simply: "Dominators," "Submissives," and "Avoiders."

I feel it is important to clarify that that I am actually not completely comfortable with the use of labels such as these. Using a term like "Dominator" appears to imply that a person is completely defined by and confined to this behavior and that it functions as a personality type. Rather, most people use all three of these behaviors at different times and at different levels. In addition, these labels are not all-or-nothing. People behave on a continuum of Dominating behaviors, for example, from mildly aggressive to violent sociopath. Only the most extreme of these personality types uses one behavior most of the time. However, these labels are much simpler to deal with when writing. While it would be much more accurate to write, "a person who tends to behave with Dominating personality traits," it becomes very cumbersome in a lengthy book. So throughout this book please remember that these terms are shorthand for a behavior or behavior pattern, not a complete description of a person's permanent and complete personality type.

Dominators Prefer a Fight Response

Unbalanced people in emotionally threatening situations react automatically based on their innate personality and socialization. When I looked around at people I knew who were Dominators, I realized they almost always responded with "fight" when they felt threatened. They have the motto: "Attack first." A Dominator personality will generally lash out with an argument, an emotional meltdown, or a cooked up drama. Certainly, the attack does not have to involve violence, but Dominators believe adopting a "tough guy" attitude intimidates most people. They feel powerful – even if it is a false, unbalanced type of power. The fight response is what they feel comfortable with, because they have somehow learned that other responses are signs of weakness. Dominators learned to keep people and their potential criticisms or rejections at bay by attacking and intimidating.

Submissives Prefer a Flight Response

When Submissives feel endangered, they generally choose to "flee" emotionally, to cower, avoid conflict, and to placate. When I labeled myself as a Submissive, it hit me like a gut blow. I had to admit that I had given up my power on a daily basis without questioning why I was doing so. I had automatically acted submissively for four decades as a way to fit in and gain acceptance. When I realized I had, through my own weakness and submission to Ray, brought on the very violence I feared, I got incredibly angry with myself. I had held the keys to gaining power and respect the entire time, yet had handed them to Ray unquestioningly. This insight made me vow to never unknowingly turn over my power to someone else.

It was no surprise, then, that I had felt like a loser most of my life. I came to understand it isn't natural to demean yourself to others. Even dogs know this – cowering isn't natural and it isn't healthy.

Avoiders Prefer to Withdraw

A smaller number of people prefer an Avoider approach. They will shrink from conflict, hide out, or become depressed or anxious because they feel they can't or shouldn't react with fight or flight. They have learned to restrict their primal emotional responses to a limited repertoire. They choose solitude and work and social environments that have minimal human interaction as a way to keep their fear to a minimum.

Avoidant types often become social loners, limiting their contact with people. It's as if these people are opting out of the social hierarchy

– choosing to not fight for a place in the social order. This avoidance behavior is seen in dog training when you begin rehabilitating an unbalanced dog. When an unsure dog doesn't know how to behave in the presence of a more dominant person or animal it will go through a phase where he refuses to make eye contact with the new pack leader. He will turn away and sit down, seeming to ignore the trainer. While this behavior may appear to be calm, the energy level remains tense, showing that the dog is deeply anxious.

Don't Take Kindness for Weakness

The need to establish a social hierarchy is innate in humans, showing up as young as age three in children all over the world. These are skills that we require to live successfully as social creatures. People instinctively want to know who has power.

It appears to me that many of us have become unhealthy and unbalanced in ways that violate the natural social order that kept us mentally healthy for millennia. The cooperation and kindness that we developed to survive as tribes is now being used increasingly to manipulate and control others for individual gain and to grab for a surface level of emotional security.

We seem to have lost the understanding of how to behave in a balanced way, mainly, as I've written, because with our growing population and geographic mobility we have also lost the power of social shunning. It is also because we've seen so many examples of insecure, unstable Dominators, Avoiders, and Submissives. As a result, we've gotten rid of the good aspects of social ranking and mutated other aspects so that our understanding of social hierarchy and correct behavior is now skewed.

My family gives a good example. Once I began to understand my family dynamics, it helped me explain the roots of my own behavior. My maternal grandmother had many Dominator tendencies. She was quite unhappy in her life to the point of being hostile, had many paranoid ideas, and very rarely expressed love or positive emotions. My mother, daughter of this angry, suspicious woman, saw those characteristics and did a U turn. She became extremely caring, kind, loyal, and nurturing, apparently rejecting her mother's lack of those skills. This was a positive reaction, but my mother took it to an extreme. She felt she couldn't stand up for herself or speak out. I now wonder if at times she simmered with resentment because she felt she was taken advantage of. My mother had overreacted to my grandmother's behavior, eliminating signs of assertiveness in her own character, but as a result became unable to stand up for herself even in a healthy way. She got rid of some of the best aspects of assertiveness because she only knew them as part of a package of unhealthy dominance. I, too, was overly submissive, overly generous, overly kind, and loyal. I gave away all my power to the Dominators in my life. A balanced, middle road would have been healthier.

Just as Reilly can run and hunt like crazy and still curl up and be sweet, we must take the best parts of dominance and subordination to fashion our healthiest, most authentic personalities.

Pack Leader Wisdom:
Watch for the primal fear responses of fight, flight, and avoidance.
These behaviors play out as Dominant, Submissive, and Avoidant behaviors.
Fear is the weakest energy.
And weak attracts weak.

CHAPTER 7

We All Want to Be Accepted

When you charge full-speed through life, you are bound to trip once in awhile. This is certainly true with Reilly. Although she is a tremendous athlete, she will, occasionally, stumble. One day she was chasing a squirrel up a tree by my driveway where there is a rock wall. She misjudged the jump off the wall onto the driveway and was moving so fast she fell and actually did a flip and skinned her nose. But since I was heading down the driveway for a run, the stumble and skinned nose didn't slow Reilly down even for a second. She was too eager to go on an adventure to consider how she appeared. Contrary to the typical human response, dogs don't look around to see if someone saw them fall. They don't chastise themselves for their clumsiness.

This self-acceptance is one reason we find dogs so appealing, one of the many lessons we could learn from these smart animals. We like dogs because they don't judge themselves and they also don't judge us.

If you ask people why they like dogs, most will tell you it's because a dog gives them unconditional love. While that is a wonderful thing, it's a sign to me the person is afraid of criticism. Dogs are, of course, very nonjudgmental. They live in the moment and don't hold grudges. This makes them very easy to be around if you are overly sensitive to the possibility someone is judging you.

I certainly love Reilly and enjoy having her in my life, but I don't rely on her to feed my self-worth. I love her solely because she is a smart, athletic, well-balanced dog, not because she doesn't threaten me. I think many people who retreat into lives made up almost entirely of pets have an extreme fear of criticism.

Jon Katz, in his book "The Dogs of Bedlam Farm," writes about what he calls Dog People, including his sister, who seem to cut off relationships with other people and focus entirely on saving and caring for needy dogs. He theorizes it is a way to create a caring childhood these people didn't have. That Freudian-based interpretation may be true, but I'm convinced it is because the dogs create an uncritical family and pack that feels safer than human interactions. These Dog

People are, almost certainly, all very nurturing, Submissive people who are harsh on themselves and unable to establish boundaries against what they perceived to be critical attacks by others. So they go into withdrawal mode, retreating into a life with nonjudgmental animals as a way to avoid criticism.

The More Parts of Ourselves We Reject, the More Important It Is to Feel Accepted

As I stood there crying and bruised, I was shaking from fear and shame. A sheriff's deputy was taking a Polaroid picture of me in my ripped T-shirt and pajama bottoms to show evidence of the bruises on my arm and face. Proof that my husband, Ray, had beaten me up.

Ray was handcuffed, screaming, and struggling with the other deputy in the doorway. Oddly, the thoughts that kept popping into my mind were that I looked like hell, that my hair was a mess and my makeup was running. That I didn't have on nicer clothes and I'd been crying for four hours. I was shocked that at age 44 I had ended up in this situation, despite an upper-middle-class childhood, college education, and professional career.

In hindsight, I realize my embarrassment over my appearance was actually an indication of my deeper emotional problems. My main worry was: "What would others think?" I now know my overwhelming concern for the opinions of others was exactly what got me into that situation. My over-eagerness for approval and acceptance had made me an easy target for a manipulative, controlling man, and for many other manipulative people in my life. Where was my concern for myself? At the bottom of the list. Maybe not even on the list. Did I ever ask myself what I wanted or how I felt? Oh, sure, I would have told you I was mad at Ray and mouthed some words about kicking him out and never letting him push me around again. But did I ever feel viscerally angry with him – or anyone else? Did I even comprehend what emotions really were? Could I actually feel an emotion other than fear or insecurity? How telling it was my thoughts were on others and their acceptance, not on my needs and my safety.

Clearly, this idea of the importance of self-acceptance and self-awareness had to have significance to other people as well.

It's Natural to Want to Belong

As I've written, considerable research has shown that as social beings humans have a natural need for social acceptance. Getting cast out of the tribe used to be a frightening possibility that might have meant death. Even if we are no longer likely to be physically cast out (unless sentenced to prison), we can be ostracized or ignored – ways society reprimands misbehaviors. I believe that the elemental fear of being kicked out of our clan and the social behaviors that served us so well for tens of thousands of years are now being misappropriated and overused by modern humans, altered into a feeling of emotional rejection. This can lead to an aroused physical state that is not mentally or physically healthy. In fact, the perception of emotional exclusion and loneliness can lead to psychological and physical illness. Fear of rejection activates the hypothalamic-pituitary-adrenal axis, which prepares the body to respond to threat. This chronic state of hyper-arousal leads to anxiety – the physical and emotional manifestation of being on primal alert at all times. To Dominators, they feel as if they must fight off a world full of threats coming at them. This creates a cycle: If you feel "attacked" by nearly every interaction with people in your life, you are on alert 24/7, your primal fear response is on hair trigger, so you overreact to minor or imagined criticism by others.

This hyper-vigilant fear can lead to "all-or-nothing" responses; when you are alert for danger, everything looks like danger. Think of a time when you walked into a spider web. You startled. If someone snuck up behind you the next moment and tapped you on the shoulder, you'd probably jump even higher than normal. Every scary movie uses this concept in its plotline because it is such a natural reaction we all understand. For many, fear of personal rejection is the spider web that triggers a cascading matrix of anxious responses.

The power of perceived social exclusion made complete sense to me as it related to Dominators. Yet as I thought about how Ray had behaved, I became confused. Since I had been so obviously submissive and weak, why should Ray have continued to attack me? He was clearly dominant and had no need to keep reminding me of that. This would be like a wolf pack leader continually growling and biting a subordinate, cowering pack member for no reason.

Ray seemed to perceive an ongoing series of threats where there were none and then he overreacted. It became obvious to me that, just as unbalanced dogs respond with inappropriate behaviors, from cowering submission to "red zone" attacks, humans also overreact to what they perceive as threats. Ray was in a low-grade fear mode all the time, on alert for threats, so that when some minor event occurred his anger was triggered. In addition, perhaps his over-reaction was due to the fact that he had invested too much in me as sole member of his pack, so that when I criticized him it felt like a fear-provoking rebuff by his only pack member.

It became clear to me that Dominators, Submissives, and Avoiders are so concerned about rejection they misperceive threats from others and overreact when they feel threatened, leading to odd, inexplicable behaviors. The emotions can hijack behavior, making us suspicious of others and driving us to react in a primal fear mode with fight, flight, or avoidance.

A balanced person not only doesn't perceive threats where there are none, but she doesn't overreact using merely a primal response. She can choose the appropriate emotional and physical response because she is calm and in control of her emotions, not hijacked by her unthinking primal brain into a visceral reaction.

Low Self-Acceptance Increases Fears

As I looked back at my personal experience, and did some reading, one key idea became clear to me: Some people are especially needy for approval and vulnerable to feelings of social rejection because they have inadequate feelings of self-worth. The tendency to self-criticize comes partly from the natural need to belong, which drives us to self-correct as a way to fit in. However, because of a lack of self-acceptance, unbalanced people feel an extreme need to look for approval externally. It appears as if large numbers of people are far too much at the mercy of others' opinions; they view criticism by others as a rejection of their intrinsic value, a devastating and hurtful threat to their very essence. Is it any wonder some people react with panic attacks, depression, anger, or other behavior disorders when they have low self-worth? They feel they have been found fundamentally flawed by others and, because they believe they have no self-worth or competence, they have no mentally healthy way to respond to that situation.

With my Pack Leader Psychology paradigm in mind, I realized that unbalanced Dominators, Avoiders, and Submissives look to the tribe for approval far too intensely, are highly attuned to possible or perceived rejection, are especially fearful of rejection and the resulting feelings of shame, and fear the sting of exclusion more strongly than a balanced person would. For a person with low self-worth, a broad natural desire to belong can spin out of control to become very personal and overwhelming.

Shame is the naturally occurring social emotion we experience when we have done something that might get us kicked out of the tribe. Shame is defined as a painful feeling of humiliation, guilt, embarrassment, unworthiness or disgrace. Although it feels uncomfortable to us, shame functions to keep us from violating social norms and keeps us honest and reciprocal in our actions.

Because an unbalanced person is especially fearful of social exclusion, she may begin a campaign of constant self-criticism and self-blame in an attempt to "fix" herself so that she fits in and is accepted by others. She becomes hyper-vigilant for critical messages, overly aware of the judgment of others, and searches endlessly for external approval. For insecure people, internal voices are running a nearly continuous commentary on their failings and weaknesses. They fear being exposed as defective and flawed, which will cause others to reject them. Carrying around unhealthy levels of self-blame can make them feel unworthy of acceptance by anyone.

Fearful People Are on Nonstop Alert for Criticism

Quite significantly, I realized that the fear of social rejection plays out in interpersonal relationships as a fear of criticism. Our natural tendency toward external shame when compounded by internalized self-shame can result in a tendency to overreact by "lashing in" at oneself in self-criticism, "lashing out" at others in an attacking mode, or avoiding others as a way to defend against criticism.

By linking a concept from social psychology to a concept from clinical psychology, both ideas not only made more sense, but also carried much more weight. Although a fear of being ostracized by the group is the primal survival issue driving behavior, this appears as fear of shame, vulnerability, and criticism in our romantic relationships, friendships, and family dynamics.

With this revelation, the idea of "the power of the pack" continued to offer far-reaching explanations for daily human interactions.

Because of low self-acceptance, many people become fearful that everyone is judging, criticizing, and rejecting them. Low internal acceptance drives a desperate need for external acceptance, causing some people to be on the lookout for signs of rejection at every encounter. Any message – real or perceived – that others are criticizing feels as if they will be cast out of the tribe and delivers a threat to their primal call for survival.

Recognizing the power of the fear of criticism was like a door being opened and a light being turned on for me.

I thought back to all the times Ray had argued with me and I observed that they mainly involved jealousy and suspicions that I was cheating on him. However, it became apparent that his real concern was that he might be embarrassed. He seemed to be thinking: "What if she rejects me for another man? What would everyone think of me? I'd be humiliated." It wasn't my possible cheating per se, but how others would perceive him that was the problem. The cause of Ray's insecurities and fears were many, as is the case with most human behaviors, but one thing seemed clear: When he became jealous and violent, it was because he felt he might be demeaned or humiliated. And because he had so closely tied himself to me as his sole pack member, and relied on me so heavily for approval, when he perceived rejection it was an especially damaging blow.

When Ray became uncomfortable about social events that felt out of his league, he would drink too much and act out as a way to manage both his insecurities and me. His drunkenness or anger would force me to leave the event early or not attend at all. How ironic that Ray was afraid of being embarrassed, yet often his out-of-control behavior earned him exactly the humiliation he feared.

This fear of social disaffiliation is actually more powerful than many other moral messages we value. For example, it is very common for Dominators, when they sense that a marriage or love relationship is falling apart, to cultivate a new romantic interest. This Plan B allows them the perfect emotional cover story when the first relationship inevitably fails. "Oh, sure we're getting divorced, but I'm in love with Miss Plan B." The Dominator would rather be seen as an adulterer, a liar, and philanderer, than be seen as being thrown over by his wife. The cover story of the new lover is more positive than having to admit he was shamed by rejection. That is the power of the fear of social ostracizing.

I wonder if Ray went around town after I left bad-mouthing me, lying, and creating tales of my infidelities and deceptions. He would rather be seen as having been cuckolded than as decisively rejected for his actual, personal failings. Couple this fear of criticism with a Dominator's inability to accept accountability and you can imagine the denial and twisted logic that can ensue.

The more I understood about domestic violence and the type of men who commit it, I recognized that these Dominators are on alert. They are on the lookout for their partners abandoning them, opening them up to feelings of shame. Even if it is a symbolic and temporary abandonment, at its root it feels like world-shaking rejection and criticism. The abuser believes: "If my wife goes to the grocery store, it feels as if she is leaving forever, and that would embarrass me in front of my peers." Then, if the Dominator can't manage his emotions well, he is suddenly catapulted into fight mode and has no skills to back down from a conflict. It all made complete sense to me since this was exactly how Ray behaved on dozens of occasions.

Many people want to protect their fragile self-esteem so much that they are willing to twist information in odd ways. Research on racial discrimination shows that it is less stressful to believe you are being rejected because of your race than to believe that others reject you as an individual.

Our self-protective mechanisms can be extremely powerful and feel good, but can be destructive if taken too far.

This topic of self-shame hit very close to home for me. As a Submissive, I had fed myself a heaping helping of self-critical, judgmental messages. Although I never had a panic attack or other extreme response, I had to admit I lived in a very low-grade flight mode for a big chunk of my life.

Without a healthy level of self-acceptance I felt the need to look externally for affection to bolster my weak self-worth. As someone who was constantly looking to others for approval and affirmation, I spent my energy focused outward, looking for threats to my self-worth. These threats were pretty low-key as things go: "Were people laughing at me? Did people like me? What should I say? What should I do?" But to my body, it only knew my brain was saying, "Be on alert!" It wasn't until later that I was able to recognize I was now much more physically relaxed because I was not so worried about approval by others.

Additionally and conversely, I kept others at bay for fear of criticism. I spent the first 45 years of my life being pleasing and appeasing on the surface to get others to like me, but also being emotionally withdrawn and distant. I now know I put up walls because I was afraid others would find me unacceptable and I did not want to consider this possibility. By keeping others at a distance, I was playing it safe, hoping they wouldn't catch on to the fact I was a fraud, an impostor, and incompetent – as I defined myself then. When you label a slight criticism as complete rejection and a primal threat to your existence you will do anything to avoid it.

I felt this false toughness would protect the vulnerable emotional part of me. But the irony is that the opposite was true. I now know that by trying so hard to keep people at bay, I signaled I was afraid of them and what they might do to me. Ironically, by trusting others, opening myself up emotionally, and showing some vulnerability, I now project strength. I show I can handle whatever comes my way – a confident pack leader attitude.

In the past, I felt I had no right to protect myself or respond incrementally to others. It was all or nothing. Either I was a Submissive doormat with the door wide open or the door was shut and locked. Of course, this made me fearful and avoidant – my options were extremely limited. I now have the ability to respond appropriately to each person and each situation, which gives me much more strength and adaptability.

Look Inside Yourself for Acceptance

Let's look a bit more deeply at the idea of self-acceptance, because its definitions vary widely. In education and the self-help press, it is commonly believed that self-esteem comes from external sources: Failure or lack of competence is blamed for low self-esteem. Some believe that, for example, if "everyone is a winner" at youth sports or if children are praised and given high grades in school they will have good self-esteem.

Because of this common definition, I ignored the issue of self-esteem for years. I was reasonably hardworking, intelligent, athletic, and successful, and I was competent at most tasks I attempted. I never considered that my internal perceptions of my worth were actually far more valuable in determining my self-image than any external, rational judgments of my competence.

Once I discovered that my self-image was causing me to look to others for approval and had led to many inappropriate decisions in my personal and professional lives, I came to redefine the concept and elevate its importance in my life and in my understanding of human psychology.

Throughout the history of psychology, the definition of self-appraisal has been researched and debated at length. In fact, a number of terms have been offered for how we each perceive our value, including self-image, self-worth, self-esteem, self-concept, self-perception, self-description, self-schemas, likability, self-approval, self-acceptance, self-regard, self-criticism, and self-doubt.

Some psychologists define self-image as internally developed and competence based, the result of a discrepancy between our real abilities versus our idealized image of what we should be able to accomplish. Behavioral psychologists conjecture that if competence on a task improves, self-esteem will improve.

Common sense, however, tells us that competence-based definitions fall short. We all know people who are talented, good looking, athletic, generous, kind-hearted, or have other skills, but still express low opinions of themselves. We also know people who can factually be judged as less competent than others, yet these individuals may have overly grandiose perceptions of their abilities and worth.

In fact, the very idea that if we increase our successes we will feel more successful points to the fallacy of this theory. For example, I was always a fairly good-looking woman. Being prettier would not have helped my self-esteem. In fact, it is the very idea that my looks were essential to gaining approval of others that was at the root of my low self-acceptance. Striving to be prettier would not likely have increased my self-worth, but rather reinforced messages that I was unworthy as I was and needed to change to be worthy of love.

Of course, the idea of unconditional self-acceptance is based on the concept that a person should value herself irrespective of achievement, looks, or competence.

Some philosophers and psychologists believe that true self-worth involves values and character, and these are concepts that arise out of behaviors and interpersonal relationships. This parallels my definition of a pack leader as a person whose values imbue their self-worth and self-assurance.

Many core human values are cross-culturally recognized – courage, self-discipline, honor, selfless leadership, and altruism – illustrating that these signs of strong personal character are the roots of a universally accepted healthy, balanced personality.

Much of the research on self-esteem relies on self-reports, which are usually biased. People want to present a good image of themselves, so they generally report positive self-comments. This points out the distinction between what is called narcissism and true self-acceptance. A secure person can assess and describe himself accurately without fear of the judgment of others. An insecure person will work hard to present a falsely positive image of himself to others.

In addition, much self-esteem research asks questions about situations when people felt competent. I believe true self-worth is tested when a person is feeling incompetent, unsuccessful, emotionally vulnerable, and socially rejected. That is when a person's real nature will emerge. If a person can continue to feel good about herself in those situations, this signifies an emotionally secure person.

Many people continue to adopt the simplistic belief that self-image is generated internally and linearly: We define ourselves and that image is reflected out into the world. In short, most people believe that self-image is what we think of ourselves based only on our own perceptions of ourselves.

However, many psychologists believe that we define ourselves not just on internal comparisons of ideal versus real abilities, but rather measure ourselves against social demands and the reactions of others.

The idea of social comparison as a source of self-image, then, can be conceived of as a double set of mirrors, with an individual's behaviors being reflected out into the world and judgments about those behaviors being reflected back by others in her life in an ongoing, dualistic, interpersonal feedback loop. We define ourselves based largely on the reactions or reflections of others, interpreted and processed through our own perceptions, continually adjusted, and continually re-reflected by others.

Many researchers now recognize that self-criticism functions as a way to help us avoid social exclusion. Because we look to others for feedback and to help us modify our behavior, it decreases the likelihood that we will be rejected or punished by others. I concur that the goal of judging ourselves is to make sure that we live up to the tribe's standards so that we do not get ostracized. When I listen to psychotherapy clients talk about why they have low self-worth it is almost always based on the opinions (perceived or real) of others. It's when that need to fit in goes overboard that trouble begins.

Many books talk about low self-worth but fail to make the connection to how this attitude might influence a person's behavior. I believe there is an important connection between low self-acceptance and the need to be hyper-vigilant for "attack."

The failure to connect low self-worth and anxiety is especially concerning in psychotherapy. Many styles of therapy treat the symptom only, not the cause. A therapist may treat the fear of crowds, but not recognize that the root cause is a low sense of self-worth, because the client feels the need to be hyper-vigilant to criticism, judgment, or rejection by others, even total strangers passing by on the street. This fear of emotional "attack" will be translated into a physical response with symptoms of anxiety. It might seem unlikely that addressing the client's low self-worth would reduce a fear of crowds, but it is very probable. Because if you are accepting of yourself, you will not be looking for approval from others, so, conversely, you will also not be on the lookout for disapproval from others.

When I consider that up to a quarter of the American population may have what are considered diagnosable behavioral health issues and many others have less-severe problems, I have to believe this is not man's natural state. I wonder: "Was an emotional overreaction to criticism and shame always normal in humans? Were humans always so anxious?" I believe that because we no longer have strong packs to belong to, the sense of social exclusion is especially threatening, which leads to this overreaction. I have to believe that acting in a more natural way – as balanced pack members who are trusting and confident, not fearful and controlling – has to be the answer.

Free Yourself from Perfect Parents

When you go through a journey of self-discovery as I have, one topic pops up repeatedly: parents. I had to, for the first time in my life, shine a spotlight on my parents, their behavior, and the messages I learned from them. Those messages are so very powerful when coming from the most important, powerful people in your life – the people you depend on for survival as a child.

This process helped me take my parents off the pedestal they and I had put them on. Although my parents were very good, well-intentioned parents, I needed to take an uncritical look at them to wean myself away from ingrained thought patterns. I came to understand that they were, of course, human and imperfect – which felt uncomfortable to admit since I had been uncritical of my parents for decades. An interesting thing happened, however. By allowing myself to look honestly at my parents I learned that if they weren't so perfect, maybe I wasn't so imperfect. Not that I had to drag my parents down to feel good about myself; this wasn't a zero-sum game. Yet unleashing myself from an automatic acceptance of everything my parents said helped me recognize maybe, just maybe, some of the messages my parents had sent me had been wrong. Maybe I wasn't quite the irresponsible loser they had perceived me to be. If they weren't perfect, maybe some of their judgments also weren't perfect. Perhaps their shame and embarrassment over my minor misbehaviors were unjustified. Perhaps their shame and embarrassment were more about their desire to fit in to their social system, rather than any actual moral violations on my part.

When I admitted that my parents might not have been perfect, it unleashed me from needing their acceptance as a means to feel good about myself. And when I stopped looking to others for acceptance it took power away from them and put it right where it belongs – in my own hands.

A balanced person looks only to herself for the approval, acceptance, and love she needs to feel worthwhile. A first step down this road was for me to admit that I had to stop looking to my parents for love and affection. I had to get over my fears of abandonment and rejection.

It was very empowering to realize my parents had actually already rejected me and I just hadn't noticed it! Yet I had survived just fine for 40-plus years. Why should I keep knocking on that door when no one had ever answered?

When you exist only for everyone else's approval, you constantly risk rejection. When you rely only on your own approval, the risk of rejection evaporates. This was a tremendously powerful awareness on the road to becoming a pack leader.

The Journey to Fearlessness Starts with Self-Acceptance

I had easily come to understand that controlling others through outright dominance is usually futile and always unbalanced. It took me a while longer to learn that controlling through the subtle manipulation of submission was just as futile. If you are looking for acceptance, it can only come from yourself, not through controlling the reactions of others. This may seem like a simple concept, but I did not truly understand it or its importance for many years.

In the past, by giving away affection I hoped to manipulate others into providing some sort of approval or validation in return. I dangled affection as a way of getting affection in return. I avoided conflict in the hopes I wouldn't ever offend anyone and they would reciprocate with no critical feedback. I worked super hard to please everyone and anyone so as to be liked. For 44 years of my life, I lived in a low-level state of anxiety, constantly worried about what others thought of me and trying to get them to like me. How freeing it is to no longer have that undercurrent running through my mind.

It was only when I was able to honor my intrinsic self-worth that I was able to recognize my inner strengths and competencies. Relying on the approval of others had gotten me into a boatload of trouble in my life. Every time I looked to others for approval, I weakened myself. By delegating responsibility for my emotional wellbeing to others, I gave them power over me, and at the same time I made them contemptuous of me. At some level I, too, grew resentful of my neediness and dependence on others for approval. And if I knew I was weak and submissive to others, how could I respect myself? I believe that self-worth is not about believing you have a special talent or attribute. Self-worth comes from behaving with character, with high moral standards, self-respect, and respect for others. Unthinking manipulative submissiveness in service of bolstering weak self-worth does not equal strong character.

I began to see that respecting myself was the key to moving forward with confidence as a pack leader. And respect does not involve overly critical self-judgment and self-shame.

While I am not a Pollyanna and know I have to look out for myself, I have attempted to be less judgmental – of myself and of others. I've come to understand that when I tell myself I am a loser, it only weakens me. It does not make me stronger. People sense that you are judging yourself and finding yourself lacking. They feel your lack of confidence and react to that weakness with, at the least, a lack of respect. Or they may discover your soft underbelly – your low self-worth – and go in for the emotional "kill." If they recognize that you are eager for affirmation, they may provide it to you, gaining power with each crumb of attention you gobble up.

I also have learned that when you judge yourself, you tend to judge others. And even if you never say anything, I believe people sense when you are critical of them, if only in your unspoken thoughts. Now I try to be positive, supportive, and compassionate. When I see someone, I try not to let my mind jump immediately to a criticism: "I don't like her voice," or "What is he wearing?" I try to look for the good in everyone and I believe this translates to a warmer persona, a more welcoming look on my face – small signs I am trustworthy, approachable, and pleasant.

By accepting others, I am signaling that I don't have to tear them down to build myself up. I am not insecure about my ability to hold my own with anyone, so I don't back down shyly from interpersonal conflict. I don't bully or cause a fight to instill fear in others and keep their judgments at bay. I don't have to appease and please to keep the criticisms from my door. When you know your rank in the pack – and it fits you – you don't have to constantly fight to defend or earn your role. Everything falls into place without effort.

I also make much less effort to fit in, to conform to others' needs and opinions. In everything from my fashion choices to my conversations I have a much healthier balance between my personality and the personalities of others.

Now am I strong enough in my own self-identity and self-acceptance to be comfortable establishing boundaries. I no longer push back against control by others, because I don't fear becoming overwhelmed or engulfed in their control tactics and persona. I do not have to temper my behavior to make others like me in an attempt to sidestep their potential criticism. I am no longer afraid of the opinions of others and that allows me to dance happily to my own tune.

The prescription is remarkably simple. If you improve your self-worth, you will learn automatically to be able to gracefully accept criticism and give up the belief that a criticism would be a fatal blow to your very existence. You will no longer feel the need to control, manipulate, and manage others in your life to keep criticism at a distance. If you base your self-worth on your latest achievements and the opinions of others about those achievements, you are looking externally for validation and will be constantly at the mercy of others. Defining yourself by others' definition of you leaves you vulnerable to their manipulation.

Most importantly, because I now accept myself, I can open my heart to accepting others.

In one of those conundrums of life, I found that the more I behaved in what I would have previously termed "selfish" ways – liking myself and standing up for myself – the more people liked me. Here was a win-win situation. I liked myself more, but was, as a result, less preoccupied with myself. Others liked me more and were no longer resentful of my self-absorbed attitude and emotional neediness. When I didn't subtly manipulate others into liking me, other people actually did like me for who I was, not for who I was trying so hard to appear to be.

Be Brave

When I was deciding where to live after my second divorce, I had a recurring dream. I pictured myself as the owner of a restaurant or bar in a small town where everyone knew me and I knew everyone who came into the place, where I was a respected member of the community, yet could be fun, honest, outspoken – an authentic person. That dream showed me I wanted to belong, yet also be accepted for who I really was. I wanted to have friends – something I had not allowed into my life. I wanted my real personality to shine, not to cave in to all the more dominant people in my life and mold myself to their wishes and demands.

When it came time to actually move, I decided not to move to a new town. Instead, I moved back to an area where I already had some friends and set out to make a lot more. I now had more tools to be a good, close friend, yet not let my friends take advantage of me. I could allow myself to be a friend because I wasn't afraid of being steamrolled or engulfed by others.

And because I no longer have irrational fears of being criticized, controlled, or dominated, I am living one of Reilly's lessons: Be brave. I am bravely allowing emotional intimacy into my life. I am allowing friends and lovers to be close but not overly demanding. I am bravely being honest with people when I feel I have been disrespected. I am expressing my emotions, which makes people sense I am an emotionally warm person and they can be free to open up emotionally as well.

I also smile at the irony that, previously, I didn't listen to my intuition and didn't accurately sense when I should be fearful. Yet I still lived in fear – fear of all the wrong things. I was afraid of not being liked, yet this fear was exactly the weakness others preyed on in me and the real reason I should have been afraid. I was busy being afraid of rejection, yet this should have been the least of my worries. I had already rejected myself, the most fundamental source of shame and criticism there is.

I now realize that by existing for everyone else's approval, you constantly risk rejection. When you live only for your own approval, the risk of rejection disappears.

A pack leader listens to her intuition to sense fear, but knows that acting bravely starts with thinking bravely about herself. Inner, emotional fears are the most debilitating fears of all. When in doubt, be brave.

When You Have Nothing Left to Prove, Your Fear of Disapproval Goes Away

•••••••••••••••••••••••••••••••••••••

A friend of mine was contemplating filing for divorce from her husband. It was a difficult decision, especially as they had only been married a short time. She said, "I'm coming to grips with the idea that maybe this marriage was just a step and I'll find another love in my life." I could see she was thinking ahead to meeting another man. But I said: "Yes, you will find another love. You'll find you love yourself."

•••••••••••••••••

Fear of Rejection is the Root Cause of Mental Health Disorders

When I began to study psychology, I quickly realized the significance and applicability of the fear of social exclusion when considering psychological conditions. It seems as if far too many people today are living with a chronic sense of inadequacy, leading to an over-activation of the fight-or-flight response. The result can be an increased prevalence of stress-related physical conditions and an array of psychological disorders and misbehaviors. Two large government studies found that 22 to 23 percent of the U.S. adult population (44 million people) has a diagnosable mental and/or substance abuse disorder. In children, about 20 percent have mental disorders with at least mild functional impairment. (Of course, many argue that the Diagnostic and Statistical Manual, the bible of the psychiatry and psychology professions that is used to "diagnose" these conditions, is overly broad in its listing of symptoms.)

Many of the disorders categorized in the Diagnostic and Statistical Manual involve some fear or anxiety related to situations involving judgment by others. For example, a common set of symptoms describe all the mood disorders and anxiety disorders:

- fearful of being embarrassed or humiliated
- self-conscious, fearful of failure
- depressed and hopeless about the future
- obsessive, perfectionist, and fastidious
- avoids public situations
- very self-critical, low self-esteem
- feels helpless and inferior
- physical symptoms such as nervousness, headaches, rapid heart rate and sleeplessness

These descriptive terms point to a person who is extremely self-critical, looking to others for acceptance, and fearful of being criticized or disapproved of by others. Quite simply, low self-worth is at the core of many psychological disorders, including depression and anxiety disorders, suicide, paranoia, addictions, sexual disorders, eating disorders, the personality disorders, criminality, and antisocial behavior. The cause is the same; just the symptoms are different. A single label could suffice when hundreds are used.

One day I thought about a friend who suffers from many symptoms of anxiety. I realized the phrase "paralyzed by fear" describes his life perfectly. He is unable to look for a job, go for a walk, meet a woman, or hang out at a coffee shop. Sadly, many people live their entire lives this way, stunned by fear and anxiety, literally in the grip of their primal freeze response, like prey frozen under the stare of a predator. However, the predator they fear is merely other people who may pass judgment.

They live with low-grade anxiety, spending far too much emotional bandwidth wondering about irrelevant issues such as: "Did the barista at the coffee shop smirk at my pronunciation of 'espresso?'" They ruminate about what they said or did today, last week, and last year. They worry about whether they can perform a task capably next month. This hyper-vigilance also leads to misperceptions that another person's behavior is threatening when it isn't or to view it as more threatening than it is.

For example, a person with Paranoid Personality Disorder, as defined in the DSM, sees rejection in very nonthreatening behaviors of others. Phobic and Obsessive-Compulsive types of people imagine threats in inconsequential or uncontrollable items from germs to tall buildings. Most psychological disorders are the result of people being in non-stop alert mode, unable to stand down from minor threats.

Pack Leader Wisdom:
Look inside yourself for acceptance.
The more parts of yourself you reject,
the more important it is to feel accepted.
When you have nothing left to prove,
your fear of disapproval goes away.
Watch for people who are afraid of criticism,
rejection or abandonment.
A fear of social exclusion signals a lack of
self-acceptance and low self-worth.

CHAPTER 8

Lead, Don't Control

I was running on a sidewalk one day and Reilly was running in the woods about 30 yards to my left. There was a road about 10 yards to my right. A woman approached me, walking her dog on a leash. She had a look of panic in her eyes. She yelled out, "Is that your dog?!" I nodded my head and smiled. She said, "Aren't you afraid she will run into the street?" I shook my head. "No, she won't." The woman continued to look shocked. Her dog was also dragging her down the sidewalk, so I knew she had no clue how to be a pack leader.

She didn't understand I wasn't controlling Reilly, so much as being her leader. If I had gone into the street, Reilly would have followed me. But since I showed no interest in the street, neither did Reilly. Of course, my job was made much easier by the fact that Reilly had no interest in the street when there were so many squirrels to chase in the woods. I am also very observant of Reilly's behavior. I can read her intention well before she nears the road. I also know that in five years, she has never once even crossed the sidewalk toward the street, much less gotten near the road. And I know that with one sound, I can tell Reilly I don't want her heading toward the road. She will turn on a dime if I yell, "Hey!" It is difficult to describe, but I don't see this as a command, but more of a reminder. I'm not telling Reilly what to do, just reminding her that we – the pack – don't go over there. She knows my intention and listens to me even when she is off leash.

When using traditional obedience methods to train a dog, one of the most difficult tasks is to get a dog to come when she is off leash. That is because these methods are based on a command and control philosophy. The owner gives a command and the dog is to unthinkingly obey. Leadership is actually more about getting a dog to think about what you want and agree with you, not obey blindly.

I also believe traditional obedience doesn't work in all situations because it fails to address a fundamental failure of most contemporary dog owners. If a dog believes it is the pack leader it is very unlikely to obey a human it believes is lower in pack rank. A dog that doesn't respect you is unlikely to obey you. Your ability to get your dog to respond to you depends on what your dog thinks of you as a person. Respect and trust must come first.

The key to off-leash training is to first establish yourself as pack leader so that the dog feels it wants to obey you. You can't control a dog's behavior and you can't make a dog come if it doesn't want to. You can show it what you want, but ultimately it has to decide how to behave.

As a leader you can't push and you can't pull. You can only BE a leader and others will decide if they want to follow you.

You Can't Control Anyone but Yourself

Early on in my journey toward self-awareness my eyes were opened to the dynamics of control in relationships. I was suddenly aware that Ray's behaviors reeked of control. Just like an aggressive, growling dog, he intimidated me so that I would be reluctant to criticize or question him. By keeping me under his thumb he felt powerful. He felt he could manage me so he could ensure a steady flow of approving emotional support and fend off any rejection.

As I gained self-understanding and distance from that marriage, I grew to deeply and primally comprehend how powerless I had felt when he was dominating and controlling me. During the relationship I didn't recognize how oppressive the control was. I later read about how a controller instinctively knows to escalate the dominance gradually, so the person being controlled doesn't notice what is happening. Over the course of months or years, the Submissive person acquiesces, but doesn't recognize what has happened.

We Are All Controllers

At first it was very easy and comfortable to place full blame for our divorce on Ray's controlling tendencies – they were obvious and hurtful in the extreme. As I developed more understanding of my Submissive personality, though, I realized I was also using control to manipulate others. A shocking admission. How could this be? I was putting my needs below others, wasn't I? How could I be controlling others when I felt constantly dominated? But I learned that it's true: Submissives are also very controlling. I was using people-pleasing techniques to manipulate others into liking me and as a way to forestall criticism.

At the time that I was cowering in an attempt to gain control, I failed to comprehend that I was also losing power by debasing myself.

My efforts to manage the reactions of others by appearing weak had given them the green light to control and dominate me.

With my newfound awareness, the theme of control kept popping up in my dealings with people, and it became very clear to me that nearly all people use some form of control in their relationships with others. It can be an overt, dominating form, or a subtle, submissive, appeasing form. Even Avoiders manage others the way they feel most comfortable: by retreating into a shell. If you are literally not available, no one can criticize you. You feel protected from rejection if you're already at arm's length from others physically or emotionally.

Fear of Criticism Drives Control

The reason for all this control in relationships is good, old primal fear – the fear of being betrayed, demeaned, humiliated, shamed, or rejected. Most of us are busy trying to manipulate others so we can manage the flow of shameful, critical messages we are so afraid of receiving. A simple need to fit in, a normal human reaction, drives our need to control, dominate, manipulate, please, accommodate, avoid, or submit to others. When our self-image comes to rely far too heavily on what we think others think of us, it can result in emotional problems.

Nearly everyone uses the unhealthy responses of Dominance, Submission, or Avoidance to manage relationships with others in an effort to feel safe and invulnerable. What stems from a natural instinct to remain part of a tribe morphs into an unnatural behavior pattern that is unhealthy for us and those around us.

Each personality type favors a type of control as a means of dealing with the threat of criticism by others.

- Dominators can be charming but ultimately fight or lash out to keep criticism away. They refuse to accept blame or responsibility and tend to intimidate and bluster to scare others into not criticizing.
- Submissives focus on forestalling criticism by overachieving, never saying "no," being nice, and avoiding conflict.
- Avoiders try to withdraw from or ignore situations that might provoke criticism.
- A balanced person will have a healthy need for social acceptance but will not be overly sensitive to social rejection or personal disapproval.

Control behaviors show up in a variety of guises, but they all have the same goal: to manage other people and reduce the opportunities for criticism.

To varying degrees and in different ways we reach out to others for approval, but also in different ways and at different times push back from others. We want to gain a thumbs up, but we want to avoid risking a thumbs down as well. We manage others and situations in an attempt to sidestep the feelings of shame and humiliation so many of us fear. When a person is insecure, she doesn't want anyone to be able to expose or exploit her insecurities.

Fear of Disapproval Leads to a Loss of Approval

So it was all coming together in my mind. I had feared rejection and criticism, but so had Ray. I had sought out affection and connection, and so had Ray. We had both wanted the same things, but it was amazing how our behaviors were so different, driven by our basic Submissive and Dominator personalities. This points to a fundamental irony about the typical relationship between a Submissive and a Dominator.

My relationship with Ray at first had the sheen of love and affection, but it was fake. Dominators want a relationship with a fantasy person, not with a real person, because a real person might criticize. A Dominator's fantasy partner would never do that.

Ray wanted to manage feelings of connectedness in a way that precluded criticism. His very use of overt control and power meant he drove me away and he lost the one thing he sought – approval.

And I never got the one thing I wanted: real affection, a real relationship. My neediness for approval set me up to be manipulated and dominated and judged, the things I was desperate to avoid.

Both of us tried to ensure affection and avoid criticism, yet our maneuvering ensured we got the opposite result.

In fact – a further irony – when we are busy trying to control others, we don't realize that while it may feel powerful this behavior is actually weakening us. With our neediness and fear, we are putting ourselves in a position to be controlled and dominated by others. I certainly set myself up to be manipulated by Ray because his affection had felt so good to me after 40 years of having none. I tried to control Ray with my Submissiveness, yet, at the time, I felt I had no power, no ability to manage his reactions.

It was only much later that I realized Ray was also in a very weak position. He desperately needed me and my attention. He also needed to keep me fearful so that I wouldn't question his behaviors. Torn between these needs and fears, Ray eventually hurt the very person who was giving him his fix of attention. He was willing to risk jail time and social embarrassment just to frighten me and keep my criticisms at bay. Ironically, Ray's fear of rejection ultimately got him rejected. And my neediness for love, attention, and affection earned me hate, violence, and disrespect. While it was painful to admit my responsibility for my situation, the powerful, life-changing insight I gained has more than made up for it.

After reading and study, I learned that traditional psychology has, for many years, posited that two fears drive many human behavioral problems related to control: fear of abandonment and fear of engulfment. These concepts sprang out of Freudian and attachment theories emphasizing the very elemental, dependent relationship of the parent-child bond. Some psychologists theorize that if our parents fail to establish a "secure base" for us as infants, we may develop a deep-seated fear of abandonment. If this fear is overwhelming, a person may spend his entire life seeking to replace parental affection and attention, which can play out as fear of abandonment.

The theory of fear of engulfment says we try to control others to keep them at bay so we don't become engulfed in their neediness. This theory proposes that people flip-flop between the fears of abandonment and engulfment, using control tactics to manage those fears. They pull you close, then withdraw and become distant.

While it certainly is best if parents form a healthy bond with children and no one likes to be engulfed in neediness, I believe there is a deeper and simpler reason for these twin fears of abandonment and engulfment. Rather, the root cause for all this mixed up behavior arises from an even more primal place: fear of rejection by the pack. I believe that fear of engulfment and fear of abandonment are two sides of the same coin. These fears play out in our daily personal relationships as fear of criticism.

One person can experience both the need to control others and the need to push back from them. Abusive relationships often feature this characteristic in spades. (No surprise to me!) Extremely insecure Dominator personalities like Ray seek out the most Submissive, uncritical person they can find. My fear of conflict made it easy for Ray to control me so he could both gain approval and avoid criticism.

Sure, my neediness may have felt threatening or engulfing to him, as some psychologists state. But I think my neediness was not nearly as scary as the possibility that I might criticize him. That is what makes the Dominator feel threatened with engulfment. If he becomes close to someone and includes this person in his pack, this makes him vulnerable to criticism. So the abuser alternates between demanding attention and closeness to bring in positive praise, and then, when he senses he might be criticized, becomes violent and angry, pushing the partner away. I experienced this "dance of anger," as some call it, with Ray. It is a very confusing emotional tango to perform, both of us searching for approval with one step forward and defending against possible criticism with one step back. Like boxers in a clinch, we hugged each other, hoping we wouldn't get punched, yet trying to land a few blows at the same time.

Similarly, some books on domestic violence and controlling relationships explain these relationships using the concepts of power and fear of abandonment. At a certain level these authors are correct. Submissives give affection to manipulate others into providing attention or validation, and Dominators withhold affection or use threats to manipulate others and give themselves feelings of power and connection. Unfortunately, most books stop there – they explain power plays, but they don't explain why people are so in need of the feeling of power. Feeling powerful does feel good. I'm sure this is a component of these behaviors, especially for Dominators. They enjoy the sense of strength that comes from having someone afraid of them. This feeling is certainly reinforced for them each time they get someone to ask, "How high?" when they say, "Jump." But what is causing these behaviors? I believe these books leave out the bottom-line reason people look to control others: Their low self-worth drives them to fend off or prevent criticism as a way to feel accepted by others. They try to use controlling behaviors and tactics to manage other people. If worried about being rejected by others, a person may develop certain tactics to help ensure a criticism-free connection – even if those tactics are unhealthy for both parties.

The good news is that by becoming a pack leader, you can overcome your childhood fears and insecurities. In fact, by looking at fear of abandonment from a different lens it becomes much more manageable as an adult. If you realize it is probably less about any childhood traumas or attachments, and more about a fear of criticism in the present, you don't have to delve into your past to fix this problem. It can be fixed by examining your present day experience.

Learn to Give Up Control

The fear of being judged and dominated showed up in my life in interesting and subtle ways.

One of the first issues my therapist in Chicago worked with me on was my lack of friends. Early on, she gave me a "homework" assignment to call one friend that week and ask for help – for anything. This was a very difficult task for me at the time. I had been blaming my lack of friends in Indiana on the fact that the people in that small town were not like me and no one had the same hobbies I did. I came to realize the fault was all mine. I did not reach out to people and didn't make friends. I stubbornly tried to do everything myself and didn't rely on others unless I absolutely had to. I sent off overt and subtle signals that I did not want people in my life. While I was pleasant and social when I had to be, and said I wanted friends, I never went out of my way to invite emotional intimacy into relationships.

Over the past few years I have continued to learn why I behaved this way – and have unlearned this behavior to a large degree. Previously, I kept a distance from potential friends because I was afraid they would make demands on me emotionally that would feel unsafe to me. Many mental health professionals use the phrase "lack of boundaries" to describe this situation. If a friend became too demanding or needy, I felt I didn't have the right or even the notion I could say "no." I believed that once I opened the door to someone, I couldn't close it even a tiny bit; I had to submit to their needs totally. So I sometimes chose the one response that seemed safe: Don't open the door at all. Of course, this left me in a very mentally unhealthy place, with no close friends who could have provided a very valuable sounding board on issues such as marriages and relationships. I had no one to warn me that the guy I was about to marry was a controlling jerk.

I am also convinced some people intuitively know they are in a weakened position, so at some level they push back or withdraw, protecting themselves from becoming victims of control. I had learned as a child that a dominating, controlling relationship was normal. This set up a seesaw behavior that played out for years. I would cling to someone who showed me attention, permitting a controlling relationship. At the same time, I would push back and remain distant for fear of being controlled and criticized by this unbalanced person.

As my insecurities about myself evaporated over the course of several years, and my eagerness to manipulate others to like me disappeared, I came to truly recognize a fact that the dog world knows innately: You can't control others. You can't control if someone loves you, wants to be your friend, or respects you. You can't control how other people view you or respond to you. You can only control how you respond to people and situations now, in the present. Some people are just not going to like you. Nor is it healthy to try to get everyone to like you – it is an overly submissive and weak position to put yourself into.

Finally it dawned on me. If I couldn't control if other people liked me or not, I no longer had to be afraid of being rejected by others. Why waste my time fearing what I couldn't manage? Problem solved. Move on.

I have also learned that I always had, and still have, power in a relationship. I have the right to do and be what I want. I am sad when I think about the years I wasted in unhealthy relationships, not realizing that all along I had the ultimate control: I could walk away. What a revelation. Ray actually had no control whatsoever.

As I had learned from my marriages, trying to control someone else leaves only a false intimacy and eventually a total lack of control. But in the meantime, I had expended huge amounts of anxious energy trying to manage my husbands, which is impossible and only leads to more anxiety and frustration.

When I look at society now, I recognize that few people live balanced lives, so they often find themselves in intimate relationships based on unhealthy power and control. When people with unbalanced Dominator or Submissive or Avoider behaviors pair off into relationships, it becomes obvious some unhealthy patterns will develop.

As social creatures, people naturally have relationships of all kinds that are at some level about power and control – who has it, who wants it, and who is giving it away. Unfortunately, I contend that nearly all adult relationships today are unbalanced in terms of power. Rather than treating each partner as an equal member, many marriages seem to devolve into a series of petty negotiations and not-so-petty fights, with each person seeking to be more powerful as a way to fend off criticism. Not only is this unbalanced for the partners, the family, and the children, it means the relationship is not emotionally intimate. Power struggles obviously do not enhance the emotional closeness of a couple, but rather severely damage it. Powerplays are based on manipulation, control and emotional distance – clearly not a way to build trust, intimacy, and respect.

The only reason some of these dysfunctional relationships appear to work is that both parties are happy playing the game and no one upsets the applecart with any inconvenient questioning of the arrangement. Both Dominator and Submissive are content because the setup lets them avoid honest communication and conflict, so that they feel safe from criticism. Neither one wants the other to discover their inner insecurities, so they are both happy to play by these rules.

True pack leaders don't manipulate and manage; they lead and guide.

Actually, the minute you attempt to control others, it proves you are an unbalanced person, not a pack leader. While attempts at control may appear to work – and some dysfunctional controlling relationships work for a lifetime – they are not healthy, balanced relationships.

Control Is Not Affection

Sadly, control can even feel like affection to some people. I learned this after a yearlong relationship with a man I'll called Pat ended. I thought we had a fairly good relationship, but about 10 months into the relationship he seemed to be very "busy" all the time. We gradually started to see each other less and less and then he stopped calling. I later learned he had started dating someone else. I was, at first, confused. We had never fought, he had never said he was unhappy with me or complained about our relationship in any way. I later realized Pat was so conflict-averse he would never have complained if something had been amiss. When I asked what he could not get from me, he couldn't really describe it. He said he wanted someone who was more affectionate. This made me a bit confused. I was very physically affectionate to him by any standard that I could think of. I was attentive to him, we had great conversations, and discussed emotional subjects in depth. I asked him questions about his life and his day and showed true interest in him. I cooked him dinner regularly and made sure he was comfortable in my home. I even designed and hand knit him an Irish Aran sweater for his fiftieth birthday!

But then I had the a-ha moment. All of these "affectionate" things I was doing were not what he defined as affection. I had smothered him with kisses and doted on him in any number of ways, but nothing registered with him, because he defined affection differently than I do.

Pat, like many Submissives, defines affection as controlling behaviors. I wonder if he would have preferred a woman who dominated him, told him what to do, and gave him clear direction: "We're going out for Chinese tonight. And don't be late like you always are. And don't wear that stupid red shirt ever again." Since this type of control was not at all my style, if this was what he wanted I was obviously not giving him what he defined as affection.

Everyone defines and feels affection differently, then looks for affection that fits that definition. A kiss, a smile, and a hug may seem like affection to you, but to your partner it has no meaning. Sadly, even being shoved around feels like affection to some people.

These varying definitions of affection cause a lot of problems in relationships, especially when honest communication is lacking. I could have poured my affection on Pat for years, but I would have felt empty and used up. My affection would have washed over him as if I had done nothing. He would also have felt rejected and unloved, despite my best, well-intentioned efforts at loving him. The concept of affection can take on a whole lot of baggage it shouldn't when control is involved.

This disconnection keeps some of us searching for love, even though love in another form is being ladled out right on top of us. It seems to me this is one reason people cheat on their partners. Sometimes they enjoy one mode of attention and love, but then change and decide (perhaps only subconsciously) they want and need a new, healthier form of affection.

This paradigm also explains the answer to the age-old question, "What does he see in that woman?" and, "Why did he go back to that woman who is so wrong for him when his current girlfriend is so nice?" When we see a woman being controlling with a man, keep in mind this is not what he experiences. He doesn't feel control; he feels affection. To him, control is not a bad thing! I believe personal, perhaps unbalanced, definitions of affection are what drive many attractions and relationships.

Sadly, most people have come to define love as the feeling that they are getting their preferred form of affection – usually a form of control. We have learned to use manipulative behaviors to draw others toward us so we can generate and sustain this feeling of being "loved."

Pack Leader Wisdom:
Watch for those who try to control others
through Dominance, Submission
or Avoidance.
They are using manipulation to protect
against criticism.
You hold the power to break free of control.

CHAPTER 9

Beware of Aggressive Dogs

My first dog, Kiva, began to snap at people at the end of his life, unusual behavior for this sweet, friendly Vizsla. I now know he was feeling anxious because I had abdicated my role as pack leader. It must have been very difficult to be a 13-year-old dog, suffering from a chronic disease, yet still saddled with the responsibility of leadership – of an unbalanced human, no less. No wonder he snapped at me when I tried to wipe his feet: Pack members don't touch the pack leader without permission. I recall one time he bit Ray on the nose and we couldn't figure out why. Now I realize Ray had put his arm over Kiva's shoulders. A hug to us, but a pure dominance move to a dog. A more stable dog would have not felt as threatened, but Kiva was weak and old, which magnified his fears, so he overreacted with a snap.

In contrast, Reilly is very trusting of me. I have absolutely no fear she will bite me if I am clipping her toenails or pulling out a thorn or dealing with 100 porcupine quills in her mouth. (Yes, IN her mouth! And, yes, she bit another porcupine the very next day. Did I mention her incredibly high hunting instinct?)

I am not afraid Reilly will bite me because she is a balanced dog who will not react out of fear. She would only bite as the last resort and when truly physically threatened. My calm energy and lack of emotional reactivity communicate that I am not threatening to her. In contrast, fearful dogs are the most dangerous and mostly likely to bite. The toughest-looking pit bull, if he is balanced, can be no threat at all, whereas a small, yippy dog may be much more of a danger.

Reilly, of course, can instantly sense an unbalanced, anxious dog. She avoids these unstable animals because she knows their unpredictability makes them dangerous.

Pack leaders aren't fearful, anxious, or aggressive. They have no need to defend their role, bully, or control other pack members.

What most people call dominance among domesticated dogs is really unwarranted aggression, and this is also true in the human world.

Don't Be Fooled by Fake Pack Leaders

As someone who married two bullies, I am fascinated by what it means to be a fake pack leader. An executive in the auto industry, my first husband, Paul, tried mightily to present himself as a strong, fearsome man. But if you looked closer, you could see he was certainly not a calm, fair leader. He relied largely on bluster and intimidation to succeed at work – a fight response. While he was a very smart, talented, hardworking man, his insecurities did not allow him to be open to criticism or to be an authentic, vulnerable person.

While Paul was very aggressive at work, he never fought with me, choosing instead to avoid all emotional conflict in our marriage. I now realize that this was because he felt that an argument might open the door to criticism of him. Better to keep that door securely shut. Just as he worked very hard to be the smartest one in the room as a way to avoid being judged as inferior, he rarely showed any emotional vulnerability.

Neither of these choices – bullying or avoidance – is the sign of an emotionally secure person who is comfortable establishing boundaries for appropriate behavior and who is reacting with a healthy range of behaviors.

Ray was different in many ways, but still unbalanced. He was much more pleasant at work and socially, but took on the bully role at home. He believed that if I was an independent person it was somehow a threat to him. Both my husbands relied on aggressive dominance rather than develop an equal partnership in their relationships.

I believe many other people are confused as I was about how an "alpha" personality should behave. I watched a true-crime TV show about a sociopathic murderer who convinced several other people to help her slowly torture a victim to death. I heard an expert criminologist describe the perpetrator as an "alpha female." I would disagree with that description. As you've discovered, true pack leaders would never viciously harm another person for no good reason, as this woman did. Just because other overly weak people submitted to this woman and went along with her murderous plan does not make her a pack leader. She is a very unbalanced, extreme Dominator.

Of course, from an evolutionary point of view, anger and assertiveness are not always maladaptive. Anger has always been a useful survival

skill when it comes to reacting to a predator's attack, overcoming ene-
mies or sticking up for your rights against someone else. What is maladaptive is that many people today believe that nearly everyone is
attacking them, leading to chronic stress and the resulting behavioral
issues, but also physical symptoms of high blood pressure, adult-onset
diabetes, heart disease, headaches and many others. The researchers
who labeled the "Type A" personality that seemed to have a higher inci-
dence of heart disease and stroke found that there was a link between
those health problems and hostility and a sense of paranoia and perse-
cution in these over-stressed, anxious people. With those behaviors, it
appears these "Type A" people are Dominators.

As you'll learn more about here, an unhealthy person who uses
dominating behavior to get what he or she wants is never behaving as a
pack leader.

Be Powerful Yourself; Don't Try to Steal Power From Others

Dominating behavior can take many forms, often alternating
between behaviors that protect against any form of criticism and – the
flipside – to gain acceptance.

The Dominator's goals:

- to avoid embarrassment, shame, criticism, rejection, or humiliation
- to control by intimidation and fear, so others are afraid of criticizing the Dominator
- to take advantage of a Submissive who is also very needy for
attention and affection
- make others feel unbalanced, uncomfortable, and fearful of conflict so the Dominator can forestall criticism
- to prevent being controlled by others who might criticize
- to seek attention

Just as in the animal world, all overly hostile people are, in their
deepest psychological recesses, very fearful and anxious. Even though
some may appear to be quite confident, strong, and powerful, insecurity
is the root of their problems. Dominators feel powerless and fearful,
just as Submissives do, they just mask these feelings carefully.

Some types of Dominators respond nearly universally with a physical fight response, using outright aggression, anger, violence, or threats
of violence to intimidate and control. Most Dominators know to mask

their domination with more-subtle control and manipulation techniques, because if they don't they will be shunned.

Other Dominators misbehave in very understated ways that signal a pushback. They may "forget" to do a chore to passively re-exert their power. Others have learned that emotional manipulation and intimidation are effective behaviors. Some use the threat of a meltdown or emotional fragility to get others to tiptoe around in trepidation.

Men seem to be much more likely to adopt an overtly Dominator role. This may be largely cultural, as we teach boys to be aggressive and exert force to solve problems. However, research has shown that the desire for higher social ranking may even be linked to testosterone levels in men.

Dominators Seek to Avoid Criticism

Fear of embarrassment is a major motivation for Dominators. Why would, for example, Ray have been concerned about me talking to my girlfriends? It is likely he was afraid they would convince me to leave him or that I would tell an embarrassing story about him. However, this points to his deepest fear – that he would be humiliated and shamed.

Even minor arguments with a Dominator illustrate the insecurity. It may be a simple fact of life that your girlfriend, a Dominator, locked you out of the house. But when you state this fact in an argument, it feels like a criticism to her. It may be a fact to you, but to her it feels as if you are piling on, swamping her weak self-worth with comments that feel hurtful and needlessly attacking. Because the criticism feels like a life-or-death threat to her emotional survival, her fight response is triggered.

Much Dominator behavior is aimed at making you hesitant to criticize. Dominators have learned that your discomfort brings the Dominator comfort. He knows that if you are off balance, you are less likely to question him. Rage makes others back down and the Dominator believes it shifts blame to his attacker.

If you feel on the defensive, have to explain your behaviors, or feel less powerful, you are likely in the presence of a Dominator.

The fear of embarrassment or shame shows up in Dominators in their inability to accept responsibility, apologize, or admit they made a mistake. To do any of these would imply they had failed – a source of humiliation. Being 100 percent correct in the eyes of others is their goal. This fear of being embarrassed is, of course, the source of a Dominator's greatest weakness. By defining themselves by how others view them, they are setting themselves up to be held hostage by the opinions of others.

Some extreme bully Dominators adopt a "tough guy" attitude and work hard to send out messages they are strong and powerful, which is far more important to bullies than being emotionally close and connected. For this behavior type, the need for control and domination trumps the need for belonging.

The Fight Response Is Like a Cornered Animal

Dominators are hyper-alert to danger and perceive threats in nearly any setting. This idea came alive for me one day when I realized both Paul and Ray did not like crowds at large public events or airports. This was interesting. I wondered if there was a connection. Of course there was! Both were dominating controllers – and they felt they couldn't control the crowd. They did not know how to tune out the imaginary threats they perceived from each person in a large area. They were on alert at all times, triggered and ready to fight, ready to respond to a glare that might be considered a challenge. They had no ability to discern that these strangers were not in attack mode and were unable to stand down their defenses and relax. While I can walk through an airport and not be stressed out, a Dominator is in primal "fight" mode much of the time.

At the extreme of the fight response is "red zone" rage. It is interesting that nearly every culture has a name for extreme anger. The Diagnostic and Statistical Manual describes some of them. "Amok" is a dissociative episode preceded by brooding, followed by an outburst of violent, aggressive, or homicidal behavior directed at people or objects. The DSM notes that the episode tends to be caused by a perceived slight or insult and seems to be prevalent only among males. This behavior is called "bilis" or "colera" in Latino cultures, "boufée delirante" in West Africa and Haiti, "pibloktoq" in Inuit, as well as "berserk" or "red mist."

After I divorced Ray, I realized that during our fights he behaved like a cornered animal. But why did he feel cornered? His anger seemed to spring out of nowhere. At the time, I didn't realize a Dominator's anger is usually triggered by a sense of being ostracized.

I certainly never intended to shame Ray, but he perceived shame nonetheless. At that point in my life I was not even comfortable with a normal disagreement with a stranger, much less any rejection of the man I said I loved. I rarely questioned his behavior or decisions. I never nagged or complained. I instinctively knew not to corner him emotionally with accusations. Instead, a red zone situation usually began with me mentioning some seemingly innocent event and Ray reacting as if I had done something very, very hurtful to him. It was always so confusing. He reacted as if I had committed a mortal sin, when maybe all I had done was talk to a colleague at a holiday party. What I didn't understand was that this innocent cocktail party conversation was to Ray a sign of personal humiliation. He perceived, somehow, that my behaviors or the behaviors of others were mocking or insulting him.

Because of their extreme insecurity, even an imaginary slight or loss of attention is perceived as a mortal wound by some extreme Dominators. And this imagined threat leads directly and immediately to the "fight" response – the favored tactic of this personality type. Then, if a Dominator goes into a rage, the response is far beyond what is appropriate for the situation.

Ray's overreactions were numerous. On many occasions, he would accuse me of having an affair. Even if it had been true, would a balanced person respond to this "threat" by screaming for hours, breaking the phone, and punching a hole in a wall? Even if he didn't want me to take a simple overnight business trip to Milwaukee, is it appropriate to chase me down the street in the rain and throw me to the ground? Dominators imagine threats where there are none and respond to the most minor threats to their sense of security as if a dozen lions are circling and their very life is at stake.

Ray was that dangerous combination of fearful and aggressive and, boy, could his "bites" cause some damage. As victims of domestic violence will attest, insecure and unbalanced Dominators are dangerous types. Not all Dominators escalate to using violence, but those who favor this response are most likely to become abusive and violent.

Although Dominators exhibit a wide range of behaviors – as all people do – when I am in doubt about whether a behavior is a fight response, I think of the phrase: "lash out." When they feel threatened, Dominators go on the attack in a wide variety of ways, either in a physical attack or by sowing emotional chaos and drama by blaming others, not themselves.

Of course, Dominators can also use flight and avoidance tactics. I remember one incident when I was driving a friend home one night and Ray was in the back seat. (He wasn't driving because he was drunk.) I think he felt embarrassed because he wasn't being "the man" and driving the car. Then my friend and I laughed about something and Ray went "red zone." I tried to explain we weren't laughing at him in any way – the joke was about something totally unrelated. But he was already "gone." He had been on hyper-alert status for an insult and had perceived an innocent joke as a threat to him. He then responded irrationally with an over-the-top amount of rage and violence. After arguing for a few minutes, he actually jumped out of the car as I was driving 45 miles an hour down a country road! I didn't even realize what had happened for a few seconds because Ray's response was so outrageous and unexpected. When I turned around to pick him up he was gone. He had run into the woods – can you get a more explicit example of a flight response than that? He knew he couldn't fight me in the car with my friend present, so he felt forced to use another primal response. Of course, that's because he didn't have an arsenal of rational, emotionally mature responses to use.

I can now see that Ray's responses were usually with the emotion of anger. He never got sad, never cried, never was depressed or worried. He never expressed a range of emotions a more balanced person would express. He certainly never turned inward in self-accusation or self-criticism. This is a sure sign you're dealing with a Dominator – they rarely blame themselves. The blame was always focused on me or external events or situations. He usually lashed out; he rarely lashed in.

Because Dominators look externally to target others, this makes psychological rehabilitation difficult. The examination of behaviors and feelings key to successful psychotherapy would be an admission of failure – a nearly impossible process for Dominators. Those diagnosed with Borderline Personality Disorder are often considered nearly impossible to treat with therapy and it seems clear it is because their emotional defenses are all aimed at fending off feedback, honest self-assessment, and accountability.

The best test for a person's personality is when she is under stress. When you challenge her, question her, push her, test her, or criticize her, what does she do? If she nearly always lashes out at you – she's a Dominator. If she backs down and lashes in at herself in self-blame, she's a Submissive.

Unfortunately, many people are well trained to avoid conflict. As a result, they tend to establish relationships that avoid stressing the other person – so they may not see the real personality until it's too late.

Dominators don't understand what it means to be a true pack leader. Through poor socialization, they have come to think a pack leader rules by fear and never shows signs of weakness. As I learned with Ray, this aggression can be unpredictable. Just as Reilly runs from unstable dogs, I should have run away from this unstable behavior.

Dominators Want a Nonstop, Guaranteed Supply of Affection

I once watched a real crime show TV show about a 14-year-old girl who was kidnapped and held in a bunker by her captive. The kidnapper would live down in this dirt hideaway with his victim much of the time. The girl had excellent emotional intelligence skills and began to figure out the key to this Dominator's mind. She saw if she faked liking him she would be able to control him. He wanted so much to believe she liked him he fell for it! He showed his insecurity by asking her for advice. Then she used her social skills to trick the predator into behaving as she wanted. She convinced him to let her out of the bunker and she eventually escaped – a good use of manipulation, and proof even extremely dislikable Dominators on the far end of the control spectrum deep down "just wanna be loved." This Dominator had kidnapped a girl to guarantee he had affection, and when he looked to her for that affection it led to his downfall.

When I first began to develop Pack Leader Psychology concepts, I could easily see how Submissives wanted and needed to be liked. I recognized this had been a major motivator for me. However, having just left an abusive relationship with what I would later label a Dominator, I had a difficult time making the connection that someone like Ray also wanted to be liked and to belong. Certainly, Dominators can be charming, as well as hard working and overachieving when it suits their need to gain approval. Ray was eager for compliments and made a big show of his good deeds and hard work in an attempt to look good.

Ultimately, however, Ray's violent, aggressive behavior drove me away, rather than bring us closer. This, to me, seemed like a rather odd way to seek positive attention and belonging. Now I realize Dominators truly do have a need for acceptance and affection, but their fear of criticism may overwhelm that need.

Dominators Are Fearful, Yet Control with Fear

For some insecure people, instilling fear in others is a way of appearing to gather up power. Dominators use a variety of tactics to threaten others, from emotional manipulation, such as threats of depression or suicide, to actual threats of violence. These threats do not even have to be spoken. Most Submissives are very alert to implied threats – a place where their intuitive powers are actually being used.

While Submissives often adopt a "please like me" motto, Dominators have a "you must like me" attitude. At times, bully Dominators seem to live by the motto: "I don't care if you like me." Still, they desperately do care if you like them. Dominators force, coerce, and manipulate others to like them.

If you watch a pack leader in the dog world, she doesn't go around growling at and intimidating the other pack members on a regular basis as a way to cement power. A balanced pack leader knows she is the leader and doesn't need to constantly prove who is boss or use threats to control or discipline a pack. A false pack leader feels she must puff herself up and remind everyone of her power with threats and intimidation or with boasts and brags.

I once worked in a clinic that treated children. Many were young boys with what is labeled Oppositional Defiant Disorder. These boys acted out, tried to dominate others, and had clearly learned to use violence and tantrums to get others to acquiesce. Their bad behavior was a power tool they used to get their way.

Intriguingly, I once had a psychology professor who fit the mold of most in the profession – very nurturing and submissive. When describing "Antisocial Personality Disorder," he told of how these people are often criminals, relying on overt threats and manipulation, alternating with charm and cunning, to get what they want. They lack empathy for others and make up a large portion of inmates in prison. The professor admitted he was very frightened by this type of person, and that he would not treat them in his clinical practice. He looked frightened just talking about them. Then I realized that as a Submissive, he would naturally shy away from this extreme version of a Dominator. He would sense the threats this person was giving off, even if he couldn't verbalize his fears. He would also not realize that by his passive, cowering behavior he was signaling to the aggressive, antisocial patient he was fearful and weak. Most importantly, this professor did not understand that antisocial people are actually very weak and insecure themselves.

Weakness Attracts Even Weaker

Dominators, while they go to great lengths to seem powerful and in control, exude a very unbalanced type of power based on a weak, fearful energy. Just don't try to tell a Dominator he is weak or insecure. Most Dominators try like heck not to show weakness, emotional or physical. They've learned – because they behave in exactly this way– that others may take advantage of any perceived weakness.

A true pack leader is not afraid of appearing weak and does not need to weaken others to appear strong. If you have true inner strength of character, your reputation is not something you need to manage on a daily basis. You don't need to bully store clerks or employees or your wife to look powerful. You just are strong – from the inside.

This concept was new to me, because I had spent my life being submissive toward others to avoid offending them. I learned that being stronger isn't a zero-sum game. By being stronger, I would not automatically diminish someone else. However, these were the only relationships I had experienced – husbands, a sibling, and numerous bosses who dominated me (with my compliant collusion), using unbalanced energy to gain power and try to weaken me. I failed to notice many of these people had their own self-interested agenda at the forefront.

When dogs are unstable and aggressive, their world becomes very small. Their owners are afraid to take them for walks or to the dog park because the dog may misbehave. The same is true for humans. Because Dominators are in attack mode much of the time, their world becomes restricted. Relationships fail, family members avoid them, they lose friends, they get thrown in jail, they lose jobs. If you know someone who has been labeled with certain psychological "diagnoses," such as Borderline Personality Disorder or Narcissistic Personality Disorder, this situation might sound very familiar.

To the Dominator, control can feel like powerful pack leader behavior, even when it is not. A person who is self-aware and comfortable in his dealings with other people would not attempt to exert an unhealthy type or level of control just to feel accepted. Self-acceptance is the solution.

You Hold the Power – Break Free of Control by Disengaging

One fall I received a phone call from my father. He was being honored by the university where he had been a professor for nearly 40 years. He asked me to join him for brunch at the president's house, then for a football game with seats in the president's box, and a recognition ceremony at halftime. The invitation was for him and a guest. When I told Ray, he reacted in what I now see is a predictable way. Rather than being happy for my father's honor and thrilled I could accompany him to this prestigious event, he thought only of himself and his insecure jealousy. His first response was to accuse me of wanting to go to the event so I could meet a man. As if I would pick up a guy at an event like that with my father standing next to me! Well, Ray pitched a fit, so I called my dad and he was able to wrangle another ticket. Ray never thought about the embarrassment my dad had to suffer in asking such a thing. He never thought about how I felt asking my father for the favor. Or did he think about it and these were humiliating hoops we had just jumped through that affirmed Ray's power over us?

Well, the day before the football game arrived and we were to drive to four hours to my father's, spend the night, then attend the event. As often happened when Ray was nervous about an event, he came home from work late and drunk. His attitude had now changed direction 180 degrees. He didn't want to go to the event and he didn't want me to go.

He seemed to have no conception that his change in attitude was appallingly rude, not to mention blatantly manipulative. So I told him I would go alone. Well, you know this solution wasn't going to fly. He pouted and argued. When he realized he really had no rational reason not to let me go, he decided he would, after all, join me. He said he had to keep a close eye on me. In case I should – what, jump a guy on the buffet table? I should have fled alone that night. Instead, after hours of delay, he finally packed a bag and we left. The entire four-hour drive was nothing but Ray arguing, complaining, whining, and generally acting like a child. And me begging him to stop, crying, pleading with him not to ruin this fine event with his jealousy and immaturity. I threatened to turn around, but didn't. We arrived at my dad's so late it was embarrassing, then Ray spent most of the night continuing to argue with me. By morning my eyes were red from lack of sleep and crying. I gave in. We left for home immediately, with me saying Ray was sick. He certainly was!

I was sick myself at how poorly Ray had behaved and at missing such a nice event for my father. It wasn't until a few years later I realized that these beliefs, as normal as they seemed to me at the time, were exactly what allowed Ray to manipulate me. I felt as if his immature behavior reflected on me. And he knew that I cared a lot about what other people thought about me, and as a consequence, my husband. Once again, I was shot down by my need for approval by others. Dominators like Ray have a highly attuned sensor for emotional weak spots. My concern about "what the neighbors will think," was my soft underbelly. So he pitched a fit, knowing I would placate him to avoid a scene in front of others.

I now recognize the solution was unbelievably simple. I should have told myself, "If he misbehaves, it is not my problem. His immature behavior does not reflect on me." I should have acted as if I wasn't concerned about how his behavior reflected on me. Instead, I cared what everyone else thought, yet I didn't care about myself. It is sad that my need for acceptance by complete strangers trumped my need for self-acceptance.

I now understand that people only have a grip on you if you allow them to. We are powerful in relationships only to the degree we can control our emotional response to the other person's behaviors.

And another ironic lesson that I learned: Dominators are frightened because they know you hold all the cards. They realize if you walk away or disengage emotionally, they no longer have power over you. Even though I felt powerless in my relationship with Ray, I actually had far more power over him than I realized at the time.

Be aware that if you adopt an attitude of disengagement, the Dominator in your life may feel very threatened because you are breaking the spell – the unspoken contract that you two had arranged. The Dominator may actually say he's "fallen out of love" with you, or criticize you for "not being the woman he married," or go into blame mode by saying, "What's gotten into you?" Notice the "attack" pattern for what it is. Rather than questioning his own behaviors he lashes out at you. He desperately wants you to go back to the relationship pattern you two had agreed to: You cowering and him snarling and growling.

Resist the Urge to Defend when Attacked

When I look back at the many arguments I had with Ray, I see a very obvious pattern. He would attack, I would defend. He would accuse, I would explain. He had no problem lying and ignoring facts. I felt compelled to correct every misstatement and factual error. I wanted to make sure he understood I had done nothing wrong, that I was a good person.

Of course, we will all be in relationships where there are differences of opinion. But arguments with Ray weren't about mistaken facts or misunderstandings. Being factually correct isn't what is at stake when Dominators argue with Submissives. What are at stake are the need to maintain power and the desire to push back against the threat of a personal critique. Winning is mainly about having the Submissive give in, because that way the Submissive will think twice about cornering and confronting the Dominator in the future. The Dominator then feels he has one less person to be on the alert for an attack from, permitting the Dominator to feel less anxious.

As a result, arguing with a Dominator is nearly always an exercise in futility. You are rarely going to convince a Dominator he is wrong. If you respond to his attack, he wins, no matter what you say. Because it allows him to distract you from the real issue: his original misbehavior.

I believe in honest communication, however, this pattern must begin early in the relationship. If you are already in an unhealthy relationship and an argument ensues, I'd suggest that often the best way to respond to a Dominator is to disengage. It may seem counterintuitive, but to the Dominator, your indifference is more powerful than any "winning" rational argument you put forth if you engage in the argument.

How you respond determines your power. When Ray began an argument, I should have changed tactics totally: Don't argue, don't reply, don't explain, don't defend. Don't battle over "the truth." This is exactly what he wanted me to do. When I defended my reputation and tried to "correct the record," it showed I cared what he thought of me and what others thought of me. I was showing him my cards.

This is the type of scenario when too many words can be a sign of weakness and submissiveness. Explaining gives away power. I now know that sometimes a single calm, concise, assertive statement is more powerful than 20 minutes of lecturing or pleading. With persistent application of this tactic, the Dominator will start to sense that he isn't pulling your strings any more.

I now recognize that Dominators use a certain style when arguing, as well. As I can attest, Dominators don't disagree with you in a respectful way or argue fairly. They use zigzag arguing tactics, changing direction every time you get close to proving them wrong. Again, remember that the facts are unimportant. What is important is that the Dominator can never believe he is wrong, can never allow criticism. Ray would allege I had an affair with a man. I would deny it and state evidence to prove it, then he would change course and complain that I had ignored him at a party three weeks ago or some other red herring misperception. I believed I had to restart my defensive arguments.

Don't be distracted by his distractions, his distortions of the truth, his jumbled arguments, his irrational thoughts. If you are in an argument and your partner says something off the wall, use the following test. If you find yourself asking, "Where did that come from?" this is a sign he is using zigzag tactics to keep you off balance and cause you to question your reality. If you feel "crazy" when arguing with a Dominator, he's been successful. You are destabilized and he gains power.

Now I know to pause and disengage. Don't go chasing after the bait and hook the Dominator has thrown into the water. Instead, go in a totally different direction. Label his tactics. Ask: "We both know that isn't factually true. Please explain what makes you say that." Or: "You seem to be saying these things as a way to keep me off balance. That makes me wonder why you are doing that." Or talk about the feelings behind the statement: "You seem to be acting very jealous. Am I correct in that pereption?"

Then wait for an answer without responding or adding anything else to your questions.

If the Dominator persists in zigzagging and lying, do everything you can to disengage either physically or emotionally or both. Most Submissives have a tough time with this because they want so much to be liked. It seems rude to turn your back and walk away. Submissives also don't enjoy it when lies are told about them and they desperately want to "correct the record." Remember: If you react and respond and defend yourself, you've already lost! The Dominator knows you care and you've been hooked. Even if you "win" the argument, you lose just by participating in this charade. It may not feel like it at first, but by walking away you'll actually gain power.

I watch Reilly disengage from unbalanced dogs all the time. When one confronts her too aggressively, she barks, then turns and runs, not in fear, but just to get away. Reilly doesn't stop and explain her behaviors, she just acts. How powerful is that communication compared to all the words, words, words we love to use?

Respect Is Love in Action

I know some people will say: "But I DO care what this person thinks. He's my husband. I love him." That is what I would have said about Ray when we were together. But I now know this: Respect is love in action. Is he showing you respect by lying about you and making up falsehoods? Is he showing respect by controlling you and demeaning you and stirring up arguments? Is he showing respect by badmouthing you, perhaps in front of the kids or the relatives? That isn't love, and that certainly isn't respect. Respect yourself enough to do what is right. It is your job as a pack leader to show him you have expectations for behavior. And being treated respectfully is the first and most important rule there is. Without respect, there is no love.

If you think someone will change "this time" because you overlook his bad behavior, realize the likely root of your "forgiveness" is your need for acceptance. You are enabling behavior, however, that does not lead to someone valuing and accepting you. Rather, your inability to stand up for yourself and demand respect is causing the person to disrespect you yet again – rewarding him for his behavior, rather than disciplining him for it. What you see as kindness, he sees as weakness.

Keep the Pack Calm

After I got divorced for the second time, I moved to another state and rented a house. I was working in my yard one afternoon while the neighbors were hosting an Easter egg hunt next door. Christie, my new neighbor, called me over and I introduced myself to her, her husband, Justin, and the other assorted kids and neighbors at the party.

The next time Christie and I met it started out as normal, neighbor-over-the-fence conversation. Very quickly, though, Christie moved from basic questions about me to an intimate discussion of her life and her problems.

Her frankness was an eye-opener for me. After only a few minutes I knew more about Christie's sex life, marriage problems, health issues, and parenting dilemmas than I had learned in years from close friends.

At first I didn't think too much of it and actually welcomed such a friendly person in my life when I was new in town and lonely. But I quickly learned Christie wasn't actually friendly. Not in the true sense. Her goal was to get attention from anyone at any cost and the more "friends" she had in her orbit, the more attention she could garner.

While she did have a talent for bringing people together socially and often held parties, it quickly became apparent that the entire reason for hosting a party was so Christie could have a stage to perform on. (To the point that she even kept all her house lights on full blast as if they were klieg lights for her show.) Parties usually devolved into Christie parading around in very few clothes, lifting her top to show you her "new boobs," telling lewd jokes, and otherwise embarrassing people.

Being with her was like standing next to the sun. Everything from her piercing voice to her bright clothing to her wacky antics said, "Look at me."

I could surmise why Christie was so attention seeking: She had been adopted as a child and probably didn't have the ideal childhood. The need to replace lost parental affection and attention was clearly so strong it was taking over her life. And even more sadly, it was causing a person who had a lot of good qualities to become so unlikeable that she alienated people. Christie was a fun-loving, generous, sociable person who could have had many friends and gotten plenty of attention in a positive way. Instead she made people uncomfortable with her crazy antics, tall tales, and emotional neediness.

I began to notice behaviors in Christie I had seen before in people, but hadn't put a label on. With my newfound awareness of human behavior, I began to, for the first time, examine her actions. More important, I began to consider my reactions and make a conscious choice about how I responded.

I'm glad I met Christie because it helped me realize there is more than one way to control someone. I recognized in the past I would have been sucked right in, unthinking, into Christie's orbit and would have been unable to set limits. I would have fallen under the control of someone like her and done everything she wanted – but unconsciously resented it, not knowing why I felt as I did. Instead, I now calmly and appropriately enforced boundaries and she got the message I was not a person she could manipulate.

Don't Demand Attention

Christie was the type of Dominator who develops a blatant need to be the center of attention, whether by being overly emotional or overly dramatic, by imagining illnesses, by sulking and acting "depressed," or by blaming others – anything they can do to be center stage. It is as if every decision and action is scripted to in some way generate attention. Their need for belonging overwhelms nearly all other functions of emotional stability.

Using their physical presence to demand attention, they often affect grand gestures and may be opinionated to the point of being offensive. Their clothes are usually bright and flamboyant. They may be very image conscious and status conscious, often wearing brand name or designer clothing. When they talk, it is loud, too much, and every topic revolves around them. If they feel ignored, they will "fight" to gain center stage and garner the attention they desperately need.

I remember attending one party at Christie and Justin's house. We had a potluck dinner spread out and as Justin stood next to Christie saying a prayer, she actually grabbed his butt, giggled, and made a sexual comment. Justin awkwardly stopped in the middle of the prayer, everyone looked up, and we were all embarrassed. Except Christie, of course. It was as if she couldn't make it through 60 seconds of a prayer without "grabbing" everyone's attention.

Drama queens tend to arrive late at most functions and have outrageous stories and excuses for their lateness. This permits a continually reinforcement of the message: "Look how powerful I am. I can make you wait for me. I can then have a grand entrance and force everyone to listen to my tale of woe." For some Dominators, even attention for negative behaviors feeds the never-ending need for the spotlight.

Don't Control with Emotions

A large swath of Dominators uses emotional moodiness – or the threat of it – to keep others walking on eggshells. They will conjure up a bad mood to control the emotional climate around them. These

Dominators don't want to be in a good mood if being in a bad mood gets them attention and the ability to manage the responses of others.

If you find yourself constantly having to be the optimist with someone, propping up her emotional responses, this is a warning sign. If she is always negative and you are always the one saying, "Oh, the trip to the beach will be OK, the weather will be fine," or "The party will be fun, let's go," then watch out. You feel that if you don't prop up her tender feelings then the moodiness will get worse. Well, guess what? By constantly trying to mollify her, you are merely training her to continue with this behavior. Giving a growling dog a treat means you'll get more growling. Guaranteed.

Because others are unassertive and afraid to confront this type of behavior, however, it continues. The Submissives in their life moderate their emotions to adapt – and, bingo, the Dominators know they have power over them. Dominators train others: "If you confront me, I'll blow up." So the pattern is repeated because the drama queen gets rewarded with what she wants: attention, control, power, and safety from criticism.

Obviously, taking responsibility for someone else's moods is unhealthy for both of you and clearly a sign of an unbalanced relationship. It can set up a situation that can spiral into increasing amounts of control and manipulation.

If you ever feel as if you can't express your own emotions and wants for fear of the Dominator's reaction, yet the other person has free reign to complain and kvetch, beware. Both parties in a relationship should be able to express their emotions appropriately. If you are holding back, you are being controlled by the threat of the other person's reaction.

If you feel you might be the Submissive partner in this type of emotional blackmail, here is a test to ask yourself: If I behaved as my partner is behaving, would I get the same response from him as I am giving? If I threw an emotional hissy fit, how would my partner react? If I moped around and acted depressed, expecting my partner to lift me out of my foul mood, what would she do? If I was overly dramatic or caused a scene, what would happen? If the reaction you predict isn't the same as your overly solicitous, nurturing response, then you've got an imbalance of power and control. Someone's driving this emotional bus and it isn't you.

An acquaintance of mine, Stephanie, exhibits attention-seeking behavior in a variety of ways. Most of the time she is the classic manic, loud, hyperactive drama queen. She dresses flamboyantly and has an opinion about everything. At times, though, she will try the opposite approach. She acts depressed, speaks in a whisper, complains about her circumstances, and looks for sympathy. It is interesting to watch people react to this "depression" act. Most people, quite naturally, ask her what is wrong, which opens a floodgate of explanations about the drama in her life at the moment. Success! Stephanie still occupies center stage. Stephanie is choosing to behave this way, consciously modifying her behavior for each situation to gain the most attention.

Pretending to be the victim of uncontrollable emotional problems is just an act in the Dominator's repertoire. Note the situations and times when these drama queens have "crises." They will often act out well-timed emotional meltdowns to achieve maximum effect – at family holidays, in large crowds, or just prior to an event. Clearly, this signals these behaviors are not symptoms of an uncontrollable mental illness. Instead, a dramatic Dominator will loudly and broadly announce his supposed crisis. Often the symptoms fade quickly when the wished-for effect isn't achieved or he gets bored with the act. Obviously, the emotional crisis wasn't so real after all.

One of the most egregious examples I heard was this: A couple had travelled to Washington, D.C., to attend one of the most prestigious of the presidential inaugural balls that are held every four years. As they were getting dressed they received a call from their 15-year-old daughter who was back home. She proudly announced that she had just lost her virginity – a blatant cry for attention timed for when mom and dad were away and not paying sufficient attention to her (so she believed).

While many dramatic Dominators might appear to be pack leaders because they are always center stage, they are actually unbalanced, so do not qualify for that title. They may be very extraverted, gathering people around them as a pack leader might, but their goals are not selfless. This entourage is merely an audience for their performances. You are only a valuable member of their pack when you are present and paying attention. If you do not respond positively to the attention-seeking behavior, then you are worthless.

Drama queens tend to disrupt the emotional or social balance of nearly all environments they enter. On one level they do this simply because they can. It's as if they want to create turmoil wherever they go because this confirms that they are the center of attention: "Look what I can do!"

In contrast, think about the wolf pack. A pack leader would never arbitrarily stir up trouble and negative energy in the pack. This would not only distract the pack from its important focus on survival, it could unleash a fight – and what leader would want to provoke a fight among a bunch of strong animals with sharp teeth and powerful jaws? Yet this is exactly what drama queens seem to do in their lives – sow disruption and chaos, usually favoring emotional crises.

A pack leader is generous and considerate, not emotionally needy. However, dramatic Dominators are anything but. When this type of person enters a room, the energy all drains to her corner. She is a black hole, sucking everyone toward her bottomless pit of neediness and negativity. In contrast, a good pack leader increases the energy in a room by sharing positive feelings and ensuring that others share the spotlight.

Drama queens enjoy the attention and energy they pull from others, largely because they can't generate feelings of acceptance and positive support on their own. They look externally for approval because they lack internal self-worth.

Be Self-Observant, Not Self-Absorbed

The emotional intelligence skills of attention-seekers are extremely shallow and weak, and what skills they do have are overwhelmed by their need for attention. It can be almost comical. Many dramatic Dominators act out so outrageously that those around them give blatant signals the behavior is inappropriate. Nonetheless, the perpetrator completely fails to recognize these responses.

I watched numerous times as a certain Dominator in my life was condescending and rude to waiters and clerks. I would see these people blatantly rolling their eyes and shaking their heads, but she never noticed. She was so wrapped up in her performance that she failed to see that the audience was unimpressed. I witnessed waiters who started out as pleasant and helpful, but in the course of a few minutes of being subjected to her domineering antics morphed into providing grudging, sullen service. (I only hope they didn't spit in my soup!)

I was eating lunch with this person in a Sunset Boulevard restaurant once and she was doing her normal schtick: Talking too loudly, gesturing too wildly, almost knocking over a glass. Since I wasn't getting any chance to speak (surprise!) I had plenty of time to scan the restaurant. I noticed that the neighboring diners, all with that super-laidback Southern California demeanor, were shooting her looks. Maybe in some parts of the country her antics might play, but in L.A., the land of cool, they definitely were out of place. But did she notice these looks? Not a chance. Her skills were limited to receiving the most superficial signals from others: "Are people looking at me and letting me talk? Great. That is the end of my need to pick up emotional signals from others."

The fact that the other person is bored, uninvolved in the conversation, or even hostile to her behavior escapes notice when she is at the height of a performance.

I believe there are more female than male dramatic types because of cultural and gender tendencies. Men are more predisposed to turn to a physical manifestation of the fight response when they are threatened. Women, through socialization, are not as likely to react with violence, but choose to lash out with verbal attacks, emotional drama, and social chaos.

A Good Conversation has Two Participants

You may notice some people rarely ask your opinion or seek to include you in conversation. These are soapbox orators, not conversationalists, and rarely want to hear your side of the topic. When a drama queen is on stage, expect only a series of soliloquies. To admit anyone else knows more than she does would be a sign of weakness.

I was at a holiday party once when a woman began talking about how her son was serving in the military in Iraq and would not be home for Christmas. We all became quiet and offered our thoughts for her and her son and wished her family well. Before we could even finish these supportive comments, a woman named Debbie steamrolled into the conversation with a long, tedious story of how her second cousin's friend served in Iraq five years ago. I was amazed at her insensitivity. How does this event that happened five years ago to someone we don't know come close to comparing to our friend's difficult situation worrying about her son surviving now? But Debbie charged ahead, concerned only that the spotlight was back on her.

In a good conversation there is back and forth. Conversations build and escalate to deeper meaning and related topics. Most of us have noticed that good conversationalists seem to ask more questions than they answer. If they answer a question it deepens and improves the conversation. A good conversation is a circle – except with dramatic types, where all conversational roads lead to them.

I watched this happen for years with a person I'll call Lenore. The worst case was when a group of us had rented a large cottage for a week. It was a fun vacation, especially because I rarely got to see two pre-teen girls that were daughters of someone I knew, as they lived across the country. These girls were pre-teenagers at the time and were fairly shy. I discussed at length with Lenore how we would finally have time to engage these girls in conversation and learn more about them. I knew I planned to ask them questions, encourage them to talk, focus on their interests. Ah, that might have been my agenda, but it wasn't Lenore's, despite what she told me.

One night all 17 of us were sitting at a large table having dinner. We were a talkative group, and even I found it hard to get a word in edgewise. But, quite surprisingly, one of the girls, Kayla, actually made a comment about the subject at hand. I quickly realized this was an opportunity to get her to open up. I asked her a follow-up question and all eyes at the table turned to Kayla. Perfect, I thought. This is what we need to do more of. Lenore, forgetting everything we had discussed about encouraging Kayla to socialize, jumped in boisterously with her own barely relevant story, steamrolling over Kayla, who immediately returned to her normal, subdued manner, staring at her plate. Of course, my glares at Lenore were unseen. An opportunity lost for Kayla, a stage regained for Lenore.

Clearly, many of us love to tell stories, crack jokes, and feel as if we are the center of attention at times. But with some people, you will notice this behavior at all times, in all situations, even when inappropriate.

Don't Imagine Illness

Some Dominators adopt what the psychology profession calls "somaticizing behavior." They will falsify or exaggerate medical symptoms. What better way to gain attention? Doctors have to listen, and it is a ready audience for yet another manipulation. Of course, many dramatic Dominators learned in childhood they got attention when they were sick, so they equate being sick with being loved.

Suicide Threats Are the Ultimate Emotional Manipulation

When I filed for divorce from Ray there was no doubt in my mind it was the right thing to do. He had pushed the abuse too far, and I could not take it any longer. But Ray continued to try to re-ensnare me in his web. He would alternate tender, loving comments with hateful, vengeful ranting. Now I know he was using every manipulative skill he had honed over his lifetime, every trick that had succeeded in the past to control women. Then one day came the suicide threat – the DefCon Level 4, Red Alert, Final Effort, Pull-Out-All-the-Stops emotional manipulation. I recall that at the time I almost laughed. Ray was the least suicidal person I knew. Even in my ignorance about human behavior I sensed that this was clearly not a realistic threat and merely a last-ditch ploy to get me back under his control. Not to say that aggressive, emotionally manipulative people don't commit suicide. The classic murder-suicide that occurs when a domestic abuser shoots his partner then kills himself is all too common. These men want so desperately to control their partners and fear rejection so strongly that they see killing the partner as the only solution. Of course, once this is done they realize they have killed the one person with whom they had formed an (unhealthy) attachment, so they then kill themselves. The suicide also likely occurs because the Dominator recognizes he would find it emotionally impossible to face the shame of arrest and conviction.

Honest Confrontation Is the Only Solution

Dramatic Dominators have learned that others back down from aggressive behavior. They know most people are afraid of confrontation and fear the "scenes" that might result. So, not unexpectedly, the behavior continues.

With some people in my life, I have decided it is very unhealthy for me to deal with them. They are unlikely to change, as my repeated discussions have proved, so it is best for me to distance myself. By continuing to interact, I reward poor behavior with my presence. I would be saying, "It's OK if you act like a jerk to everyone, because I'm not correcting you."

Pack leaders correct behavior early and often, just as they would correct a dog trying to dominate by biting or jumping up and insisting on attention.

A SUMMARY OF DOMINATOR BEHAVIORS

Dominators may act aggressively and maybe even confidently, however, they are, at their core, insecure, have low self-acceptance, and are desperate for acceptance and attention from others. Their neediness for belonging is often characterized by attention-seeking tendencies with manipulative dramatic or emotional behaviors or through jealousy and control of a partner. Many Dominators have a strong tendency to define themselves by others' opinions. Because they have low self-worth they are often unable to accept blame, they can't apologize when at fault, and can't accept responsibility for their actions. Because of this and their belief that they are dominant over others, they tend to feel privileged and entitled. At the extreme this can lead to cruel, violent, and criminal behavior. At the least it fosters a lack of empathy for others. Substance abuse issues are a key sign of low self-worth and the need to self-medicate anxiety, but indicate a lack of accountability for personal behaviors.

Characteristic behaviors of Dominators include:

BLAMING
- unable to accept blame or responsibility
- unable to apologize or admit fault
- lacking in self-awareness, self-reflection
- opinionated and reluctant to change opinions once set
- fail to conform to social norms, violate laws
- feel they are special, have a sense of entitlement
- have disregard for others or lack of empathy for others
- have a lack of remorse
- arrogant, haughty
- self-centered, feel they have special talents, expect special treatment
- irresponsible in many areas of life
- unwilling to work or do chores

CONTROLLING
Dominators use many forms of dominance to gain control. By controlling others they feel they can ensure they have a steady stream of attention and a feeling of acceptance.
- manipulative, exploits others
- deceitful, dishonest
- uses conflict or the threat of physical or emotional conflict to keeps others off balance
- jealous, fearful of abandonment by intimate partner

PREFERS THE FIGHT RESPONSE
- physical violence, intimidation
- anger and aggression
- emotional threats
- reckless, impulsive, irritable
- doesn't handle frustration well
- short attention span

ATTENTION SEEKING
- dramatic, emotional behaviors
- may lie or exaggerate achievements to seek approval
- loud, opinionated, bossy

- falsify or exaggerate physical symptoms to gain attention and sympathy
- emotional threats, such as suicide gestures or false moodiness to gain attention
- can act as "star" or "victim," but the goal is always to get attention
- demeans or criticizes others to appear more powerful or successful

Range of Dominator Behaviors in the Diagnostic and Statistical Manual (DSM)

If you or someone you know has been diagnosed with one of the following disorders, it is a sign of a Dominator type of personality using primarily "fight" responses.

Anti-social Personality Disorder
Conduct Disorder (under age 18)
Borderline Personality Disorder
Schizoaffective Disorder
Somatization Disorder
Factitious Disorders
Histrionic Personality Disorder
Narcissistic Personality Disorder
Delusional Disorder:
Shared Psychotic Disorder
Oppositional Defiant Disorder (under age 18)
Attention Hyperactivity Deficit Disorder

Pack Leader Wisdom:
Dominators use the "fight" response
to protect their low self-worth.
Dominators lash out and are reluctant
to be accountable as a way to avoid criticism.

CHAPTER 10

Be Subordinate, Not Submissive

I was constantly amazed at the synergies I experienced while writing this book. At one point I was developing two key ideas: that Submissives used a form of control and that everyone defines affection differently. At just that moment I experienced these concepts firsthand in my life, when I had the opportunity to care for a stray dog for a few days. Piccadilly was a very sweet pit bull with a beautiful harlequin coat. She was so submissive that she'd show you her belly at first meeting. She snuggled up to everyone and enjoyed being petted and scratched. I thought she would get along well with Reilly. Boy, was I wrong!

Reilly never warmed up to Piccadilly and, in fact, spent the entire time avoiding Piccadilly, leaving the room if she entered, giving up her favorite bed, backing away from treats, and generally being avoidant.

Piccadilly made no overt dominance moves toward Reilly. She did not put her head over Reilly's shoulders or jump on her back. She did not charge, growl, or eyeball her. I was watching carefully to make sure no fight broke out, but I never saw Piccadilly act aggressively. She tried to play, but Reilly – who loves to play fetch and catch – gave up the toy instantly if Piccadilly wanted it.

Piccadilly spent her time following me around incessantly, trying to crawl onto my lap, getting in the way, and generally being sweet, as most people would define it. But to me, it was quickly obvious that Piccadilly was too sweet. Her demeanor was as if she was trying to send two messages: "I'm not a threat. Like me," and "If I can get you to like me, I can get you to do anything I want. I'll have you wrapped around my finger. I can control you."

Since she had been a stray in a big city with lots of feral dogs I'm certain Piccadilly learned these habits as a survival technique. She instinctively used her "go along, get along" tactics to avoid getting into fights. The lowest, most submissive members of a pack pay constant attention to the more dominant members as a way to pay homage, but also to be on the alert for changes in status or aggression.

However, her sweetness felt to me like manipulation, which it was. She used her insistence on being petted as a way to signal, "I'm not dominant"– yet she actually was trying to control me. She attempted to act weak so she would not appear to be a threat to anyone. Her fake submissiveness covered up the fact she was really a stubborn dog. When I tried to get her into the shower or into a crate her real character showed up.

Boy, did that hit home with me. Sounded like someone describing me from a few years ago.

I immediately and intuitive realized Piccadilly's behavior was evidence that Submissives really are controllers at heart. They behaved as they did to get people to like them, but also to get people to do what they wanted – subtle forms of manipulation. This form of attention-seeking behavior feeds the Submissive's needs and calms insecurities.

After just 48 hours with Piccadilly, I felt worn out. The tension between the dogs was obvious with their body language, but I, too, recognized I was tense. The energy level in the house had escalated because of this clingy dog following me everywhere, looking to me constantly for attention and affection. I became aware that everything I did made the dog react. With Reilly I can get up, empty the dishwasher and bang a pot, and she won't come running at every sound and with every movement. With Piccadilly, she tuned in to my every twitch. I could never get away from her neediness. While many people would have loved having this 100 percent affection and attention, to me it was stressful. I couldn't even do yoga without Piccadilly literally getting in my face.

This nonstop barrage of neediness felt like I was being sucked dry. Piccadilly was playing me constantly to get me to acknowledge her.

This incident confirmed that being overly needy is a form of control.

Reilly once again had taught me an important lesson. She sensed Piccadilly was much too needy and unbalanced. Piccadilly masked her manipulation and control in a false submissive style. I was fooled for a while, but Reilly wasn't.

You Don't Always Have to Give or Give In to Get What You Want

Piccadilly appeared to be giving me affection, but to me it felt manipulative. I began to think: Was this the effect I had on others when I had been Submissive? Even though I had been self-sufficient and independent in many ways, had I given off signals I was emotionally dependent? Did my eagerness to please have an effect on my past relationships? Was this how Ray and Paul had felt when I was around? Did my neediness drive Paul to become emotionally avoidant? I had thought I was giving affection, but was it over-the-top, unhealthy, and laden with manipulative agendas?

I thought back to times with my husbands and boyfriends. If they looked hungry, I offered them food. If they looked bored, I suggested we go out. If they looked tired, I suggested they take it easy. I was super-attentive, thinking I was being helpful and loving. Instead, I was smothering. My nonstop focus on the other person was not healthy for either of us. The evidence had shown up in a stray dog.

After experiencing Piccadilly, I understood how they felt. Just as I felt drained dealing with Piccadilly's neediness, it was obvious a needy wife could have the same effect on a husband. I couldn't help but realize that my behavior had probably pushed both Paul and Ray away from me. Who wouldn't push back against someone who constantly looked to others for validation? While I was never verbally needy, never asked for a compliment or insisted on hearing, "I love you," I'm sure I gave off those vibes 24/7.

And I had to fully admit that my neediness had some role in driving Ray to become violent. Of course, he must take full responsibility for his actions as an abuser. Nothing I did was worthy of a punch. OK, so I was overeager: I cooked great dinners every night, kept a clean house, worked two jobs, and paid all the bills on time. That clearly doesn't earn a person bruises! But I now could see how my desire to please created a tension and instability Ray could not handle because he came into the relationship so unbalanced.

Submissiveness is Learned

The roots of my Submissive tendencies became very apparent during therapy after my second marriage fell apart. As my therapist asked me questions to get a complete family history, my answers to those questions opened my eyes to my family and our dynamics in ways I had never considered before. When I took stock of my parents and their behavior toward me, I realized that what I considered to be a "Norman Rockwell" family actually was somewhat dysfunctional emotionally.

One of the most shocking moments was when I first admitted that my parents had never said they loved me in my entire life. My grandparents had never said it either. I am not blaming my parents and living in the past, however I mention this fact because I had not considered this aspect of my childhood before I entered therapy. I had always labeled my parents as perfect. I had not criticized their parenting once or examined the lessons they had taught me. They had been firmly on an unquestioned pedestal.

Before my mother died, I recalled she had once given me a side-door compliment: She told me some of the nurses in the hospital had said I was a wonderful daughter because I visited so much and took such good care of her. I remember how nice it was to hear that from my mother because even this very indirect compliment was so rare. That was perhaps the most loving statement my mother had ever made about me and I could recall it years after it had happened.

It made me realize this lack of parental expression of love would cause someone to go seeking affection from just about anyone who would give it. No wonder I was so emotionally needy!

I also looked back at my childhood and realized I had unconsciously adopted a Submissive persona as a way to try to get my parents' attention. I can't imagine how I could have been a more obedient child. I never even went to a party or drank in high school. I went on about two dates and never even kissed a boy until after high school. I was president of the honor society, first chair in band, editor of the school newspaper, and nearly a straight A student. The list of my accomplishments was extensive, but despite being a desperately "good girl" and a hard worker, I do not remember being praised. My parents believed giving a compliment was the road to perdition and damnation. Getting a big head was a real sin in our house. My brother and I were not allowed to talk back or misbehave – we were one of the last generations raised with the idea children are to be seen and not heard, to speak only when spoken to.

This lack of praise continued even when I was an adult when I would have been able to take their compliments without learning "bad" behaviors. But when I was accepted to an honors program in college: No comment. Honor roll my freshman year in college? Yawn. Award-winning reporter my senior year? Not a word.

I certainly didn't get a big head from my upbringing. Just the opposite. Painfully shy would have been a better description of me throughout my high school years. For 40-plus years I was self-deprecating, suffered from low self-worth, and was certainly never an attention-seeking type of person.

It was an important step for me to admit that as a child I hadn't gotten the love and attention I needed to feel strong and confident. I then had to take the even-bigger step and admit that I was never going to get that much-wanted love from my parents. By that time my mother was dead and my father, well into his 70s, was not going to change his ways and suddenly start acting emotionally effusive. Once I could admit that, I was able to move on. I could stop looking for approval from others and generate love and support from within myself.

While "good girl" characteristics are to be valued if done for the correct reasons, I now realize that I was acting this way mainly because I felt it would earn the respect and praise of those around me. Now if I do something, it is because I want to, I enjoy it, or I know someone else will enjoy it – not to earn approval.

Of course, Submissive personality traits earned me the opposite: disrespect in relationships, friendships, and on the job. I was unconsciously setting myself up to be dominated by controlling, aggressive people.

The lack of praise from my parents did more than give me a poor self-image. It taught me not to trust my own instincts. When my therapist called what my parents did a lie, I was shocked. But their lack of expressions of love and of proper praise were essentially lies. As a result I experienced a huge disconnect throughout my life about the most fundamental elements of my personality, my capabilities, my intellect, my morals, and my character. I was doing all the things I'd been told to do, so I rationally knew they were correct. I also felt, intuitively, I was a good person (and I was). But the very people I was working so hard to please seemed tremendously unimpressed by my efforts. I was told, by their silence and their dismissal, that my own brain, gut, and emotional reactions were wrong. That my sense I was doing good things was somehow out of kilter with the rest of the world – a world I could intellectually and logically see agreed with my perceptions. (Being on the honor roll is a good thing, right? It seems so to other parents.) Parents are such a powerful influence on our lives we are willing to suspend our belief in what the entire universe is telling us and believe what our family says.

The lesson that I should disregard my intuition was taught in other ways.

My parents consistently gave me very mixed messages. On major life decisions, such as where to go to college, what career to pursue, what jobs to take, what city to live in, and which men to marry, they stayed totally and completely silent. They gave me no help, no advice, made no attempt to discuss these issues with me in any way. They signaled I was competent to handle these difficult decisions on my own. However, during summers when I came home from college and was working the closing shift at a fast food restaurant, I would occasionally go out to breakfast with my friends after work, coming home at 2 a.m. This caused huge screaming matches. No matter how much I assured them it was safe and innocent and we weren't drinking and having sex, my parents ranted and raved. What was this telling me about my judgment? That at age 18 I couldn't discern that going to a diner with a group of friends I'd known for years was not likely to lead me to become a sex-crazed, drug-using, criminal freak? (Or whatever fears my parents had.) My parents were not showing me respect for my own ability to make a small decision – a decision that at age 18 I certainly could handle. I had given them no indication to that point that I was misbehaving in any other area of my life. And they trusted me to make the major life decisions without any input. How confusing! Was I completely responsible or completely irresponsible? Was I trustworthy or not?

These mixed messages signaled to me that my thought processes weren't correct: "See, you think you're doing the right thing and you're still getting screamed at by your parents." If that doesn't make you question your judgment, what will? I would spend the next few decades of my life distrusting my own intuition about myself and others, my talents, and my ability to deal with the world. How fascinating that I would be super-competent at all things practical and logical, and incredibly incompetent at anything involving emotions and relationships. Proof that if you raise a child to value one behavior and devalue another, you will succeed. Treat a person as if she is something and she will reward you with being exactly that.

My life shows how to raise a child who seeks approval at all costs: Withhold love and praise and honest reflections. She will learn being disapproved of is the worst thing that could happen to her, priming her for a lifetime of searching for others' approval and avoiding criticism, rather than developing her internal self-worth. She'll seek endlessly to please others, setting up an unhealthy and potentially dangerous scenario for her personal relationships, work relationships, and friendships. She will distrust the most valuable asset in her emotional repertoire – her intuition.

Submissives Say: "Please Like Me so I Can Like Myself"

Just as Piccadilly was trying to manipulate with wriggling and snuggling, Submissives send the message, "Please like me so I can like myself," with their body language, their eyes, and their words. They look for approval and acceptance from people around them, hoping others will offer the love and affection they can't give themselves. These "pleasers" are constantly seeking attention and affirmation by being nonthreatening.

Submissives have an unbalanced energy and project weakness immediately, dangerous traits in both the dog and human worlds.

Just as a dog may cower in the corner over some inconsequential sound, Submissives see threats in things that are in no way truly threatening. Their biggest fear is to be criticized by others, so they fear conflict, negative emotions, and the angry response of others.

Remember the difference between submissive and subordinate: Being subordinate is not a negative behavior. We can't all be pack leaders, nor do some of us want to be. Some people are quite happy to be followers in the pack – and that's a good thing! When you are subordinate you are still a balanced pack member, you're just willing to have someone else be the pack leader.

However, overly submissive dogs and humans do not just accept their subordinate place in the pack and live confidently in that role. Submissives constantly adjust their behavior, accommodating themselves to others in a misguided attempt to try to control the responses of others. These behaviors are manipulative because the goal is not altruistic, but an attempt to curry favor.

Just as Dominators try to "distress" others as a way to gain power, Submissives try to "de-stress" those around them. I would work hard to try to reduce the anxiety and discomfort of others by avoiding conflict and drama. Of course, this meant that I had to ignore my own discomfort – emotional and physical.

The typical Submissive exhibits a range of traits that put her in a very weak position in the world, including:

- low self-worth and self-acceptance
- an excessive need for external acceptance
- "good girl" and perfectionist behavior
- fear of conflict and criticism
- reluctance to express emotions
- fear of being controlled
- lack of emotional boundaries
- overly responsible
- weak emotional intelligence skills
- very reactive to others' emotions and behaviors

Being "Too Good" Gets You Treated Bad

Submissives do not usually seek attention by blatantly strutting into the spotlight, but would rather sidle onto stage by being good. Submissives are often overeager worker bees in many areas of their lives, earning good grades, working hard, and pleasing others. Because they base their self-worth on their latest achievement, it is a sign they are looking externally for validation.

Having had an extreme case of "good girl syndrome" when I was younger, I see how this behavior pattern continued throughout much of my life. It started innocently enough trying to please teachers, parents, and other authority figures by always having the right answer. Being wrong would feel like rejection, because I was raised to believe I got acceptance for being "right" or "good" or "quiet." So what worked as a child, must still work as an adult, right? I kept trying to earn affection and control others with my obedient, correct behaviors.

Looking back, I recall many instances where someone would ask me a question and I would immediately jump in with an answer, usually involving my experiences or knowledge. Although I was shy, in these situations I tended to talk too much, giving people way more information than they really wanted. I never stopped to consider what the person was really asking.

Many years ago a female colleague unexpectedly invited me to lunch. Soon she asked if I planned on having children. I rambled on about why I wasn't. Only in passing did I ask her if she was planning to have children. I now realize she was using me as a sounding board to discuss whether she should have children. Instead, I turned it into a lengthy essay on the topic, rather than recognizing her emotional need to open up, discuss this intimate topic, and engage in a meaningful conversation. I was so eager to impress her with my informed decision-making skills that I totally missed an opportunity to connect with her and be truly helpful as a good listener. I was all fact and no feeling.

The need to be a "good girl" can show up in small ways. One day I came to the realization that I said the phrase, "I know," in response to others' suggestions far too often. It had become like many speech patterns – a space filler I didn't even think about. When someone gave me advice or a recommendation, I would automatically say, "I know." I didn't say the phrase harshly, but rather with a nod of my head and an acquiescent tone. (Always the pleaser!) I now see this phrase was loaded with unintended meanings. When someone gives you a well-intentioned suggestion, saying "I know" implies you don't need help because you already know the answer. It shuts down the conversation, rather than open it. A better response might be with a reflective question: "So you think if I join a health club I'll meet athletic men?" Or how about a thank you and compliment: "Thanks for thinking of me! What a good idea. I'll check out joining a health club tomorrow."

I saw that being right and "in the know" all my life was a very ingrained habit even affecting my speech patterns. And with these small phrases I unwittingly sent Submissive signals.

Submissives generally get along well with others, but this is because they make such a concerted effort to do so. The tendency to scan for responses affects how Submissives communicate. As chameleons, Submissives are constantly observing other people for hints as to what is expected of them. I was always trying to give a response I thought someone wanted, rather than saying what I really felt.

Submissives are fearful of being different and work hard to fit in with the crowd. Because of this they tend to bend with the wind. Depending on the social situation their personality may shift – bubbly with a boisterous person, quiet with a somber person. Matching the energy style and level of someone you are interacting with, called mirroring, can be a socially helpful way to connect with someone, or can merely be a means to garner approval.

With these personality characteristics, many Submissives can usually claim very strong caring skills – they are often nurturing, loyal, and generous. You'll find Submissives in the caring professions such as nursing, teaching, and social work.

Perfection and Risk Avoidance are Ways to Avoid Shame

Submissives are often perfectionists, constantly overachieving so others will not judge them harshly. Some Submissives use an obsessive attention to detail and perfectionism as a way to structure their lives to avoid failure. They attempt to find fault with themselves so they can make a correction before others discover the fault.

Risk avoidance and perfectionism have, of course, the same basis: fear of criticism. These people say to themselves, "If I stay organized and under control, nothing can go wrong and no one can find fault."

Many Submissive and Avoidant types set rigid limits in their life as a way to avoid risk and failure. I have a friend who was on vacation and wanted to go for a walk. He was used to walking for miles, still he got in his car and measured out a 2.6-mile route. This seemed a safe distance that he could walk without failing. He didn't want to just set out on an unknown route, go too far, and "fail." He knew that would trigger a series of self-blame messages or give others an opportunity to criticize him. So he avoided those risks, rigidly limited his daily walks to that same, exact 2.6-mile route. His self-esteem was safe.

Submissives may also experience anger and frustration when others don't perform up to their perfect standards. This is because the Submissive resents the double standard – even if it is a standard that he has established for himself alone. I used to get very angry with colleagues I believed didn't respond fast enough or acted unprofessionally. It was only later that I realized it was because I felt I was exerting X amount of effort and thoughtfulness – yet they were working less diligently and still getting approval.

Don't Be the "Prey" in Relationships

Paradoxically, while Submissives are on the alert for criticism, they can also close their eyes to or under-react to inappropriate behavior by others.

While my overeager habit as a "good girl" may have been merely annoying to friends, it was actually harmful to my career and, of course, my intimate relationships. In those settings, I failed to consider this: "What signals am I sending when I eagerly answer questions so quickly?" To Dominators, these messages are gold. These signs of weakness say, "I am a victim you can prey on."

Just as some Submissives learn to avoid conflict, many Dominators learn to use conflict as a way to destabilize and manipulate others – especially those who fear conflict. What a happy coincidence.

The irony is that by being so desperate to please others and gain acceptance, Submissives end up with the opposite result. By grasping blindly, they risk attracting a Dominator who will not accept them for who they really are, leaving them in a constant void, unable to connect meaningfully with others.

Or worse, they will be targeted by one who will control and manipulate, sometimes with physical violence. Just as wolves hunt the weakest elk in a herd, Dominators are easily able to pick out the emotionally weak in a crowd.

Now I realize that self-acceptance is the key. Until you get to the point where you don't have to have someone in your life, you will attract someone who shouldn't be in your life.

Value Intuition to Gain Insight

As I think back to when I met Ray, I almost chuckle at the irony of the situation. I had left a husband who couldn't give me a single compliment or tell me he loved me. I met Ray who smothered me with compliments on every date and told me he loved me three weeks after we met. (Warning, warning!) It became a running joke with Ray and me that when he would give me a compliment I'd laugh and say, "Oh, what a line." Of course, I now know it was exactly that – a manipulative ploy. And I knew it then too, but at an intuitive level I didn't acknowledge. My immense need for affection strong-armed my weak emotional intelligence. Submissives often can't tell the difference between honest praise and a "line" being laid on them. I should have listened to my actual words, even if I couldn't listen to my inner voice.

For most of my life I lacked strong emotional skills – I didn't know my own needs, emotions, feelings. I didn't hear my own intuition. This is because I was taught both that my feelings don't count as much as the needs of others and because intuition itself isn't valuable.

I strongly believe Submissives can't fully access their intuitive ability because they are so externally focused. Submissives scan the environment constantly for signs someone doesn't like them or something isn't right, so that they can "make things right." Being overly aware of what others are feeling and thinking, they fail to notice their own emotional signals. Busy sending out "please like me" signals, they don't spend enough emotional energy attending to their own feelings.

This not only leaves them unable to judge their own wants and needs, but also limits their ability to judge the intentions of other people accurately. Because Submissives are busy cueing in on external behavior, they fail to really stop and understand the unspoken motivations of others. The very intuitive skills that would allow them to differentiate between a friendly person and a manipulative one are shouted down by their efforts to scan the environment for a positive response.

In addition, Submissives have lost the ability to manage what emotions and energy they project because they've been taught to be nice at all costs. By taking the lessons of caring and cooperation too far, they may become doormats to others who seek to take advantage. If you are unable to project appropriate emotional cues at appropriate times, you may be unable to stop projecting fear, making you a target for manipulation or abuse.

I believe Submissives learn to distrust and deny their intuition, ignore their emotions and senses, and under-react to threats – all in an effort to avoid offending others. This lack of intuitive and emotional skill puts Submissives in a weakened position socially. If you can't predict how another person might behave you are operating without an essential source of information.

Submissives "Lash In"

A sure sign of my past Submissiveness: self-criticism. I turned aside compliments and dismissed praise. I was, after all, taught by my parents not to get a big head. My sense of humor centered on self-deprecating comments – a clear signal I had low self-esteem. How sad: I wanted everyone else's approval but withheld approval from myself.

Because I had such low self-worth, if I was criticized I took it to heart. I vowed to study harder, fix myself, be a better person. (Contrast this with Dominators who usually lack the ability to be accountable for their actions.)

Another indicator of Submissive behavior is the tendency to perceive criticism even if there is none. A friend not returning a phone call, a person ignoring me at a party, not being invited to an event – I viewed all of these as rejection, when there may have been perfectly good explanations.

As I discussed earlier, Submissives have an inclination to avoid close, intimate friendships. For years I had a network of friends and colleagues I enjoyed spending time with, but I had a very difficult time calling them to ask them to go shopping or go for a walk. I certainly could never bring myself to call and ask for a favor or advice. Every time I considered picking up the phone, I thought: "Oh, it's dinnertime. I better not call," or "It's Friday night. They're probably out." I now realize I didn't want to disturb them, as if my call was not important enough, as if I was not important enough. Of course, reaching out to friends, even asking them a favor, shows you need and like them. What a simple concept, but one I failed to understand for years.

I also had a very difficult time asking for help from family and friends. I would struggle with difficult tasks by myself, when a phone call would bring an extra pair of hands. Somehow I learned the lesson that asking for help was a sign of weakness. I think Submissives need to relearn the real signs of weakness. It is fascinating to me that Submissives send "I am weak" signals in many primal ways, yet are reluctant to ask a favor for fear of appearing weak.

My habits at self-deprecation over the years created a cycle that kept me from recognizing the truth about myself. Because my self-worth was so low, I tended to dismiss or overlook compliments and positive messages: "They can't possibly mean me!" I also repeated internal messages to myself about my inadequacies, reinforcing my already low self-image. While I was so busy telling myself I was worthless, I wasn't able to tune in to the signals others were sending me – a missed opportunity to hear real, accurate messages about myself and my abilities.

This cycle is difficult to break. It is tough to stop repeating mantras about your inadequacies that you have told yourself for years and that you perhaps first learned from your parents. The key for me was realizing that by cowering submissively I was giving away all my power. And I had learned where that got me.

Submissives Avoid Conflict to Avoid Criticism

A need to be dependent emotionally, if not also physically and socially, results in the Submissive defining herself not as an independent, worthwhile person, but as someone good only as defined by someone else. I have to believe that if you don't recognize you have worth as a person, the threat of rejection will seem especially devastating.

When I was very submissive, new relationships were anxiety-producing because they put me in an uncomfortable situation. I wanted others to like me, yet I was thinking subconsciously: "What if I befriend him, then he criticizes me? Or what if decide I don't like him? I'll be in a position of having to reject him. And that's not 'nice.'" This double bind means Submissives desperately want and seek approval, yet they may at times be afraid of reaching out to other people for fear of being dominated and betrayed.

I was trained not to critique other people to their face, even those who were looking to harm me. I didn't show anger, even in situations where I should have been raging mad.

Submissives have usually spent their lives entrained with a Dominator, whether a parent, sibling, or spouse, so that they have learned to walk on eggshells. Most Dominators have learned how to manage criticism in a way that gives them power – by biting back. Submissives have learned when they do or say something "wrong," the Dominator will react – either with drama, emotional withholding, arbitrary punishment, or emotional or physical abuse. Correcting or disciplining a Dominator can bring a dramatic scene, and with it the feeling of fear, which Submissives strive to avoid.

Dominators overreact when someone tests one of their boundaries, attacking immediately if criticized. Submissives do the opposite, underreacting when setting personal limits. They fail to speak up when challenged, they give in to others' demands, they surrender their physical space, and they may tolerate abuse. Because of a lack of self-respect they let others disrespect them.

Since Submissives have a hard time saying no, involvement in a group or organization usually means they take on too many responsibilities.

These "yes" people tend to over-work, over-promise, over-volunteer, and over-commit to gain favor.

While Submissives make great casual friends and colleagues, this reluctance to confront others and a tendency to ignore their own feelings and needs can lead to issues in their close relationships. Lack of open communication is essentially a form of deception. Submissives, by avoiding conflict, are sending signals they are being less than honest – a signal that others can also lie to them without repercussion.

Submissive Parents Are Never a Good Idea

If being Submissive as a dog owner is a weak strategy, then being Submissive as a parent is certainly going to put you in a one-down position. Not only does this make you an ineffectual parent, it is also extremely damaging for your child. I've seen many families where the parents look to the children for affection – a complete and very unhealthy role reversal. They try to become friends with a child, asking the child's opinion, and involving the child far too much in decision-making. Divorced parents also do this when they demean the ex in the hopes of gaining the child's affection. The child, with her very sensitive intuition, realizes she is now responsible for providing emotional support to her parent. She learns a very frightening lesson: That she is now, at an emotional level, the leader. By heaping this duty on a child, the parent may have set her up for a lifetime of insecurities and possibly driven her into a role as a super-nurturer, someone who is overly responsible for the needs of others. She will learn to feel responsible for feeding others their self-worth, but may never fully develop her own confident self-image.

Parents should never selfishly make a child responsible for the adult's feelings of acceptance. Pack leaders always do what is best for the child.

Only You Are Responsible for How You Feel

For me the road away from my Submissive behavior is ongoing, but I have made tremendous progress in many areas of my life. I now acknowledge that no one else is responsible for how I feel. As a result, I don't spend as much time worrying what others think of my abilities. I don't sprinkle my speech with brags about my accomplishments, talents, travel, or experiences. I don't worry whether my clothes are OK and don't constantly fidget and fix my appearance. Where I used to find a mirror or reflection everywhere I went, I now go hours without checking my hair or my hemline. I spend very little time wondering whether I will offend someone or have offended someone. Where before I would walk into a room watching others for their approval, I now enter situations not judging, not worrying about being judged.

What is so powerful about the Pack Leader Psychology paradigm is that these behaviors changed with no conscious effort on my part, without my attention to individually reversing each habit. I didn't recite affirmations or post reminders on my mirror. These behaviors merely disappeared naturally once I slipped the bonds of Submissive traits. As I became more of a pack leader, the anxieties, fears, and insecurities that seemed such a natural part of my life eased away unnoticed, leaving a much more authentic, confident, and self-assured person.

My experience is an example of why using affirmations to change individual behaviors does not work. You must change the attitude underlying those behaviors first.

The journey to self-awareness that I took is one I wish every Submissive person could undertake and succeed at. The main reason I wrote this book was to help free Submissives of their fears and their controlling relationships. I sincerely wish every unbalanced person could find inner strength and become a balanced pack member – or maybe even a pack leader!

A SUMMARY OF SUBMISSIVE BEHAVIORS

Think of the Submissive personality type as a cowering dog – overly needy for approval, driven by a fear of rejection, seeking to manipulate and control others with niceness. The mantra for this type is: "Please like me so I can like myself." While Dominators have little sense of responsibility toward themselves or others, Submissives often have an exaggerated sense of responsibility. They want others to like them, so they feel the need to "make everything right." They also have a lack of boundaries, making them so conflict averse they hesitate to express their needs or wants. These two traits often show up in a fear that they will do something to harm others. Submissives can act with avoidance. They may push back and isolate from family and friends at times, mainly to avoid control and to avoid the possibility of being criticized.

Submissives are much more likely to experience physical symptoms of anxiety due to their chronic flight and avoidance reactions. They commonly experience sleep disturbances, as well as rapid heart rate, GI disorders, headaches, high blood pressure, and other physical conditions.

Characteristic behaviors of Submissives include:

SUBMISSIVE
- prefers to be dependent on others socially, emotionally, financially, physically
- appears fearful, helpless, weak
- afraid of being alone
- reluctant to make decisions

BLAMING
- self-critical, self-blaming, self-deprecating
- fearful of failure
- preoccupied with possibilities for humiliation, shame, or embarrassment
- works to avoid potential embarrassment, may relive past embarrassing situations
- perceives criticism where there is none

ATTENTION-SEEKING
- overly concerned with the opinions of others
- overachiever, productive, hard-working, perfectionist
- may lie or exaggerate achievements to seek approval
- eager for external praise and recognition
- helpful and loyal to a fault, unable to say "no"
- conforming

CONFICT AVOIDING
- reluctant to express opinions or needs
- acts as a mediator
- "walks on eggshells" in relationships, deferring to the needs of others
- avoids emotional, conflict-laden situations

CONTROLLING
- uses "niceness" and "goodness" to try to win approval and acceptance of others

Submissive Personality Types in the Diagnostic and Statistical Manual (DSM)

If you or someone you know has been diagnosed with one of the following disorders, you are a Submissive personality type:

Anxiety and Stress Disorders
Panic Disorder

Generalized Anxiety Disorder
Obsessive-Compulsive Disorder
Obsessive-Compulsive Personality Disorder
Phobias
Post-Traumatic Stress Disorder
Acute Stress Disorder
Hypochondria and Body Dysmorphic Disorder
Mood Disorders
Depression
Dysthymia
Bipolar Disorders I & II
Cyclothymic Disorder
Major Depressive Disorder
Recurrent Mood Disorder with SAD
Dependent Personality Disorder
Avoidance Disorders
Schizoid Personality Disorder
Schizotypal Personality Disorder
Avoidant Personality Disorder
Paranoid Personality Disorder

Pack Leader Wisdom:
Submissives use the "flight" response.
Submissives avoid conflict and are appeasing
to avoid criticism.
Submissives lash in with self-criticism
and self-blame.
Submissives say: "Please like me so I can like myself."

7 LESSONS ON HOW TO BE
A PACK LEADER

Given that many of us have been raised in a society that does not value social connections and that we may have also been raised by parents without an understanding of the need for strong leadership, is it possible to overcome these handicaps? As Reilly taught me, it is much better for your emotional health to be raised among a balanced family pack. But I am evidence that it is quite possible to change completely, from an unbalanced personality type to a more emotionally healthy person. Anxiety, depression, aggression, resentment, avoidance, and hostility do not have to be a daily part of your life.

The following lessons are taught naturally and effortlessly by wild animals and balanced human parents. The rest of us have to learn them the hard way: through education and reading, thoughtful self-reflection, and honest self-observation. We must have the courage to break free of old habits and try new behaviors, the fearlessness to give up long-held fears, the self-compassion to ignore some messages from parents, and, most important, self-acceptance and self-respect. Accepting the intrinsic worth of our own unique, authentic self may be the hardest part of the journey, but is the most important first step.

LESSON 1

Be Authentic

When Reilly goes hunting, she certainly doesn't hesitate. She runs full speed through woods, plows through snow banks, hurdles over ravines. She swims like an otter through ponds and crashes through dense swamps. If she sees a deer, she doesn't waver, but tears after it with 100 percent effort. She never backs down from a kill, unless I call her off, and she doesn't seem to be afraid of anything. Reilly goes at full speed until I put her back on the leash. She also plays joyfully, jumps to catch a flying disc with glee, and romps with other dogs with abandon. Reilly certainly doesn't hide her light under a bushel basket, as the old saying goes.

However, she also is not afraid to be vulnerable. She curls up sweetly under my desk and snuggles with me when I sit and knit. When she steps on a thorn, she stops, lifts her paw and waits for me to remove it. Reilly recognizes that she is not the pack leader, but she is no less of a dog for being subordinate to me and she knows this.

Reilly is proudly the best Reilly she can be.

Be Competent and Confident of Your Competence

For years, I hid my competence. I was taught not to be boastful or big headed, so I underplayed my talents in every aspect of my life. If someone gave me a compliment, I ducked it. I was afraid of intimidating others, of appearing more talented than someone else. So I worked very hard and was very competent, but I didn't brag about it and was uncomfortable if others noticed.

I now recognize that I was living in a confusing double bind. I was supposed to be hardworking and talented, but I couldn't admit to those capabilities.

I even noticed the way I talked was an effort to be less threatening to others. Even if I knew an answer or had a good idea, I talked with hesitation. I hemmed and hawed and tap-danced around my opinions so as not to be overpowering. If I was in a meeting and someone asked for ideas, I sat on my hands. I now realize I was constantly strategizing on how to behave and communicate so as not to offend someone, even if that meant I looked less intelligent or less competent.

Of course, I now realize this attempt to be less threatening was part of my Submissive strategy: "I'm not smarter than you. So don't hate me." By diminishing my capabilities I signaled my insecurity and weakness. All that strategizing leads to anxiety. By downplaying my talents, I wasn't acting as my authentic self. I was trying to match my capabilities and personality to those around me, trying to fit in and be liked.

As I had friends read drafts of this book and as I talked about the changes I had made in my personality in becoming a pack leader, several people who had known me for many years mentioned to me that they had never seen the Submissive side of me. They had mainly known me professionally and I had behaved decisively and confidently. What this says to me is that I was not living authentically. Which was the real Harper – the insecure introvert or the confident extravert? My interior and exterior selves did not match and were not integrated. That alone can cause anxiety as there is a continual questioning of what your real desires and beliefs are.

I also have come to believe that people may behave in different ways in different aspects of their lives, yet their inner insecurities will be more visible in their interpersonal relationships. In these relationships with their "pack mates" the fear of social disapproval is more of a concern, therefore they may react more emotionally to any perceived threat of rejection.

Living more authentically is not something I consciously set out to do. There were no self-help exercises or meditation mantras to help me on this journey. Authenticity came only through self-acceptance.

When I truly gave up trying to impress others and gave myself the permission to be imperfect, I freed myself from self-judgment and from the need for approval of others.

I now try to truly balance my behavior. I confidently express my natural capabilities without being arrogant or full of myself. If someone is offended by my capabilities, that only speaks of their insecurities. Besides, because I am comfortable in my own skin, those around me are more comfortable. No matter how nice a Submissive may appear to be, most people would prefer to associate with a confident, competent, authentic person.

Learning this lesson is a prerequisite to learning Lesson #2: Be Assertive. Without inner self-acceptance you will remain dependent on others for their approval and fearful of their criticism and will be unable to respond with the appropriate level of assertiveness. You will either cower in submission or lash out in hostility and anger because you feel you are at the mercy of the opinions of others.

Pack Leader Wisdom:
Hunt at full speed.
Don't hesitate.
Be yourself.

LESSON 2

Be Assertive

In addition to her unstoppable hunting drive, Reilly has one talent that makes her an excellent bird dog: She retrieves to hand every time without fail. She truly loves to retrieve and will play fetch with a ball or disc until my arm wears out. One day someone was visiting and asked me what command I use to tell Reilly to fetch. I realized I don't give her a command and never have. I do occasionally say "good fetch" to her when she brings the toy back to me, but it's praise, not a command.

I then thought back to how I acted when I trained my first dog, Kiva. Of course, I didn't know anything about pack leader concepts and I certainly wasn't calm and assertive. I was, I now see quite clearly, anxious and submissive. But I also did what traditional bird dog training books said to do: Give a command and praise. So I yelled "fetch" at Kiva when I threw the retrieving dummy, a canvas "bird" used to train dogs. And when he ran out to the dummy I yelled "fetch" over and over. When he headed back to me I repeatedly yelled "good boy, fetch, good Kiva!" I never could get him to retrieve to hand consistently.

Gee, his response is no surprise to me now. (It is amazing how obvious things become when you look at situations from a new perspective.) My screaming and eagerness for Kiva to perform were nothing but pure anxiety. What dog would respect someone who is behaving with such high levels of fear. It's surprising he didn't run in the opposite direction.

For Reilly, her reward is my calm, pleased demeanor and the primal joy of "hunting" the ball. I realize my behavior is completely counterintuitive to most people. It probably appears as if I don't care if Reilly fetches. Shouldn't I praise effusively and pet her and get very excited when she retrieves so well? Actually, no. This excitement is just felt as weakness by the dog.

As I continued to learn from Reilly on how to be a pack leader I realized further nuances on the concept of being calm and assertive.

"Deliberate" is a word I like to use when I describe calm assertiveness. When training Reilly I project an attitude that says: "This is just how it's going to be. Period. No arguing or debating with the pack leader. This isn't a democracy and you don't get a vote." While this sounds harsh, it is how a balanced pack leader operates. Pack leaders are firm and decisive in their actions. As long as they are fair, the rest of the pack is accepting. Their deliberate nature also engenders trust because it is a predictable energy.

Even something as simple as letting Reilly out the back door in the morning can be a practice in deliberate behavior. Early on I noticed that when Reilly went to the door, I would hurry over and immediately open it. I decided she could certainly wait a few seconds and that this would be good training. Now I stroll over, take a breath, and pause, surveying the backyard. Then I open the door and make her wait until I release her. The whole process is done at my pace and my choice. This simple exercise shows her that I am in control.

Deliberate does not necessarily mean slow. When I first growled at Reilly it was done instantly. But it was deliberate. When Reilly chases an animal, I don't react slowly. I yell "come" instantly, but it is firm, not fearful.

People Only Have Power Over You if You Let Them

A few months after I separated from Ray and moved to another state, I came home one night and began to fix dinner. I was humming and singing and suddenly realized I had not been this relaxed in the last few years of living with Ray. The awareness of this simple fact suddenly changed my happy mood. Waves of anger, then grief, alternately washed over me, along with massive amounts of relief. By its absence, I was finally able to recognize what I had ignored for so long – that a slow drip of tension had filled every crevasse of my life. I was now relaxed in a way I hadn't been in…how long? Years? My whole life?

I was relieved to no longer live in fear, to no longer dread Ray's arrival home. I no longer had to consider every word I said for fear it would trigger an outburst. I was queen of my own domain and it felt great. The grief and anger, though, were powerful counterweights to the relaxed pleasure I felt at my freedom. I had let a very mean-spirited, hurtful man control and dominate my life. Although I had felt very much at his mercy, I regretted that I had been complicit in allowing him to have power over my life.

This was the first step for me in understanding a very important concept: The victim of a controlling relationship actually has all the power. Your ability to assert yourself and walk away from a relationship gives you power.

How shocked I was when I realized that although I had felt power-less, totally at Ray's mercy, I had held all the cards the whole time. By being loyal and continually giving Ray endless second chances, not only was I encouraging his behavior, but I was also giving away my power. By just ceasing to care about Ray's reaction, by disengaging from him, I could have actually acted assertively. That's all it would have taken. The fighting and pleading and trying to convince him I loved him all made me less powerful. I had control the whole time.

Of course, this made perfect sense, I told myself. Everyone knows one of the axioms of negotiating is, "You must be able to walk away from the deal." If a buyer is too eager to buy something, she will likely pay too much. If you fall in love with that sweet sports car in the sales brochure, by the time you walk into the showroom you are at the mercy of the salesperson. It is only when you can emotionally distance your-self from the purchase that you can negotiate powerfully.

As a Submissive, I signaled to the Dominators in my life that they had control over me because I cared. I cared what they thought about me and I wanted their attention and affection. And Dominators know you care. Imagine the control they have over you just because you've shown you worry about their opinions. Someone only has power over you if his opinions have the power to define you.

Obviously, as social creatures it is appropriate to show a certain level of concern for the opinions of those around us. But this concern should be truly selfless, done for no other reason than because you understand the other person's needs and care about him. Instead, many people are concerned about how their actions will bring something back to them: usually attention and approval or as a defense against crit-icism. This puts them at the mercy of the very people they are "loving" or "helping."

If your insecurities make you fearful, and if the other person isn't an emotionally mature person, it can easily lead to an unbalanced, unhealthy relationship with the other person taking advantage of your weakness and neediness. As I've learned the hard way, Dominators have a finely tuned prey instinct. They can sense within minutes whether they are going to be able to control you, if that's their agenda. They will size you up at a primal level before a word comes out of your mouth.

A Dominator knows she has power over you because you care and because your self-worth isn't strong. Once she solidifies her power advantage, she can jerk you around on a short leash.

Of course, a balanced pack leader would not take advantage of someone's affection in this manner.

You must give up your need for power and control in a relationship to break free of these cycles. "Walking away" from the control dynamic you both have created can be the most assertive choice you make. I'm not advocating ditching a relationship at the drop of a hat. You don't have to physically leave to have this power. All you have to do is be emotionally autonomous, with good self-acceptance, and without fear of criticism, so you don't rely on the other person for approval.

Another way to look at it is from the pack leader perspective. When pack leaders show leadership, anxious dogs become calm. If you change your behavior, the other person's behavior may also change. If you step up and assert yourself, the other person will respond with more respectful, less dominating behavior.

To be clear, however, this is very different from forcing the other person to change. I know I fell into this trap of incorrect thinking. I kept hoping that if Ray would just stop drinking, stop beating me up, stop doing drugs, and stop being irresponsible, then everything would be OK. And it was easy to focus on his misbehavior, because it was blatantly unacceptable.

However, my misbehavior was partly the cause of his misbehavior. I was allowing him to act out by my unassertive tolerance. Codependence is a word often used in self-help books. I had heard that word, but it meant nothing to me because it is so vague. When I pictured myself as cowering and showing my belly – now that got my attention!

Because I didn't reprimand him, Ray knew he could continue with his disrespect. But the solution wasn't that I should control Ray's behavior or punish him. All I needed to do was assert myself. He likely would have changed all on his own, just as a dog stops misbehaving when an owner steps up and becomes the pack leader.

Most important, I learned that if I could walk away from the primal fear of rejection and criticism – my biggest fear – I could unleash myself from the very thing keeping me enmeshed in unhealthy relationships. Only by giving up the desperate search for affection from others was I able to find the strength to have healthier relationships. When I relied on others' opinions of me to define my self-worth, I gave away my power. It took me two divorces to learn this, but at least I have moved forward.

Be Calm to Let Your Intuition Speak

I always believed I was a calm person. I am not a worrier. I tend to be a very positive, forward-thinking person who doesn't dwell in the past. I don't have any phobias, obsessions, or other anxiety-based behaviors. I am not an attention-seeker, stirring up dramas or having emotional meltdowns. I'm also very decisive in personal and business matters. I have no problem making major decisions and don't wallow in regret. Physically, I've always tried to carry myself with confidence. Despite all those positive characteristics, I now recognize that in the past I wasn't calm at my core. I was too busy worrying what everyone else thought about me.

Being calm now permits me to sense the energy of others. My intuitive reactions can percolate up into my consciousness, giving me lots of great information about other people and situations. Many people are running at "high alert" all the time, so anxieties, fears, and insecurities over imagined situations are overwhelming the real information flowing in from their instincts and emotions. They may miss out on a wealth of valuable facts about threats from people trying to manipulate them. I know I sure missed these signals in the past.

Over the last few years I have learned to project a more deliberate energy. In the past I was always a bit on the hyper side. Now I practice slowing down my physical actions. When I walk, I try to stride. I gesture less frequently and with a slower pace. I have even noticed I am slowing down my eye movements. At a social event, for example, I used to let my eyes dart around a room. Now I try to be deliberate about where I look and let my eyes linger – really see the room and make eye contact with people.

I've learned that being scattered and hurried in my physical behaviors tells my human pack I am anxious and eager to please, that I am merely reacting immediately to what others want, rather than considering my response.

Being calm and assertive has many benefits to a pack leader, but it also calms those around you. A pack leader can walk up to a tense situation and, just by his or her presence, calm the situation. Unlike Dominant drama queens and bullies, a balanced person doesn't inflame a situation by perceiving threats where there are none.

You Can Be Assertive AND Be Liked

How did I learn to be more assertive? It took several years and is still a work in progress. I am unlearning more than 40 years of deeply engrained submissive behaviors, thoughts, and feelings that were rehearsed thousands of times each day.

First, I had to overcome my fear of offending others. Not an easy task. That fear had ruled my life for decades. But as I came to understand I couldn't control others or make them like me, and as I grew to like myself, I looked less to other people for affirmation. Gone was the overarching goal of my life: "Like me so I can like myself."

When I came to see that being assertive with Reilly was a good thing – she wanted and needed a pack leader – my eyes were suddenly opened. This insight was truly life altering. Being assertive with people might also not be such a bad thing. I could be assertive and people wouldn't be offended. They might actually like me more! Being assertive stopped being negative and started being a very, very positive thing.

Eventually I came to fully understand the distinction between the words aggressive and assertive. Aggressive people are anxious and insecure people; assertive people are secure and confident.

I have since learned how to identify true assertiveness. Assertiveness isn't about control. In the incident where I growled at Reilly for taking my shoe, I did not take the shoe away from her. In fact, if you pull an object away from a dog, you are not being assertive. Ideally, you should wait until the dog chooses to drop the object.

Assertiveness is merely claiming what is rightfully yours – whether it is respect, privacy, physical safety, or a shoe. It isn't right or wrong, it just is.

I believe Submissives tend to act unassertively in many human interactions because they feel they do not have a right to claim what is naturally theirs or expect respect. It is important to erase any beliefs you have that being assertive is rude or demanding or selfish or hostile. If someone is regularly and unfairly angry or dominant when you claim respect, then inspect her motivations.

Assertiveness is also not anger or frustration. As you've learned, the rule when training dogs or disciplining children is never to do so with emotional reactivity.

I also came to understand that we all need skills in being assertive, in standing up for our own rights. Even a natural follower must not roll over and automatically show everyone her belly.

I am sure some readers are thinking: "What if everyone went around assertively grabbing what they wanted and doing what they want?" Clearly, assertiveness does not mean we are each out for our own good no matter the cost to others. While individual needs are important, assertiveness is honestly striving toward one's own potential within the construct of society's moral codes. An authentic existence requires a social dimension that brings an inevitable tension between the needs of the individual and the needs of others.

For me the most important distinction is that a truly assertive person is acting without a manipulative agenda and without fear. I am amazed now to experience situations where, in the past, I would have either not spoken up or would have done so hesitantly or tearfully. Now I am pleased that I can calmly state my opinion and feel good about it during and after. That's how I know I'm being genuinely assertive and not aggressive or controlling.

....

Actions DO Speak Louder than Words

If you've ever owned a dog or seen someone else discipline a dog, you have probably experienced this scene. The dog is misbehaving and the owner gives a series of rapid-fire commands in words: "Petey, come. Come, get over here, stop it, now come over here, right now, I mean it."

All these words, usually said at a high pitch and fast pace, communicate very clearly to the dog that the owner is fearful that the dog will not obey. I compare these word-happy people to yippy dogs who yip-yap at everyone who comes near. Eventually you tune them out.

Most dog training techniques emphasize the use of word commands, which is not good pack leader behavior. Unfortunately, some owners do nothing but talk to their dogs, babbling commands anxiously, yet not enforcing them. Telling your dog, "no, no, no," and not enforcing your command merely reinforces what she already knows – that you're not the pack leader. What dog will eagerly obey an anxious, ineffective person? Have you ever seen one of these yapped-at dogs obey their owner? Exactly.

Balanced dogs don't over-communicate as humans do. If you watch a pack of dogs, there isn't a lot of "talking." The leader doesn't scurry around getting in each dog's face, reminding that she is the boss. Quite the contrary. The pack leader is often the calmest one of the pack, serenely going about her business.

Being a writer, I sure felt comfortable using words to communicate. I am glad that Reilly taught me to communicate with my more primal side. I now see that there are times when I absolutely must act rather than talk. One day Reilly and I were hiking in a woods and she was 20 yards ahead of me on the trail. Over a hill came two golden retrievers with the owner a few yards behind them. When the two dogs saw Reilly they very aggressively charged her and by their behaviors I knew instantly I had to act. Reilly sensed the threat and ran into the woods. Both dogs pursued Reilly, despite her clear behavior that she was trying to avoid a fight. The first dog, which outweighed Reilly by 30 or 40 pounds, plowed into Reilly with its chest and rolled her. The second dog was right behind. By this time I had run up and shoved the second dog out of the way with my leg. The more dominant retriever was growling, hair on end, and was trying to pin Reilly. I didn't hesitate. I deliberately shoved my way between the retriever and Reilly. With my arms and legs outstretched I blocked both dogs and ran toward them, herding them back toward their owner. They quickly realized I was the boss and ran off. It was a very tense situation that could have quickly gotten out of control if I had not intervened, as these dogs were clearly packing up in an unbalanced way to attack a smaller dog.

Yet where was the owner of these two bully dogs? Standing unassertively in the trail, calling them with words. They were, of course, ignoring her. She clearly was not the pack leader of this dominant pair and her lack of assertive actions – as well as their aggressive behavior – proved it.

With dog training, owners should communicate in the proper tone, body language, authority, and with active intervention.

Stop Talking and Act

Humans are verbal creatures and have evolved an amazing capacity for language. Just as we often do with dogs, when humans relate to other humans we tend to rely on words to express ourselves. We talk and talk, hoping our knowledge and bluster communicate that we are powerful, when words really are a weak substitute for real leadership.

Real leaders often do more listening than talking, more observing than acting. But when it is time for action, the words and watching stop.

As I looked back at my life through the prism of a pack leader, I recognized I had talked way too much and for the wrong reasons. As a Submissive, I used words to impress people in an attempt to make them like me. I would say something, anything, to show I was smart, capable, eager, hardworking, pleasant, and nice. Always nice.

I would also listen only to the words of others, not watching for body language or other physical clues that would have tipped me off to their real agenda or emotions. I was, of course, so focused on my needs and agenda I wasn't truly observing the other person. My anxious waterfall of words was all about me and certainly not an honest conversation.

In a more self-aware hindsight, I realize all those words flowing out were a sign I was not only eager to please, but anxious and uncomfortable. Now I recognize a long stream of words as a big power giveaway.

In building my pack leader skills I focused on listening more than talking. On speaking calmly and deliberately. On pausing before answering a question. I now see that how much I talk – or don't – is an important way of verbally claiming space and communicating that I am a leader. I have stopped sending the signal I am eager to please with my outpouring of words.

Respect Is Love in Action Redux

Sometimes actions are really and truly the only way to communicate, a very powerful part of discipline and communication. Actions do speak louder than words.

When Ray behaved particularly badly one time, I moved out of the house for a week and didn't tell him where I was, didn't call, didn't contact him at all. After that he quit drinking and being violent for five months. However, when I went back to him (big mistake!) I had not changed my day-to-day behavior, so it continued to communicate that I would not really stand up to him in any meaningful way. I kept treating myself as the powerless one, when really I had all the power – I could walk away and disengage from him and he would no longer have the control over me he thought he had. That is powerful communication.

I now value acting, not just talking, in my relationships. Now if a date were to show up two hours late I would send a powerful message: When he arrived, I would not be home. By acting, the message becomes very clear. I communicate that I am in control of the situation and I decide how I am to be treated. Establishing a consequence for his action and then enforcing that consequence is very powerful. I can talk all I want about how much I dislike his being late for dates, but until I do something, it's all just talk.

I also learned via that abusive, aggressive ex-husband of mine that some personality types just do not hear when you speak – they don't want to hear you. Dominators shut out incoming information if they sense a criticism, a threat to their weak self-worth. They erect a psychological wall and moat, protecting their shaky castle with every defense and offense they can muster. Their logical listening skills will have left the building because to hear the truth would feel too frightening.

Many Dominators lack the empathy to see others as real people. They view others in an idealized way, as a means to get what they want, so that when that fantasy viewpoint is challenged, they are reluctant to acknowledge their perspective might be wrong.

With this type of person, especially when in a "red zone," actions are about the only message that is understood. Of course, I now know I should have acted and left Ray at once when he became abusive. All my words and talking and patience and second chances were a huge waste of years of my life.

Behaviors are morals writ large for all to see. Behaviors expose ethics, attitudes, feelings, thoughts. Listen and observe with your primal powers to receive the full range of communication, rather than just the words.

· ·

Exercise First, Calm All Day

German Shorthaired Pointers are notorious for their high energy levels. This breed may have the highest need for exercise of all of the Continental gun dogs. Reilly needs an hour run in the morning, with at least 15 minutes off the leash running full speed through the woods. She then needs another 30 minutes later in the day – minimum. In the summer she spends nearly all day outside in my one-acre yard, waiting for woodchucks to emerge from under the neighbor's shed and stalking squirrels. I usually play catch with her every day for another 15 or 20 minutes. In the summer she is outside when I am gardening and mowing the lawn; in the winter, when I am shoveling the snow. And this routine just takes the edge off this built-for-speed dog. On weekends, we often go for a much longer run or hike in the woods or on a golf course so she can run off the leash and really burn it up. When I am doing errands, I often put Reilly in the car so she can have a bit of excitement just driving around town. On hot days I take her to a local river and she swims upstream – an aquatic doggie treadmill.

If I follow this routine with Reilly she is calm around the house, sleeps through the night, follows commands, and does not misbehave.

Without proper exercise dogs actually seem like different personalities. I remember watching a TV show about dog training (not "Dog Whisperer") and a family had a German Shorthaired Pointer that pinged around the house destructively. She bulldozed over the toddler, crashed into restraining gates, spun around excitedly, knocked pots and pans out of the owners' hands, and would not calm down with any traditional obedience training. My instant analysis: That dog needs more exercise. A lot more exercise. This is not a breed for someone who wants to take a casual stroll around the block once a week with the baby carriage. (Unfortunately, that TV dog trainer missed the prescription for exercise entirely.)

Unexercised dogs develop anxieties, such as barking, chewing, "separation anxiety," and other nervous or obsessive behaviors.

Having watched that poorly behaved GSP on TV, and having observed other dogs, I know what would happen if I didn't exercise Reilly enough. It wouldn't be pretty. As I say, either I give Reilly her exercise, or she'll take it.

Cesar strongly recommends dog owners lead their dogs on a walk each morning. This not only burns energy, but also completes a hunting ritual for the dog that is instinctive. When the pack leader leads the pack in a hunt, this establishes the leader's role and gives the pack a task to complete, fulfilling a primal need.

When I started making the connection between Cesar's teachings and my own theories about human behavior, I immediately saw the validity of one of Cesar's sayings. He says dogs need "exercise, discipline, and affection." And they need them in that order. Exercising a dog makes it calm enough to listen to discipline, and affection is a reward for calm behavior. Can this idea translate to humans? Absolutely.

Exercise Reduces Anxieties

I have been a runner all my adult life – more than 30 years. I have also been a downhill skier, volleyball player, and I can still walk 18 holes of golf carrying my bag. I have completed a daily yoga practice for more than a 15 years. I do all my own gardening, lawn mowing for a one-acre yard, snow shoveling, and housework. I clean gutters, spread mulch, and haul out the trash. I watch TV very rarely in the winter and almost never in the summer. This isn't to brag about my fitness level, but to show the level of exercise I regularly get.

I believe a major part of being a balanced person and projecting the correct physical presence comes from exercise. If you are physically fit and carry yourself as an athlete, you send a message that you can take care of yourself in a tough situation, that you have the energy and stamina to deal with the world. If you are obese or frail or weak, you send the opposite message: "I am helpless, so you can trample all over me." Is this the message you want to be sending?

In the pack, dogs react to energy and intention, not just physical strength. This is also true in the human world, especially because we value strength of character, not just physical strength. So the good news is even if you have physical disabilities or illnesses or aren't a world-class athlete, this doesn't discount you from becoming a pack leader. Even those of us who aren't bound for the Olympics can try to be as strong as we are able.

Vigorous aerobic exercise should be part of everyone's day for well-established physical health reasons. But I can emphatically state from experience that exercise improves emotional health as well. Aerobic exercise, such as running, vigorous walking, biking, or swimming, relaxes the body and the mind. When you are physically tired you are much less likely to be worried or fearful. I challenge you to be anxious after running 5 miles. It is physically and mentally impossible. Visit the finish line of a marathon. Not much anxiety there, I guarantee you. I have been on numerous ski trips. Go to a big mountain ski resort and sit in the hot tub or ride a bus back to the hotel at the end of the day. Let me tell you, there isn't much nervous energy. Everyone is exhausted after a fun day of high altitude fresh air and snow riding. You don't hear arguing, bickering, or sniping.

Daily aerobic exercise brings the calmness essential for balanced behavior. I believe one prescription for many human behavioral problems, such as anxieties, obsessions, compulsions, depression, and phobias, is a vigorous exercise program. In fact, exercise has been shown in studies to be more effective than psychoactive medication at treating depression. Research also consistently shows that meditation and other mindfulness activities are extremely helpful at reducing anxiety.

Quite simply, if you are well exercised and calm, you may be less likely to lash out in anger at yourself or others.

I am sure many behavioral health professionals will pooh-pooh this claim. I understand many psychological issues are complex and also need more than just exercise to treat them. I can personally attest to having been helped immensely by psychotherapy at one point in my life. However, exercise is a very meditative activity, especially if done outdoors. Just as it is with dogs, I believe people are meant to travel, to cover ground. I think there is a primal sense of accomplishment and fulfillment at having completed a physical activity, even if it is walking two miles or shoveling snow off the driveway. We used to have to hike off to gather or kill food, so who's to say this primal need isn't still programmed into our DNA? We have no evolutionary coding for being couch potatoes and playing violent video games.

Calm Your Body and Mind to Access Inner Wisdom

I also believe that when well exercised and calm, you have a better shot at accessing your intuition. If your mind is whirling with thoughts and anxieties and worries, you are not as likely to hear that tiny, intuitive voice warning you of danger or opportunity.

Unfortunately, the very insecurities that could be helped by exercise also keep people from exercising. I believe many people don't exercise because they are fearful of the judgment of other people. They may worry they won't look good, won't wear the right clothes to yoga class, won't know how to lift weights correctly at the gym, or will otherwise make a fool of themselves. Once again, self-criticism and low self-worth sabotage the journey to a calm mind.

•••••••••••••••••••••••••••••••••••••••

Claim Your Space

When I leave the house, Reilly wants to go with me. Correction: She really, really, really wants to go with me. (Going for a walk or car ride is so much fun!) But I don't want her charging the door when I am juggling my purse, briefcase, coffee mug, and lunch. So I turn and face Reilly, walking her away from the door. It only takes one step or one small "hey" command and I break her focus on the door, so she stands and behaves well.

The same trick works when someone knocks on the door and I don't want Reilly charging. I turn and face her, standing tall right in the door opening. Reilly now knows not to crowd the door, but if she didn't I would also step decisively toward her and look directly at her. Of course this is done calmly and deliberately, without a word spoken. I can also extend my hands and use my legs to make myself seem bigger. These moves aren't to push the dog away or threaten her in any way. This merely is part of a body language and demeanor that communicates – without words – I own this space around the door and she is not to approach. It signals I am the pack leader and have to give permission for others to enter this space. Within minutes of an owner using this technique most dogs are not surging toward the door. They are quiet, but alert, when someone knocks.

Claiming physical space is a sign of assertiveness that dogs expect in a balanced pack hierarchy. It is a natural sign of dominance when one dog pushes his way into another's space or into another's food bowl.

Contrast this with how most dog owners behave: If their dog is surging to get out the door, they will bend over, grab the dog's collar, and pull him back. They may yell "no" repeatedly.

In this scenario, because you are physically behind the dog and bending down, it signals you are not the pack leader. It doesn't teach the dog you are claiming the doorway as your own. It only conditions the dog to lunge forward when you are holding the collar.

More important, your attitude is the key: You must communicate that you are in command. The people who try to hold their dog back are usually anxious and giving lots of commands, but they are not in command. When you are a pack leader, you are calm and don't need to say a thing.

I once watched a person try to keep Reilly from pushing out the door. His "command" was more of a request. He was backing outside closing the door behind him saying over and over in a questioning tone: "Reilly stays? Stay? Reilly, you're going to stay?" No surprise – it didn't work! Dogs respond to energy, physicality, and tone of voice far more than words. Your intention tells them everything they need to know. And stepping toward a dog is always very powerful, using your body to physically occupy a space and be larger than the dog.

However, this tactic cannot be done hesitantly. As with all pack leader behavior, you must act deliberately, as if there is no doubt in your mind that you own the doorway. It isn't an aggressive or angry behavior. In fact, calmness is required. I like to think of it as, "It's just the way it is." This isn't a right-or-wrong, good-or-bad situation. It is just the fact: I own the doorway.

Other ways to claim the space: A pack leader should never walk around a dog. If your dog is lying in a hallway or in your way in the kitchen, do not walk around him. Make him move. This may seem mean, but it is a great lesson to him that you are the boss. In the same way, if your dog has toys or bones, you should control when he eats them or plays with them.

I didn't always know how to claim my space. With my first dog, when he barked too long at something outside the house, I would yell at him to stop, as would most dog owners. (Relying on words, as we humans do, rather than actions.) Reilly never has been much of a watchdog, mainly because she doesn't see herself as pack leader. But she will occasionally bark a few times at something outside the house or when someone knocks at the door. When I first got her I didn't want to discourage her watchdog abilities, but I also didn't want her to bark excessively. How could I communicate this to her? I thought about what a pack leader would do. Now when she barks, I calmly and deliberately walk to the window to investigate. I stand tall and look very obviously out into the yard to see if there is danger. The energy I radiate is: "Thank you for alerting me, but I am in control because I am pack leader." I pause, then say "good dog" calmly. Reilly doesn't continue barking, because I have taken control of the situation, assessed it, and said everything is safe. I now can depend on the fact that if she barks more then a couple of times or barks after I approach the window, there really is something out there. And that's what you want a watchdog to do, not to bark endlessly at every breeze and sound. (Dog training tip: For those who are rushing around yelling at a dog to stop barking, to the dog this just sounds like more anxious "barking." The dog senses you are upset, so it barks some more – because there really must be something wrong if the pack leader is upset!)

Claiming the space may sound very aggressive to those who haven't experienced it. On the contrary, it is not. The feeling is more nurturing than bullying. It is encompassing, not restricting. It is educational guidance, not shameful punishment.

When I claim my space I am not worried about hurting my dog's feelings. That is a human attitude about discipline totally foreign in the dog world. Discipline isn't hurtful; it is actually respectful. Dogs expect the pack leader to establish boundaries and enforce discipline. They want guidelines on how to behave. They want a pack leader to be in charge. As a result, they don't have to question how to behave or who is in charge and this brings predictability, respect, and trust to their world.

Claim Your Space and Claim Respect

I believe that when we claim our space we are claiming respect. Start owning your space first with self-respect and then by insisting on respect from others.

When I taught Reilly not to charge the door, I was only claiming what is rightfully mine: To be shown respectful behavior in this little piece of the universe around me. Reilly's desire to go outside does not give her the right to barrel me down and jump on the door. Her desire to go outside does not trump my desire to calmly and safely open the door. Charging the door is disrespectful and I'm only telling her that. I act respectfully to her and it is only fair that she acts respectfully to me.

As I was learning about this topic, I noticed I tended to give up my personal space very quickly if someone moved into it. I would be the first to step out of the way in elevators and the first to give way on a crowded sidewalk. My whole life I have been very aware of others around me and of their personal space. I believe this sent the message: "My need for space isn't as important as your need for space." I was literally accommodating others and their "more important" needs.

I then observed how dogs project submission. A dog will express her lower status by holding her head low, by cowering, and making herself appear smaller and so less of a threat.

But in a balanced dog pack, blatant submission is a sign of unhealthy weakness. If you watch a balanced, subordinate dog enter a pack, the signals are different. Her head is neutral – not slunk down low and not forward with aggression. Her tail is not up in alertness or down between her legs in submission, but in a neutral position. The energy she projects is not tense and fearful, but just aware and open, looking to see what happens, eager to meet others.

Anyone who has studied human body language knows that how we sit, stand, gesture, and stare communicates volumes to others. Just as dogs make instant judgments about the status of dogs they meet, the physical energy and posture we bring into the world and into our human relationships are the first, immediate clues we present to everyone we meet. As very verbal creatures, we attach great significance to our words, but tend to forget the power of our bodies when communicating.

If you are weak, insecure, and frightened, this will be reflected in your physicality. Submissives do not claim their space, and as a result do not claim the respect of others. Dominators have learned to cover up their fear and not let it show in their physical appearance.

If you are Submissive you may use a weak physical presence to signal, "I'm not a threat to you. Please like me." A slouching posture, fluttery hand gestures, nervous tics, giggles, and rapid speech patterns are a few of the signs that say, "I don't want to take up your space or your time. I'll just try to keep out of your way."

I'm sure we all know the type of people I call "bobbleheads," because they nod their heads at everything you say, as if to give you the impression they are such good listeners and such good "agree-ers." However, with this submissive message people may sense weakness and lose respect.

I once dated a man I'll call Bill, who gave off very obvious physical signals that he was submissive to everyone he met. He talked very quickly, using numerous clichés, jokes, and pat phrases repeatedly throughout his conversations. His hand gestures were very effeminate, as was his entire physicality. Like a dog afraid to appear threatening, he approached people with his head low and forward, with a slouched posture, as if to make himself smaller and less threatening.

Once when we were walking in a park, we stopped to talk to a young man. I watched Bill seem to shrink before my eyes. His posture got even weaker, and he talked in a hyperactive, rambling way. It was as if I was watching a very submissive dog approach a stronger dog, although this young man didn't even came close to qualifying as dominant. But that didn't matter. Bill immediately gave off physical and verbal signals that he was not challenging for the position of top dog – even against a scrawny stranger.

I should note, however, claiming your space does not mean aggressively invading another person's space. Like a belligerent dog charging up to another, Dominators may use this tactic as a way to unnerve others. We have probably all experienced the bulldog type of person who barrels right up and invades personal space physically and verbally. This is using a physical presence to intimidate or keep someone off balance. If you find yourself backing away from someone in a social situation, this is, of course, a sign she is invading your personal space. The only way to fight back is to stand your ground and to calmly state your discomfort with the other person's behavior. She may not consciously realize what she is doing, but it is still an attempt to keep you off balance and uncomfortable and must be stopped.

As I began to pay attention to my body language, I noticed that because I am very tall, I find it difficult not to hunch over when I stand. It is a constant battle for me to remember to stand up straight, with my head in line with my spine. I tend to crane my head forward, as if eager to hear what people are saying. This is clearly a sign of submission and weakness to others. I realized that if I wanted to be viewed as a pack leader, I had to stop slouching. I continue to work on a strong posture without tension, with my chest out, chin up, and eyes up.

I used to express nervousness by fidgeting. Some of this fidgeting was simple toe tapping and wriggling. But I now realize I would constantly readjust my hair, check my clothes, look in mirrors. My desire to look good was a sign I wanted to fit in, to be accepted. Anyone seeing these nervous glances would, on a primal level, have correctly interpreted these gestures as insecurity. Now if I find myself in a situation that makes me nervous, I consciously focus on relaxing. I have cut back on my random gestures, and if I do gesture I do so more slowly and deliberately.

I occasionally slip back into my habitual behaviors, but I try to be aware of how I present myself to others.

Research has shown that our physical behaviors do influence our emotions. The physical act of smiling makes people feel happier, studies show. So it seems obvious that acting as if you are confident and physically strong, claiming the space that you are entitled to, may loop positive messages to your brain and help you re-imagine yourself as a respected pack leader.

Pack Leader Wisdom:
Relax to let your intuition speak.
Watch for actions, not just words.
Respect is love in action.
Exercise calms the mind and body.
A calm mind can access inner wisdom.
Claim your space and claim respect.

LESSON 3

Be Honest

Most dogs Reilly meets are not very well socialized to dog behavior. Consequently, they approach too aggressively, which appears to Reilly as a dominant move.

Reilly instantly reacts, barks, growls and lets them know they are out of line. If you listen closely to her communication, it isn't a bark of anger or aggression, but rather contains a sense of outrage. ("Hey, you!") Reilly doesn't bite or attack, but moves away from the other dog. If the dog quits acting dominantly, Reilly approaches and all is forgiven. The dogs sniff, wag, and start to play.

Dog communication is instant, honest, and direct. Reilly isn't afraid to tell dogs when they are behaving incorrectly, but she doesn't over-react. She communicates exactly what she needs to – they are in her space and acting poorly – and then she moves on.

Balanced dogs will often reprimand dogs that are behaving fearfully. Reilly was off leash in a field one day when a large Rottweiler, also off leash, came up to play. Everything was fine until the Rottweiler's owner tried to leash his dog and leave. The Rottie snarled and began biting the owner's arm and the leash, jumping up on the owner and disobeying. Reilly went from calm and playful to standing and watchful. Then she began circling this scene of owner and snarling dog, barking at them anxiously, something I had never seen her do before. She was telling the Rottie to calm down, to quit being dominating. It was a clear example of a balanced dog telling another to quit behaving inappropriately: Honest, prompt communication if I ever saw it. Sadly, there wasn't enough time for Reilly's lesson to have any impact on the dog.

Watching Reilly communicate with and discipline dogs taught me a lot about how to deal with conflict.

The growling incident in the early days of training Reilly helped me understand how important communication is – with dogs and with people, of course. In that incident I did several things correctly, even though I didn't know it at the time. I responded immediately, reacting with instinct in a flash to communicate that Reilly's shoe-nabbing behavior was inappropriate. Yet I responded without anger or frustration. I educated her about my "rules, boundaries, and limitations," that the shoe belonged to me, and I was claiming it. I stayed "in her face" literally and figuratively, physically not retreating until she dropped the shoe. Afterward, I didn't feel bad about the incident. Instead, I felt empowered. What I did not do was pet her and apologize for disciplining her. I just picked up the shoe as if it was the natural thing to do and went about my business.

After learning about dominance dog training, I had to admit I had been afraid of hurting my first dog's feelings when disciplining him. With Kiva I had failed to provide proper guidance. I was too nice and had failed to step up and take charge as a pack leader.

However, by failing to be assertive, one can end up nurturing unbalanced behaviors and anxiety – leading to an unhealthy situation for both owner and dog. Aggressive dogs will learn they can take advantage, but they will remain anxious and fearful because they lack a pack leader who explains and enforces correct social behavior. Submissive dogs will grow even more submissive and anxious, also because the owner is not showing structure and guidance.

Throw out your "person-centered" concept that if someone is strong, it means someone else becomes weaker. Toss away your idea that if you speak the truth, it will devastate others. By communicating strength, you strengthen those around you.

Honest Communication is Assertiveness in Action

When I growled at Reilly I didn't immediately associate it with my human relationships. That insight came later. But, boy, what lessons it held on many, many levels. It taught me a lot about communication, and not just about growling!

As I learned more about pack leadership, I learned that in the dog world, a lack of boundaries is seen as inappropriate submission. This is the dog that immediately rolls over and shows his belly. As I applied Pack Leader Psychology ideas to my life, I could see I had been immediately showing my belly and the way I communicated was a big sign of my submission. For much of my life I had difficulty being assertive. I hesitated to tell others how I felt, to stand up for myself, to give directions to employees, or be honest in relationships. I would communicate, but in a very soft, tentative way.

By not standing up for myself on everyday issues and on major problems, I had given others the green light to take advantage of me. How had I not understood this basic, primal concept?

Of course, I now realize that at some level I did understand exactly what I was doing. I wanted approval so badly that I unconsciously held my tongue, hoping not to offend. I didn't establish any boundaries because I was so eager to have everyone like me.

When matched with a Dominator in a relationship, this pattern suits both people. I did exactly what my husbands wanted me to do, which is to not criticize or correct. My passive pleasing was my way to avoid criticism, and this suits the Dominator's fear of criticism just fine.

Parents Must Teach Healthy Communication

It became obvious that much of this training came from my childhood, which was at a time when being properly behaved was drilled into children. I was taught to be polite, respectful to adults, and well mannered at all times, which seem like good ideas on the surface, but if taken overboard are very dangerous lessons to teach a child.

When you are taught to be nice at all costs, you learn many unhealthy lessons about dishonest communication:

1. I was taught that the truth was somehow uncomfortable, scary, and impolite and if I spoke the truth someone might become uncomfortable, scared, and wouldn't like me.
2. I learned I didn't have the right to stand up for myself and ask for what I wanted, because this might be seen as too needy or demanding. I was taught that I shouldn't be "difficult." My upbringing lead me to believe my needs were worth less than those of other people.
3. Instead of asking directly, I manipulated others into giving me what I wanted. I learned to appease and please as a form of communication.
4. I learned not to disagree with someone because it might provoke an angry response. I put this imagined reaction by others above my own needs and feelings, as if protecting others' feelings was more important than protecting my own. If you were raised by or around someone with a tendency to react emotionally to conflict, you might have learned that when you asked for something they "bit back" at you. This was their way of controlling you and teaching you not to demand anything or criticize.
5. I learned to lie. Even if I didn't tell an outright lie in a situation, I learned to soft pedal my communication so as not to offend. I

often lied by omission – withholding or downplaying the truth to avoid hurting someone's feelings. Delaying confrontation is another symptom.

6. I learned I didn't have the right to refuse someone else's request.

7. I learned to overestimate the negative reaction I might get if I was honest with someone else. I envisioned the worst results from an honest conversation, imagined screaming and tension, doors slamming.

8. I learned to be afraid of facing my own imperfections and admitting any vulnerability. If I was honest about my fears, others might swoop in and use those fears to attack me. In that yin and yang of neediness and self-protectiveness, I felt that if I denied my own weaknesses I could defend myself from attack by others. Of course, I probably learned this fear earlier in life when someone did exactly that – attacked a weakness I exhibited.

I later came to understand that a lack of assertive communication had been the source of all my problems. I had tap danced around major problems in all my relationships – including my relationship with myself. I had ignored many, many elephants in many, many rooms. With my first husband, I watched his drinking problem escalate for years and didn't say anything about it. Then, when it had gotten serious and I was considering divorce, I would make brief, tentative comments. I laugh now when I realize how futile this was. This was a guy who barely noticed I was alive. Do you think that my polite nudges were even heard, much less acknowledged and acted upon?

I now know I absolutely should have laid down the law much more firmly and much sooner. His excessive drinking wasn't just affecting him; it was affecting me. It was disrespectful to me and I should have said exactly that.

Of course, what drove this fear of being honest was a tremendous lack of self-worth. If you feel you shouldn't ask for what you want, you instead attempt to manipulate others with emotional drama, niceness, or aggression.

When I learned my self-worth is intrinsic, not driven by the opinions of others, this enabled me to be more honest with myself and with others. Once I realized I had the right to stand up to someone when she attacked me it helped melt my fear of honesty.

Just as Reilly never questions whether she is able to do anything, I have learned I have to strengthen my self-worth so that I believe I can handle anything – even honesty.

Unmask the Conspiracy of Silence

As I learned firsthand, Dominators get away with much of what they do because Submissives and Avoiders are hesitant to confront them. This reaction, or rather lack of reaction, is common for most people when faced with behavior that doesn't fit accepted norms. Because people generally conform to society's unspoken rules about courtesy, we often don't know what to do when we come across someone who openly flouts those codes. Many freeze like frightened rabbits, which merely validates the rudeness.

While silence may feel like a safe solution to a Submissive or Avoider, this enabling behavior merely teaches the Dominator his behavior is acceptable. He is able to step into your space physically or emotionally and get away with it, because you did not say anything in protest. And when he gets away with it once, he may push those boundaries more next time.

Don't let fear of conflict and social exclusion drive decisions to discipline others. This is such an important lesson for everyone: Reacting to aggression with submission or avoidance only nurtures the Dominator's unhealthy "attack" mode. Communicating honestly, promptly, and forthrightly about boundary violations is absolutely essential in breaking the chain of maladaptive behavior – for both people.

When you walk on eggshells, afraid of a Dominator's reaction, the Dominator is training you to fear him and keep quiet and, thus, gains power merely from your silence. What an easy way to dominate – the Submissive does all the work! Unbalanced people use the code of silence to their advantage, gaining even more power and ensuring complicit subjugation. If someone is holding back and biting her tongue, then someone else is probably getting the upper hand. Silence is consent, as the old saying goes, and normalizes inappropriate behavior.

Individually and collectively, we seem to have an increasing need to avoid and deny certain issues and situations. Not discussing the fact that the emperor has no clothes merely postpones the inevitable moment when the uncomfortable truth is revealed. And, in the meantime, it gives those weavers and tailors of deception all the power.

As I have written, our human tendency to avoid confrontation stems from our social need to belong and get along. Stirring up trouble might get us kicked out of the tribe. When we live in a small group, we need the ability to overlook some behaviors. Picking on every fault is rude, so we choose to selectively ignore things: Tact is a mild form of the taboo against speaking out.

In a dysfunctional world, though, this view that speaking out is a form of criticism becomes super-sized. We are trained (especially Submissives and Avoiders) to avoid embarrassing others. That wouldn't be nice, after all, and you might not like me if I am honest about your faults or behaviors.

Evolutionary psychologists have a term for the opposite type of communication: "altruistic punishment." By honestly and promptly confronting inappropriate behavior, we enforce social norms. For example, when you glare at someone talking loudly on a cell phone in a restaurant or shush someone chattering in a movie, you are engaging in altruistic punishment. It is altruistic because it may not even help you all that much – in fact, you may be yelled at or worse. But it may help the next person. You are working toward making society a bit more cooperative and less selfish. If we don't do this, how do these people know their behavior is inappropriate?

I believe using the fear of social rejection as a positive force is the most powerful behavior modifier we have.

Honesty Is Frightening to Some People; They Are Afraid of What They Might Hear

Submissives have developed an unspoken social contract with the world: I won't criticize you if you won't criticize me. Unfortunately, most Dominators sense the neediness involved in this type of bargain, yet don't hold up their end. Dominators know Submissives are fearful of the truth and use this reluctance to speak out to their advantage. The Dominator is permitted to dodge criticism and avoid responsibility, enabled by the Submissive's desire to keep the peace. Needless to say, the Dominator isn't likely to hold back when it comes time to yell, criticize, or emotionally abuse others.

People develop these tactics of lashing in or lashing out because they are afraid to hear that confirming message that they fear: "I don't like you." This message would confirm their existing self-judgment that they are unworthy – and may be ostracized.

Many marriages and relationships are built on a shared agreement to avoid conflict based on feelings of low self-worth and shame. Called confluence, this agreement to never disagree leads to game playing and a lack of intimacy, but feels safe for the participants. The need for silent cooperation is at its worst in situations where family members don't speak out against incest, domestic violence, substance abuse, child abuse, or sexual abuse.

Children, who are just learning how to corroborate their personal experiences, are especially at risk for the reality-altering manipulation that is avoidance of communication.

Treat Others as Fragile and They Will Believe They ARE Fragile

Silence has an even more-powerful component. It can unleash a sense of fear by its very existence. If we're not talking about something, the topic must be really, really scary. This creates a spiral: The fear generates tension and anxiety, which generates more stuff we can't talk about, and we have to remember all those topics that we can't discuss, which generates more tension. Eventually there is a minefield of eggshells to be navigated on a daily basis, at the cost of a lot of psychological energy.

I also believe that lies of omission lead to a lack of trust in relationships, which causes anxiety. Trust is a fundamental component of cooperative social cultures. Subtle and not-so-subtle lies deceive others and break the bond of trust.

I now know that by cushioning my comments, the topic at hand becomes more consequential, rather than less. By attempting to soften the blow, it communicates that the blow needs to be softened. When you treat someone as if she is too fragile to handle a message, she will begin to believe she really is too fragile to handle honesty.

Pack leaders state the truth respectfully, promptly, fairly, calmly, clearly, and concisely without wiggling, dodging, soft selling, or backpedaling.

Silencing Praise Is a Lie

Silence can damage in many ways. Just as we must tell the truth about misbehaviors among us, we must also tell the truth about correct behavior. On an obvious level, if we don't praise others for the good stuff they do, how will they learn they should repeat these behaviors? Without honest feedback, how do we confirm a correct sense of reality?

If we don't praise when it is appropriate, it teaches others to deny their intuition – a subtle lie about their abilities and perceptions.

While I do not recommend that we praise just to assuage insecurities, I do think well-earned and well-placed compliments give us an accurate portrait of ourselves and our talents. Withholding this valuable information causes people to become insecure, to question their abilities, to needlessly redouble their efforts. If no one ever tells you that you are good enough, you may keep plugging away trying to achieve that goal, never realizing you are already there.

Lacking real input from others, a child has a difficult time understanding how others perceive his behaviors. Social interaction is a teaching tool, if what is taught is truly reflective and not judgmental, false, or manipulative. Honest reflection allows a child to fully experience his authentic self within a supportive social context.

As I look back at my life, I realize I grew up without much honest feedback on my behavior, driving me to question my abilities and endlessly strive to be better. I then moved into a marriage where I also never got a compliment or praise or admission of love, adding more unstable ground under my feet. (Some Dominators may use withholding of praise to weaken Submissives and get them to continually question their abilities.)

As a culture, we seem to be very reluctant to give appropriate praise to family, friends, and colleagues, however one of the most powerfully positive behaviors we can offer is to support and recognize each other's talents and actions.

Honest Communication Is Respectful

It became obvious to me that healthy communication helps build respect. To earn respect, I had to establish boundaries for myself and for those around me. When I communicate clearly with others it says: "I respect myself enough that I have minimum standards of behavior for people in my life. I don't allow others to trample on me."

I learned that when I attempted to please everyone it was disrespectful to me. The cost to my self-respect when I acted like a doormat over the years was insidious, but monumental. It was a death of a thousand cuts when every day I acquiesced, kowtowed, and submitted to the needs of others. Heck, I even gave in without question, without a fight. Such weakness!

I am now nice to those around me only when they respect me. If a date were to show up two hours late, I would say, "That is disrespectful," and I would educate him about how I feel. In the past I would have said and done nothing – communicating that his behavior was OK.

To Earn Respect, Stand Your Ground

Avoiding conflict can feel safe – for the moment. But what do these little omissions and white lies say? I believe that holding back, tiptoeing around topics, and being "too nice" are actually lies – lies people can sense intuitively. They feel at a primal level someone is not telling them the whole truth. And if they sense someone is lying, will they trust that person? Dishonest communication and lies of omission are disrespectful to others.

As I have learned, honest communication is an essential tool if you are going claim respect for yourself and show respect for others. If it is worth saying, it is worth saying directly and forthrightly. Being honest saves everyone time and emotional energy: Others know exactly where you stand because you've drawn your boundary clearly.

Communicate, Don't Manipulate

One of the most difficult things I had to admit to myself was that failing to provide honest communication is more than fearful; it can be a form of manipulation. As a Submissive I had been avoiding conflict as a way to get what I wanted – a feeling of acceptance. By being too nice and less than honest, I had tried to manipulate others into liking me and providing the affection I craved. I had been communicating strategically, trying to control how others reacted to me. No wonder I had struggled to maintain relationships of all kinds. People could sense I was trying to manipulate them.

When I avoided conflictual communication with others, I communicated that I was uncomfortable with honest feedback. This not only stifled my emotional growth, but the growth of those around me. They weren't dealing with a real, authentic person, so if they felt anger or resentment at me, they were forced to manage it on their own because I had built a moat of silence and denial as a way to fend off potential criticisms.

Once I let go of the need to try to control how others responded to me, it opened the way to more honest, real relationships unlike any I had experienced in my life.

An ongoing series of small lies or withholding of the truth can sabotage a relationship just as surely as a major lie. When we are not truthful with ourselves or with others, it means the relationship is built on a falsehood.

Honesty can have beneficial effects on many relationships. Constructive conflict handled appropriately can bring people together – it doesn't have to drive them apart. Manipulative non-communication will surely poison a relationship.

If you are the type of person who uses fear and intimidation as a tool to "win" arguments, be aware that this is not the same thing as the honest, direct communication of a pack leader. One reason some Submissives are uncomfortable with confrontation is because they have been around so many who use confrontation inappropriately – not as a way to educate about how to behave, but as a means to sow turmoil, weaken, intimidate, and increase anxiety in others.

Communicate Immediately

Anyone who has trained a dog has learned you must discipline immediately after an event. Yelling at a dog an hour after he has upended the trashcan does nothing – except confuse the dog and communicate that you are upset and anxious. You must catch the dog in the act and immediately show him that the trashcan belongs to you and he is not to touch it.

It is no different with humans. I now see that the timing of my reaction to that tardy boyfriend, for example, is key. What does it say when I cut him some slack and go out to dinner anyway, but on the way home I say timidly, "Could you please show up on time in the future?" It communicates he can be late and I will tolerate it. Some men will spot it as exactly what they are looking for: A sign of a submissive woman they can control.

Some experts on domestic violence believe that these small delays in communication early in a relationship are the green lights a Dominator reads correctly as signals that the partner is afraid of conflict. It is then a slippery slope to even worse behavior, driven by intimidation and control. Once a man learns he can disrespect in small ways without consequence, he may conclude he can escalate that disrespect.

Discipline is Education, Not Conflict

With my new pack leader mindset, I began to rethink my fear of criticizing others. Let's say I wanted to tell my boyfriend that when he shows up late for a date it bothers me. In the past I would have dreaded and avoided this conversation because it seemed so negative. I would have felt as if I was giving him a slap on the wrist.

But how would a pack leader think about this situation? The conversation didn't need to be one-sided, with me as the hammer. It could involve me calmly informing him that when he is late it makes me feel unimportant in his life and feel as if my time is not valued. I could also express some positive thoughts: I was looking forward to seeing him, and when he is late it makes me disappointed. My tone and attitude would be as if I were explaining to him about how I felt, rather than criticizing his behavior. The distinction is a subtle, but important, reframing.

As you've learned, discipline is education, not punishment. To a pack leader, proper communication is educating my boyfriend about how his behavior made me feel, not punishing him to make him stop. For those who have been socialized to avoid conflict, it becomes less frightening to consider once you realize assertive communication involves education, not punishment.

Also remember: Pack leaders lead, they don't control. With dogs, you can't make Fido stop barking, chewing, or pulling. You have to express to him his behavior is unacceptable to you and disengage when he behaves inappropriately. He then decides how to behave.

This style of communication also puts the responsibility right where it should be – on the misbehaver. Submisssives, however, tend to take on responsibility for controlling and correcting the misbehavior, rather than acknowledging it is up to the other person to decide how he or she behaves.

Unassertive Communication Causes Pent-up Hostility

After a couple of years of communicating more like a pack leader, I realized one day how much less anger and hostility I had in my life. In the past, if someone had made an unreasonable request, I would have either complained to myself or I might have become slightly snippy with him. While I always considered myself very pleasant, I now realize it was a pasted-on, overly pleasing manner – done to get people to like me. So when someone didn't return my phone calls or didn't do a job correctly, I might get angry. But I didn't let that anger out in direct, honest conversation. Instead, I might simmer, rehash the perceived slights mentally, and gather up resentment. Which certainly did not endear me to other people. While I would never have been considered an angry person – because I had been so busy being nice – my low-grade resentment was almost certainly noticeable to many people.

In hindsight, I learned that when a person is too submissive and doesn't communicate honestly, promptly, and freely, it can result in an ongoing pattern of allowing others to bulldoze. Resentment can build because you feel you can't or aren't allowed to defend yourself – because you are such a "good person." Eventually this resentment becomes unsustainable. We may lash out at others inappropriately because we have held our tongue, denied our own needs, and been too people pleasing for our own good. The flight response will eventually turn into a fight response if we are pushed far enough into that emotional corner.

Eventually, I developed enough self-respect to state clearly how I wanted others to treat me. Just knowing I had the option to respond assertively made me happier and less resentful. I didn't always express myself in every situation, but just recognizing I had the ability was empowering. And when I did respond, it was more appropriate because I didn't take every issue as a personal criticism.

I can't help but wonder if this lack of prompt communication is what causes someone to go "postal." Is it because for perhaps years the person has ignored his own needs and wants and did not exert reasonable boundaries around himself? Then when pushed just so far he over-reacts with the fight response, becoming violent "unexpectedly." Of course, it seems clear that these people are over-reacting due to a misperception that they have been unfairly criticized.

Compounding the problem is that this type of person may be a social loner for whom work colleagues are the only social group he or she knows; when fired the sensation is that of being cast out of the only pack they know.

Are occasional violent outbursts the price we pay when we don't insist on honest communication and self-respect?

Re-Learn to Communicate Honestly

As a Submissive who was looking to become a pack leader, I knew I needed help in being more assertive with my communicating if I was going to manage the Dominators who came into my life. I had to develop skills to be firmer about educating others about my rules and boundaries using direct, honest communication. Here are some things I learned:

1. Speak the unspeakable. Avoiding topics gives others power. State the facts. Or talk about the fact a topic is being avoided – a very power-shattering move.
2. When I feel myself getting worked up I generally choose to be calm and assertive. I take a deep breath. Pause. Think first. Consider my words carefully. Talk slowly and deliberately.

3. I remember I always have the power. I drive this bus. I don't let the Dominators rush me, control the tempo, or get me riled up. I don't respond to their escalating energy. I also remind myself they are insecure and fearful, which helps me develop compassion for them, rather than fear of them, a powerful shift of the power dynamic.

4. If I feel nervous, I make a conscious effort to be deliberate in my physical actions. I avoid fidgeting. I look the other person in the eye and hold the eye contact. I know gesturing randomly will defeat all my deliberate, well-chosen words.

5. I state my position, then stop talking. Arguing endlessly merely shows weakness – that you feel your side of the argument needs to be stated over and over. Pack leaders do not waste energy arguing with weak, unbalanced members of the pack. Silence can be much more powerful than words.

6. Don't follow the bait trail. Ray used confrontation as a power play in this way: He would start an argument about one topic, but when I had a good response – bingo – the conversation was suddenly about something else. I would then dodge over and respond to that comment, but he would change the topic again. I was left only responding to his moves. This first proved to him he was in control, "Look how I can make her jump through every hoop I put up." It was also an attempt to distract me from the fundamental issue that his behavior – the cause of the argument – was unbalanced, controlling, and inappropriate.

7. Take the offensive. When you respond only to comments and attacks, you are in a defensive posture. Now that I am less afraid of conflict I do something I call "name it." When a Dominator starts dodging and weaving with his distract-and-delay arguing tactics, I calmly talk about the communication process itself. I label what he is doing for what it is: a control move. I state that I feel he is attempting to manipulate or control me with these tactics. Then I stop talking. I don't get bogged down in responding to all his devious false arguments.

8. Once I've stated my position and heard a response – and that response isn't acceptable to me – I act. Acting can include sitting silently and looking calmly at the other person. It may mean calmly but decisively leaving the room. I use my intuition to decide which is appropriate. (If you believe the other person may become physically violent, be very careful about what action you choose. The key is to act calmly.)

9. I act as if I deserve respect – which I do! I analyze all the behaviors sent my way to see if they are disrespectful. I listen to my intuition during an argument. If I feel I am being disrespected, it is very powerful to state what behaviors or words I perceive as disrespectful.

10. Live in the moment. Avoid retribution or grudge holding.

11. Be prepared to disengage emotionally or physically. Arguing with a Dominator is exactly what the Dominator wants. It shows he has power over you. It shows you care about his attention more than your own self-respect. It shows you can be manipulated. When you don't argue, it communicates self-control. By disengaging, you show the Dominator he or she has no power over you. Even if you must deal with the Dominator and be in the same room physically, you can pull away emotionally. Continue to treat the Dominator with respect and civility, but divest yourself emotionally.

12. Don't be invested in how the other person behaves. Her mood swings or angry outbursts are not your fault or responsibility and do not reflect on you.

Dominators instinctively avoid tussling with a balanced person. All their lives they have learned to find Submissive victims because they want someone who can be easily manipulated. Bullies always seek out weak individuals who are easier targets to prey on. By using honest, direct communication tactics, you will send a message that you are not a weak victim.

By Communicating Strength, You Strengthen Those Around You

One of the odd riddles I solved as a pack leader was that if I have confidence in myself and am forthright and honest, this is a signal that others, too, can handle anything – a subliminal vote of confidence I give them. What relationship isn't improved with a shot of respect from the other person?

Looking back at relationships with my husbands, this was a shocking admission. Could it be that because I did not directly address Paul's drinking problem he learned that this issue was big and scary and difficult to deal with? And if the person closest to him felt it was impossible to discuss with him, how could he even think about changing it? If I didn't even have the strength to confront Ray about a huge issue like him beating me up, how could he confront it himself? Through my fears, I was telling these guys I was also fearful that they were, indeed, weak. That they couldn't handle the truth. That the truth was too big to handle. My weakness was feeding their weakness. My lack of confidence in myself was fueling their lack of confidence in themselves. My dishonesty helped them stay dishonest with themselves.

....

Live in the Moment

When puppies play they often escalate the level of excitement until it is too rough. An adult dog may tolerate it for a while, then when a limit has been reached, will growl at the pups or nudge them away. The pups back off and learn that their behavior was inappropriate. But the pups go on playing and the adult goes back to sleep and they're all still friends after this incident. There is no other meaning or baggage or shame attached to the growl.

Dogs confront each other and move on. No one becomes resentful at being disciplined. The discipline is done fairly and with a purpose: to teach appropriate pack behavior. It isn't performed to humiliate or embarrass. Dogs establish boundaries for proper behavior in the "now," but they don't imagine bad behavior into the future. When bad behavior happens in the future, they don't re-live and re-hash all the past incidents. Dogs live in the moment.

Anxiety Does Not Live in the Moment

For so many people, life is a chronic, anxious treadmill of worrying about a litany of minor and imagined events and occurrences on a timeline extending backward for decades and forward for decades. The psychological diagnostic categories used by the mental health profession are loaded with anxiety disorders, compulsions, obsessions, and personality disorders that feature a common sign: These people worry mainly about whether they will live up to the expectations of others. They worry if they said the wrong thing or obsess about whether they locked the door. They worry someone might be offended or that they might have made a mistake. All of these concerns are focused inward – these people are "lashing in" at themselves, worrying if their performance or capabilities are adequate, were adequate, or will be adequate in the future.

Given a high enough level of fear, this pattern can lead to thoughts that seem uncontrollable to the person experiencing them. This kind of person imagines all types of potential behaviors, some even extreme. One man imagined he might stab someone, even though he'd never come close to being violent. He then developed a phobia of knives, as if coming close to a knife would trigger him to behave inappropriately. Or a woman might worry she will start swearing out loud in church, even though she never even swears to herself at home.

Most of these overanxious people are Submissives; their thoughts are nearly always centered on doing the right thing. They are overly concerned about hurting others, making mistakes, or offending or disappointing others in the future.

If you spend your life focused on a time other than the present, and on actions that might happen, you are not a pack leader. You are much too worried about pleasing others, and you may be doing it to such a level you are risking your own health. If you have ever had a panic attack, depression, or other anxiety disorder, you need to live in the moment more. Let go of your need to manage and control others' reactions and opinions. Your anxieties will likely fade away.

In contrast, if you are quick to anger or afraid others are out to take advantage of you, you are also not living in the moment. You are fearful of the possibility of being rejected or criticized to the point that your defenses are on alert at all times. You are unable to relax and enjoy life.

Communicate Now

I have come to believe that "Live in the moment" is a great way to think about honesty and assertiveness.

We have a lot to learn from animals, because we usually do the opposite: If there is a problem in a relationship, we don't nip it in the bud. Many, especially Submissives, wait far too long to discipline, hesitating until really angry and upset. Waiting too long increases the likelihood of overreacting and escalating the discipline to a point where it is uncomfortable for the other person.

Move Past the Past

When people adopt a dog rescued from a traumatic past or poor living conditions, they often wonder if the dog will ever behave normally. If a dog has been beaten, it may cower fearfully. But nearly all dogs will recover and learn to be balanced, happy, and outgoing if they have one thing – and, no, it's not love. They need a strong, dependable, patient, fair pack leader. There is no other magic formula for rehabilitating a fearful dog. Time and patience are essential, but anxieties will fade, even in a severely traumatized dog, once it recognizes it can trust its pack leader.

Compare this to the human world where anxieties are running rampant. Emotional and behavioral problems are on the increase in the past few decades and most are caused by low self-worth and resulting anxiety. So many people seem to live their lives on edge, alert to every potential threat. I read about a woman who didn't like her husband kissing her in bed in the morning, because she startled to his touch. She was crabby first thing in the morning and really didn't even like to be touched much any time of the day. She mentioned she had been abused as a child. Clearly, this woman reacted with a "flight" response to what was certainly not a threat. If her first reaction every morning is one of fear, it seems obvious her "threat-meter" never turned off – even when she slept! What kind of stress must she be living with if, since childhood, she never truly relaxed, even when asleep?

This woman is clearly not living in the moment. It is not my intention to diminish her experience, but while her traumatic past is painful, it doesn't have to linger and disrupt her entire life, to the point where she can't cuddle with her husband. Certainly, this inability to move on emotionally is not at all healthy. Research shows that our brains are actually set up so we naturally forget negative experiences sooner and more thoroughly than positive ones. It is also natural for our brains to "rewrite" our histories so that we remember neutral or negative experiences as more positive than they were. This is our brain's way of managing fearful memories – it erases them or paints them over in more pleasant colors. But when a primal fear response is triggered over and over, it seems as if some people's brains instead flip, remembering the negative events more often and more clearly.

Why is it that one person who experiences a bombing, hurricane, or crime can go on to live her life in a healthy way, and another who experiences the same event is an emotional wreck? It is interesting that research on post-traumatic stress disorder finds a large percentage of those who develop this condition had other mental health disorders prior to the trauma, usually depression, anxiety disorders, or phobias. They were likely very Submissive, fearful people even before the traumatic event, and are now unable to adapt to the frightening experience. To me, a balanced person can manage a traumatic event much more easily than someone who comes into the event with an emotional system already swamped by fears. Anxious people add the event to the long list of "threats" they see in the world, and the new experience overloads the system, leading to diagnosis of a disorder like PTSD, depression, or other emotional condition.

The important question is: Why is it some people can't seem to move past the past? Why do some people harbor and even nurture anxieties about everything from previous events to a fear of spiders? I can't help but conjecture that it is our society's structure – the lack of trust among people due to unpredictable, unbalanced behaviors – that makes us so loaded with insecurities and anxieties. If a dog that has been beaten, starved, and chained to a doghouse can recover and behave normally once it has a trusted pack structure, what other explanation could be possible for why so many humans now seem unable to adapt emotionally?

In addition, if a person has learned to look for acceptance outside himself and this becomes a mode of operating 24/7, he may spend his time and energy scanning the environment, looking for signs someone is rejecting him or criticizing him. It uses brainpower and energy to be on alert. No wonder the result may be fatigue, insomnia, and irritability. No wonder stress-related diseases are on the rise. By never shutting down we never relax and just exist – in the moment.

It isn't a coincidence many disorders labeled by the mental health profession list sleep disruptions as a symptom: sleep loss, light sleep, decreased sleep efficiency, decreased sleep time, and disruptions of REM sleep patterns. These are all signs the body is still on alert, because the mind keeps sending it signals to worry and be anxious. Reilly's lesson would be: Live in the moment and let go of your anxieties.

Let Go of Control

In the past, I failed to live in the moment largely because I was busy trying to control other people. I was afraid of confrontation because I was afraid of the reaction I was so sure I'd get. I projected into the future to imagine other people would dislike me, then moderated my words and behavior, hoping to appease and avoid criticism.

To me, "Live in the moment" means not only to be more centered and present, but to let go of attempting to control other people's reactions.

I'm sure a balanced wolf pack leader does not try to manage every wolf in the pack at every minute. She shows the pack the way and provides guidance, then lets each member follow according to his own habits and patterns. A pack leader communicates, "We're going hunting over in the valley," and heads off. She doesn't look over her shoulder to make sure each pack member is tracking exactly in her footsteps. She just assumes they will all get to the valley in some way and does not worry about the exact trail they take. And she certainly doesn't spend any energy wondering if the other wolves like her!

So many people are busy, instead, controlling, manipulating, and establishing power plays in an attempt to set up a future that ensures they receive the required amounts of acceptance from others. Think of the wasted energy, anxiety, and frustration.

I stopped this treadmill and got off only as an unintended benefit of other changes I made. By gaining self-acceptance, self-respect, self-worth and authenticity, I no longer looked to others to provide emotional support. I stopped over-thinking what he said or what she did or whether he looked at me dismissively. I stopped worrying if someone might criticize me. I didn't waste time harboring grudges about the past, planning to seek vengeance in the future, expecting events, or hoping for reactions I could not control.

The synergy was amazing as Reilly's lessons continued to mesh together and helped me move beyond my Submissive behavior. Because I live in the moment, I no longer perceive threats from others that were probably never there. Because I am more balanced, I don't see someone else's misbehavior as a personal attack I must react to with either a flight, fight, or avoidance response. I recognize someone's reaction is just a reaction, just an opinion, and not a threat to me. I can now disengage, continue on with my life, and not be entangled in feeling emotionally hijacked by a situation. And when I am less anxious, others around me are less anxious, which means less anxiety feeds back to me. Because I am less anxious, others don't see me as Submissive, so they don't take advantage of me, which also makes me less fearful. It's a win-win-win!

"Live in the moment" is a powerful prescription that can benefit many parts of your life and the lives of those around you.

Pack Leader Wisdom:
Honest communication is brave, respectful,
and strengthens both parties.
Watch for those who manipulate,
rather than communicate.
Watch for the unspoken truth.
Watch for those who are afraid of honesty.

LESSON 4

Be Respectful

Reilly and I had arrived at a campground where my dad and his new wife were already camped. Their two dogs, Keet and Bounder, ran up quickly to where I was standing. This would appear to most people to be a natural behavior for dogs. We'd normally encourage this, pet them, squat down, say hello.

Reilly had known both dogs for several years, but when she saw these two dogs behaving this way she ran toward them and barked several times. Her bark might have sounded menacing to most humans, but I interpreted it as a warning. She was alerting me, as well as disciplining the other dogs for their behavior. Reilly was saying, "You're being disrespectful to my pack leader and to me." But Keet and Bounder didn't understand they were displaying inappropriate dog behavior. They had been socialized to approach other dogs and people directly.

Most people, if their dog barked a warning in this situation would have scolded the dog. Think of the dog's confusion: "I was trying to be a good pack member, warn my pack leader, and discipline these two poorly behaved dogs, but I got yelled at!" Although I correctly recognized Reilly's behavior for what it was, most people fail to and then train the behavior out of their dog, instead creating inappropriate and unbalanced behaviors. Not me – I say "good girl!"

A balanced dog behaves in other ways that are confusing to those not familiar with the dog world. When Reilly and I are around other dogs, the owners often say, "Your dog doesn't say 'hi' to my dog." If this occurs when Reilly is running off leash at a park I just say, "She's busy doing her job – hunting." While this is true, these people don't understand Reilly is merely behaving as a respectful dog would. A balanced dog does not run straight up to another dog with an enthusiastic greeting. Reilly and other well-socialized dogs know this is inappropriate and threatening. Reilly just is not friendly in a "people" way or in the way most domestic dogs behave. She doesn't run up to, lick, and jump up.

To balanced dogs, it is more important to be respectful than friendly. In the animal world, respect is used to honor the hierarchy of the pack. And respect is shown with physical actions.

One day a neighbor girl named Rayann was in my yard with Reilly. Rayann knelt down and put her arm over Reilly's neck in a human hug. Reilly jumped back and gave a couple of quick barks. I recognized Reilly's barks weren't aggressive. Reilly was merely telling Rayann: "Hey, what are you doing? You're a stranger. You can't put your arm over my neck." In that type of situation, a less balanced dog might have gone into fight mode and attacked Rayann.

This kind of story explains why some dogs don't like it when kids and strangers approach and pet them. Many dog bites are due to humans who do not understand how to approach a dog respectfully. But people mistakenly put a human explanation on it, "Oh, you moved too quickly and surprised the dog." No, the dog wasn't startled. Dogs are much more perceptive than humans and their reaction time is four times as fast as ours. In actuality, the person's direct approach was a physical challenge of dominance toward the dog, a sign of disrespect, and a disruption of the pack protocol. Remember that a stranger or even lower member of the pack does not approach and certainly doesn't touch a superior pack member unannounced and without permission. A balanced dog will bark. An unbalanced dog may bite.

Family pets communicate about respectful pack order, but their owners often don't understand the language. A woman named Shelly once told me a story about Phil, an 18-month-old Shar-Pei and German Shepherd Dog mix. Phil was a rescue dog and had been to obedience classes and seemed to be getting a fair amount of exercise. He was generally a good dog, but Shelly admitted he had one behavior problem. Phil was fine around all of the family members, except that he growled occasionally at Alex, the youngest girl in the family. I asked when this happened. Shelly said she just didn't understand it, because it happened when Alex hugged Phil and tried to cuddle with him. It was instantly obvious to me why it was happening. Phil was actually reprimanding Alex with his growl. Because of Alex's weak, needy energy, Phil saw himself as above her in the family pack. Alex's hugs, which she meant as love, were to Phil an unacceptable act of dominance and a sign of disrespect. Phil's growl was only telling Alex she was not respecting a more superior member of the pack.

This example illustrates how clearly dogs define their pack hierarchy and how much they value respectful behavior. It also shows how many dog owners have a very unhealthy relationship with their dog. They don't understand the need for a pack hierarchy and the respect that accompanies that ranking. It may seem very normal to our human eyes to hug and love on a dog all the time, but it isn't.

If an owner is overly concerned about being liked, and not concerned with being respected, this communicates very weak energy and a sign of submission. Ironically, in trying to be a dog's friend, an owner loses the dog's respect. Respect is the real power in the dog world and is the key to getting a dog to like you. If you are a pack leader, dogs treat you with respect. Love and friendship then flow out of respect. Dogs value having a strong, balanced pack leader who treats them with respect because they know this brings pack harmony and security.

Many dog owners are reluctant to discipline and become the pack leader because they are afraid of hurting the dog's feelings. This is a clear sign owners are more concerned about being liked than being respected. They are looking to the dog to boost their self-esteem and feed their need for acceptance – something a true pack leader would never do. If you give a dog love but no discipline, he won't respect you.

Fortunately, dogs live in the moment. They quickly forget your past lack of leadership and will trust you if you can make the transition to respected and respectful pack leadership.

Respect Is the Basis of Balanced Relationships

One of the most powerful lessons I learned from Reilly was the power of respect. Although humans have a more complex and deeper emotional repertoire than dogs, I have come to believe we have the same need for respect. Respect for ourselves and for others is a fundamental attitude of pack leaders. Respect truly is the basis of all healthy, balanced relationships. Love and friendship flow out of respect, not the other way around.

I can attest that all the years I went about my life searching for affection and respect, I nearly always got exactly the opposite. I ended up with one husband who disrespected me to the point of violence and physical control, another husband who drank to the point where he didn't remember our conversations. Bosses and co-workers treated me like dirt and – probably the worst disrespect of all – I treated myself very poorly, repeating self-shaming messages on a loop in my brain.

In trying to be everybody's friend, I actually failed to gain respect.

As a pack leader, you cannot be looking for love, affection, or to be liked. Those may be a result, but all you can expect from other people is respect.

Control Is Not Respectful

In the past, I am certain I did not know how to distinguish between respect and fear. I interpreted bully behavior as leadership. I didn't recognize that bullies are actually fearful and insecure, using intimidation to control others. (The fact that I missed this simple lesson in human dynamics is amazing, but true. However, I was raised not to judge or question other people.)

I now see that pack leaders are confident and calm. They are leaders, not Dominators. They do not use manipulation or force to gain power. They do not profit from frightening or controlling others. Controlling someone else involves a fundamental disrespect. Verbally demeaning someone is an attempt to gain a small amount of power by disrespectfully weakening the other person. And, of course, verbal abuse and physical abuse are unforgivable violations of a basic moral right – the right that our physical and emotional safety and boundaries be respected.

Respect Is Love in Action

I now believe when difficulties arise with human relationships it is often due to a lack of respect – either a lack of self-respect when a person is overly submissive or avoidant, or a lack of respect for others when someone attempts to dominate and control in inappropriate ways.

It is a mystery to me that so many people say they "love" their partners and family but do not behave respectfully toward them. They tease or denigrate their spouse in front of the children. They berate their children in front of friends. Those whom they should love the most, they show the least respect. Expecting relationships to be successful in this milieu is folly. Humans have forgotten what dogs know instinctively – that respect and trust come before love, friendship, or affection.

It's interesting that many of us have a hard time defining love: What is it? How do you know if you are in love? These have been questions for the ages. However, most of us with a bit of emotional awareness can sense when we are not being respected. After being in several disrespectful relationships, I have finally learned that respect is an essential precursor to love. Actually, respect is far more powerful and important than love. Respect should be carefully earned and maintained, and sincerely treasured.

I believe that once someone in a relationship stops showing respect to the partner, the relationship is in big trouble. It is very difficult to regain that position of respect. Because, let's face it, if someone has consistently been disrespectful to you, you have no good reason to respect him back.

Remember "reciprocal altruism?" You need mutual trust and respect to trade and share resources fairly with others, and this includes sharing love! The Bible's Golden Rule is all about mutual respect: Do unto others as you would have them do unto you. All religions have a fundamental tenet on reciprocity. Treat others with the same level of respect you would like to have shown to you.

John Gottman, a well-known marriage and relationship researcher, has identified four main causes of divorce: criticism, contempt, defensiveness, and stonewalling. In his fascinating studies he videotaped new couples interacting normally and then, based on nearly unrecognizable body language, Gottman had a fairly high success rate predicting whether the couple would divorce. The absence of respect seems apparent in Gottman's four behaviors.

Gottman believes that contempt is the best predictor of divorce. This points to the notion that even if you don't agree with everything your partner says or does, you should still show respect for that person if he or she is not harming you or demeaning you with their actions.

I read that arranged marriages often work better than love matches. Why is that? It has been said that in an arranged marriage, partners have to look for things to love about the other person. I believe this brings a level of respect to the relationship. In typical Western marriages and relationships, partners seem to spend a lot of time looking for complaints about each other. Every flaw so carefully mined and brought to the surface increases the level of disrespect. Love cannot flourish if it is sown in a bed of disrespect.

When you examine your relationships and wonder if the person loves you, look past the words to the actions. Do you both respect each other and treat each other fairly? The equation is simple: If you aren't treated with respect, you aren't loved.

Claim Respect in Relationships

In the past, I sent signals that communicated that I could be taken advantage of; I failed to earn the respect of the men I attracted, so they felt they could manipulate and even physically abuse me. I now believe because there are so few balanced pack members in the world who value respect, we must be constantly vigilant for those who might disrespect us.

Just as when training a dog, you must claim respect from other people. Claiming respect means expecting others to treat you with respect and then calmly reminding them when they don't do so. It is not asking too much to be treated with respect. It isn't selfish and it isn't demanding, but a fundamental right of every human on the planet.

Submissives need to recognize that being too accommodating isn't the way to gain respect. Would you respect someone who went along with whatever you said?

Unfortunately, I see disrespect all around me. American culture strongly emphasizes casualness over respect. We scream at family members on talk shows and children swear at their parents. We wear baseball caps to church and tank tops to funerals, not just fashion statements, but also symbols of a lack of respect. We have lost the social graces so much that a stranger asking for the time sounds like a holdup rather than a polite request – "Hey, what time is it?" not, "Excuse me, ma'am, but could I please bother you for the correct time?"

At the same time, we have lost the ability to respectfully disagree with others. We can't talk politics or religion unless we scream at each other on TV or in person, but we are afraid to even scold the neighbor's child for fear of retribution or a call to the police.

Self-Discipline Is a Form of Self-Respect

I believe many people send signals that they don't respect themselves, sometimes with physical behaviors as obvious as slouching and mumbling.

I also believe exercise can help you on the road to being a pack leader or at least the strongest member of the pack you can be. Being physically strong makes a person feel more physically capable, which signals competence and confidence.

It is well proven one of the advantages of children being involved in athletics is they learn mental toughness. Why should this lesson stop after graduation? We can all benefit from improved confidence throughout our lives. The courage we gain from challenging ourselves physically can translate to mental toughness.

I continue to downhill ski at the age of 50-plus not only because I enjoy it, but also because I feel it continues to teach me confidence. To be a good skier, you must attack the hill and ski aggressively. You can't be afraid of the speed, but must learn to manage it appropriately. Skiing fearfully and tentatively only adds tension and this makes it more difficult to respond quickly while flying down a steep hill. Good ski technique is fluid, rhythmic, and flowing, which is impossible when tense.

Physical strength leads to mental strength and the opposite is also true: When you are mentally strong, you have the determination to become physically fit.

If people see you as a flabby marshmallow, will they come to the conclusion that your character is also a bit flabby? It may seem unfair, but this concept is merely following the laws of nature. For thousands of generations we have used our first impressions and snap judgments as important tools in keeping our tribe and ourselves safe from threats. You can argue it isn't fair, but you can't argue with the fact that our intuitive judgment of others does depend on the physical appearance of those we're judging.

Self-Respect Is Self-Love in Action

When you are significantly overweight, it sends an immediate non-verbal message to everyone who sees you that very clearly says, "I don't respect myself." You are saying to everyone, "I don't care if I'm healthy or if I am physically weak and unable to care for myself." Being over-weight is a clear signal you have weak energy and a lack of personal accountability.

When you disrespect your body by overeating and under-exercising, it also says you have no self-discipline. If you don't have self-discipline, how can you possibly expect to provide strong leadership to others? If you don't even have the moral strength to back away from a candy bar or get out of bed and go for a run, how can you have the moral strength to be a leader, to show your children how to behave, to discipline an employee?

Without self-discipline and inner strength, what signal does this send about your self-respect? It may be painful for some people to hear, but respect starts with you and your own inner voice disciplining your-self. In addition, I believe that when you have addictions, you recognize this as a weakness and criticize yourself for it. How can these messages be self-affirming? If you feel you can't trust yourself around a beer or a brownie, how can you develop a feeling of self-worth? If you have a fundamental lack of trust in yourself, how can you respect yourself? How can you believe others can also be trusted and respected?

Respect Yourself First

It has been a long road for me, but a fundamental lesson I have learned is that loving and respecting myself were the first steps to earn-ing the love and respect of others. By respecting myself, I no longer felt the need to rely on parents, friends, lovers, or a boss for approval. I've learned I am worthy, not because others say so, but as a basic, intrinsic fact of existence.

·······································

Reward Good Behavior

I heard this story from a dog breeder years ago. It still makes me laugh. An older woman bought one of the breeder's adorable, velvet-coated Vizsla puppies. As will happen, it grew from a seven-pound puppy to a 70-pound dog. After about nine months she called the breeder asking that he take the dog back. When the breeder asked why, the woman said the dog was growling at her. Turns out the puppy had growled once and the woman had given him a treat "to make him happy." No surprise: That training worked! The dog began growling more and more. The breeder wisely realized this woman had no business owning a powerful hunting dog and took the dog back.

Many dog owners reward a dog with affection at the wrong time – when the dog is misbehaving, yet the owners rarely recognize this for what it is. If a dog is circling nervously because someone has entered the house, many owners will reach down to pet the dog. Small dogs often jump up on the owner's lap when the dog chooses, then the owner pets the dog, rewarding this dominant behavior. Many dogs are afraid of thunderstorms, but what do owners do? They pet the dog and talk to it, thinking they are soothing it. This is not what the dog needs. To the dog, you are rewarding its misbehavior with affection, signaling that weak, anxious behavior is OK. The rule is: Give no affection until a dog is behaving with calm, subordinate behavior. Set your expectations high, then reward the behavior you want to encourage.

These are examples of the conditioning response: When you reward behavior, it gets repeated. When a dog is being anxious, you must behave like a calm, in-charge pack leader.

Of course, the root problem here is that you have not been the pack leader and the dog feels he has to assume that role. Reilly has no fear of loud noises, because she doesn't feel responsible for protecting her pack from them. That's my job. She very rarely barks and barks only once or twice when someone knocks at the door. She is not anxious and I do not reward her if she acts nervously. Reilly only gets petting and massaging when she is calm, so she learns that is the correct behavior.

In contrast to the human view that constant praise will help relieve anxiety, take a look at the wolf pack's concept of praise. Being part of the pack is the main reward. A pack can throw an unbalanced member out of the pack, so fitting in is important. If the pack leader isn't getting in another dog's face (this isn't a cliché, it is literally how a pack leader disciplines), a more subordinate dog is happy. No news is good news. The pack leader also doesn't scurry around to each dog and give a lick and a bark of encouragement every day. The calm contentment of the pack snuggling together at night or snoozing in the sun brings satisfaction. Belonging is the biggest reward.

Give Affection as a Reward for Respect

Many of us make the same mistake with our human relationships that many dog owners make with dog training – we give affection at the wrong time, for the wrong reasons, and before it is earned.

With Ray I gave away my affection much too soon in the relationship because I was so needy for affection. Then, when he realized he could do anything he wanted, he began to misbehave. Each time I forgave him it was a reward for his bad behavior. If I had been more disciplined in response to Ray and others in my life, I would have insisted on being respected first before I gave my love.

Both Submissives and Dominators use unbalanced behaviors to troll for affection, rather than claiming respect. Submissives have a tendency to give affection as an enticement before it has been earned. Dominators quickly discover this eagerness to please and take advantage of it. They may escalate to demanding affection – but they certainly don't ever provide respect.

Affection Must Be Earned with Correct Pack Behavior

In terms of social hierarchy, being too accommodating drops a person down in the power structure. Earning the respect of others raises a person's rank.

The idea of praising only when appropriate has special importance for parents and dog owners alike. Many traditional dog trainers believe in giving heaps of praise. You hear dog owners eagerly shouting, "Good job, Scruffy. Good dog, good dog." In the same way, I see parents catering to their children, appeasing them, and praising them for the slightest good behavior. Excessive, excited, emotional praise merely nurtures instability and anxiety. It shows a child that a parent is reactive, that the child's behaviors can please a parent or they can disappoint. This overuse of praise during discipline and teaching tells the child he is dependent on others for his self-worth, that his behaviors can change how his parents feel about him.

I praise Reilly, but not effusively and not often. I save praise for when I am teaching her a new behavior, and I give it calmly and deliberately, not excitedly. Her reward is to be respected and in the presence of a respectful pack leader.

Pack Leader Wisdom:
Watch for those who lack self-discipline;
they lack self-respect.
Watch for those who are disrespectful to themselves;
they are probably also disrespectful to others.
Respect for others begins with self-respect.

LESSON 5

Be Instinctive

Anyone who has owned a dog has probably marveled at this feat: A dog can often sense when someone is due home long before the person is within scenting or hearing distance. Kiva would often wake up and start pacing 10 minutes before Paul came home, despite the fact that Paul's schedule was very erratic. He rarely came home at the same time every day and, because of his travels overseas, he often didn't come home for days at a time. Yet Kiva seemed to sense when he was near.

People are often amazed that animals can sense these things, but I'm a believer. I am also jealous. I wish I had such strong instinctive powers.

I have learned to trust Reilly's intuitions, which – naturally – seem to focus on when the deer will show up in the backyard and where the skunks have holed up in the rock pile. OK, so these are more a function of her scenting ability, but I'm still impressed!

Reilly does, nonetheless, have the ability while hunting at full run, hot on a scent, to stop in midstride and seemingly recalibrate. She will be gung-ho on a smell, absolutely crazed with hunting fever, then freeze in that classic pointer pose. I know she is scenting the air for clues on where to go next, but I have to wonder if she isn't also re-grouping, opening her senses to all possibilities, listening to her intuition for where that prey went. How much of her hunting ability is scenting ability and how much is intuition?

Animals have access to their intuitive power in ways that we would be wise to emulate.

Trust Yourself and Your Intuition

From Reilly, I have learned to trust my instincts. But to do this I had to trust myself. I had to stop questioning my abilities and insights.

I have over the past few years had many experiences that showcased the power of intuition, a source of information I had completely disregarded for most of my life. It started when I had the experience of growling at Reilly shortly after I had adopted her. That growl was a purely instinctual reaction. I felt in awe of the power I experienced. "Wow," I thought, "where did that come from?" I had never reacted that way or responded so instantly and instinctively. My usual mode of operation had been to see only the surface facts, then over-think a situation.

For someone who over-relied on intellect in decision-making, I was later amazed to admit that most of my poor choices had not been due to lack of smarts, but lack of instinct. Ignoring my intuition lead me into two bad marriages, several inappropriate career paths, and many other unfortunate decisions. As I look back at my life I recall situations where my intuition had been sending me messages I just did not acknowledge. That was because I was busy using my limited intuitive abilities merely to sense the other person's opinions of me. "Does she like me?" was the only question I was asking of my perceptions. My opinion of her didn't enter into the equation, so I didn't even listen for my reactions.

I now recognize the key to avoiding unhealthy relationships is to rev up my intuition. I have allowed my intuitive voice to break out of the hole I kept it in for decades, a hole tamped down and crusted-over with messages that only intellectual knowledge is good, that my own feelings aren't to be trusted, that others' opinions are more valuable than mine.

The change in the past few years has been remarkable. My intuition now is so accessible to me that messages come hard and fast when I meet new people. It's almost overwhelming to me when I am with someone who is unbalanced and carries negative energy.

Because I am no longer dependent on the other person's opinion of me, I am able to take some of my intuitive energy and use it to sense my reaction to the other person: "Do I feel this person is honest and trustworthy or a lying manipulator?"

A revolutionary element of this new skill set was realizing that I was able to control my interactions with others. I wasn't responsible for their feelings toward me, and I didn't have to like every person I met. I didn't have to be emotionally entrained by every guy I went out on a first date with or every nasty boss I had. I could interact in a polite manner with someone, but I did not have to feel compelled to "catch" every emotion she sent my way. I could stand back, listen to my intuition, and make internal assessments of a person ("What a sleazy lounge lizard") and continue a conversation, knowing I could control the boundaries of the relationship.

I now have the information I need to be promptly honest with people when their emotional behavior is inappropriately controlling or disrespectful. I can immediately say how I feel, rather than waiting to process my reaction intellectually at a later date. If I feel manipulated, I speak up right away.

Now when I am in a new social situation the difference is noticeable. I am very comfortable just joking and talking with the person standing next to me. At a cocktail party, I just say the first thing I think of to a stranger, usually a joke, and the next thing you know we've been talking for an hour. I am relaxed because I know I have a tool that will help me assess this other person. I also have learned the best way to get this tool to work is to relax. When I am anxious, my intuition can't shout over all the fear messages an over-reactive brain is pumping out. I now have the self-acceptance to recognize I have both the intellectual and intuitive skills needed to manage an interaction, so I don't become fearful.

Foster Your Ability to Read Others' Intentions

Many of our behaviors are governed by instincts most of us are not consciously aware of. Our "sixth sense" of intuition is a tremendous ability developed over tens of thousands of years of evolution as a survival tool. In contrast, the Western culture has intellectual, philosophical, and religious traditions that gang up against intuition and feeling, in favor of reason and logic. This stems from the religious belief that human nature is nasty and frightening, so we must use our moral strength and rational mind to overcome those scary emotions and that out-of-control id, as Sigmund Freud postulated.

Sadly, it seems that in many cultures today we are raised not to value, access, or trust our intuition. We are not taught to pick up on subtle physical or emotional clues that someone is not in a healthy state of being. We fail to recognize when behavior is rooted in unbalanced energy. By being so focused on words, concepts, and facts, we have become unpracticed at identifying nonverbal signals using our intuition, senses, and emotions. As a result, in the same way that most humans have lost the ability to understand dog behavior, I believe we have lost the ability to read the physical and emotional energy given off by other humans. Our ability to understand our intuition's interpretation of other people has atrophied from disuse. These signals can tell us much more and are often more-accurate messages than words. Humans send millions of subtle messages without speaking – but is anyone listening?

Even if we do recognize our intuition, we most likely disregard it because of our social training to do so. I once went to a party given by my friend, Patty, where I met her new boyfriend, Adam. I immediately did not trust him. My radar told me he was exactly like Ray, with the potential to be controlling and perhaps abusive. He also clearly had a drinking problem. I didn't say anything at the time, but I noticed that my friend, Vanessa, was acting very on edge that night, which is not like her at all. I guessed that she, too, felt very negative energy coming from Adam, but I let it slide. A few weeks later Vanessa asked me what I thought about Adam. A-ha! I could tell immediately just from her question that she shared my feelings about this guy. We had come to the same conclusion. And it turns out several other friends felt the same way. Of course, then we debated if we should say anything to Patty – because we didn't want to be considered nosy or judgmental. Patty later broke up with Adam because he was controlling, abusive, and an alcoholic.

I now say: Listen to your intuition, which is generally driven by an innate moral sense. If you are a Submissive, you especially need to improve your instincts when dealing with people. Become more aware of when someone is behaving in an unbalanced way and trying to take advantage of you or someone else.

This is important because every time a controller gets you to back down it's a lie you tell yourself. By permitting this deception, you are essentially denying your feelings, which is a denial of your reality. If you believe the lie often enough that your senses have no value, then you begin not to know what to trust, what is real, and what is true about your feelings and perceptions. Self-doubt is a very powerful weapon that the controller has now gotten you to aim at yourself. Controllers want their reality to intrude on yours because it weakens you and gives them power. By getting you to ignore your valuable intuition, it's doing the controller's work for him.

Behaving instinctively also means sometimes reacting to others to remind them that their behavior is inappropriate. Previously, I found myself listening to lies, half-truths, or misleading statements and letting them stand. Each time this happened, it told the other person I was not strong enough to stand up for myself and push back against an obvious falsehood. When I hear a small voice in my head now, rather than turning down the volume, I turn it up. If my instinct tells me a person or a message or a situation is inappropriate, I listen and react. If I feel I am self-censoring my instinct, it is a sign I am not in tune with how others are treating me.

You may ask: "How do I really know if it is my instinct talking or some other impulse? How do I know if I am correct? Is this person lying or am I just reacting for some unknown psychological reason?"

It is very difficult to tell if some people are lying, often because they have perfected this tactic. But I do think instincts will correctly inform us if we open ourselves to this powerful tool. However, even if you aren't certain of someone's intentions, you can always watch and wait, filing your instinctive reaction away to compare against future behavior.

Parents Can Teach Intuitive Skills

One lesson my parents failed to teach was one that most Western parents don't teach: the value of instinct and intuition. Despite their strong religious beliefs, my parents were not at all in tune with their true spiritual side. Being very academically inclined, they felt everything of value could be described in a scientific journal or encyclopedia. As I grew older I dismissed anything "New Age" as useless and a scam. After I became aware that my fact-based decision-making about people had not been tremendously successful, I opened my spirit to the value of relying on my intuition. In fact (pun intended), my intuition is now a valuable and reliable decision-making tool in my life, and honoring it is a skill I continue to practice every day.

I strongly believe a certain style of parenting taught me to deny and distrust my own emotions and intuition. My parents were constantly worried, "What will the neighbors think?" They were very concerned about their children embarrassing them. What did this teach me? That how others feel and think is more important than what I feel. That my emotions should be discounted to those of the neighbors, the church group, and the bridge club. And when you're a child and realize your parents value the opinions of the bridge club over their own children, how do you learn to trust yourself? This is one of those seemingly innocuous parenting lessons, yet it teaches children to discount their feelings and value others' opinions over their own needs and wants – sometimes with a dangerous result.

Intuition is the window to our emotions. If we don't trust our intuition, we can't read or access our emotions and we can't read the emotions and intentions of others. Knowing your own emotions is the first key to building emotional intelligence.

Think about how you would communicate if no one could talk. Your ability to read the energy, eyes, facial expressions, emotions, and actions of others, and your ability to use those same tools to communicate would escalate quickly.

Balance Instincts and Knowledge

Humans have, perhaps, a unique capability in the animal world to add a powerful component to their intuition. We have the capability to learn from the past, to read a book, to pull information from other sources, and use those facts to alter the present and future. With the human capacity for rational thought, combined with intuition, we have a powerful force for dealing with our world. I believe that as humans we have not used both these resources to their fullest. We tend to devalue intuition and overvalue knowledge, facts, and experience. By bringing these two elements into better balance, we can all become more balanced and powerful.

When you trust your intuition to tell you if a person is to be trusted, you have a useful weapon to pair with your intellect to help process information about people in your life.

....

Be Observant

When Reilly sees another dog a long distance away, she has already begun to notice the dog's traits and behaviors. She is looking for clues to the dog's personality and social rank as a way to predict its behavior.

When balanced dogs approach each other, they are observant. They sidle up slowly, rarely approaching face-to-face. They sniff, they sense, they size up. Only when this ritual is complete, and they determine if this new dog is a threat, do they begin to relax and let down their guard.

Being Observant Starts with Observing Yourself

As a reformed Submissive, I know that in the past I had been nearly unobservant of any signals other people were sending me. I had very under-developed emotional intelligence skills. Quite simply, I was a terrible judge of human character. My parents had told me it was wrong to judge others or suspect their motives, so I let this very valuable skill atrophy. (They also taught me a confusing double standard: Others can judge me harshly, yet I have no right or ability to judge others!)

So I closed my intuition down and ignored the signs others sent me – signs that often were warnings they would prey on me.

I now realize that being observant is one primal survival skill that may not help keep me alive, as it helped keep my ancestors alive, but it will help keep me mentally healthy. I now try to enter every new human relationship by being fully observant of the other person. This does not equal being judgmental. I am merely watching, not necessarily critiquing or categorizing. I am keeping my senses completely open and neutral. By being observant, I feed my intuition the information it needs. Of course, this receptive attitude makes it easy for my intuition to send a warning signal if it needs to.

Now I also can manage my reactions, choose my behaviors, and not always respond automatically to every jerk on my chain. Previously, my behavior was limited to: "Be nice. Be pleasing. Give in." Now I allow myself to behave in a variety of appropriate ways and in whatever timeframe I feel is necessary. What a powerful tool!

I have also come to believe in the value of being observant of myself. Self-reflection is the key to self-development. Until I gained the ability to step outside myself and observe what I was saying and doing, and not saying and not doing, I couldn't truly see myself in action in my relationships with other people. Until I clearly saw my behavior, I was unable to break out of the patterns I was repeating.

I now can be in a conversation and use part of my awareness to pay attention to my actions, my feelings, my thoughts, and my words. I can be observant at a different level – watching the conversation as if part of me was a video camera recording the scene. This simple sensation, called metacommunication, was quite new to me when it first happened a few years ago.

For example, one day a friend and I were driving down the highway and I mentioned I had for a few weeks felt an intuitive urge to go visit my first husband, Paul. I hadn't seen him in almost 10 years, however we now lived within a few miles of each other. For some time I had felt odd not knowing how he was doing and sensed I should reconnect with him. As we passed his exit, we impulsively decided to turned off the highway, drive to his house, and knock on the door. I know this was a bit unusual, but as I didn't have his phone number, it seemed like the best thing to do. Despite the surprise visit, he was quite cordial, invited us in, and we talked for a few minutes. It was a bit of an awkward situation, so, naturally, I felt awkward. But after a few minutes, I said to myself – take a step back. So I did a few seconds of observing. I realized I was sending out nervous energy. I was talking too much and too fast, I was gesturing too much. I told myself I was giving away my power. Why was I doing that? Old habits?

At one point a thought flashed in my mind, "Oh, what I'm wearing (an animal print blouse) is too loud, too sexy. I would never have worn something like this when I was married to Paul." I almost laughed out loud when I observed that thought and labeled it for what it was – an old message, an old habit clearly in need of erasing. So I stood up taller and wore that gorgeous blouse with confidence. I took a few deep breaths and relaxed my eyes and my body. How interesting that I was then able to recognize that Paul was also very nervous – which was certainly a natural reaction given the situation. But I asked myself, "Was he always this awkward and I had just never seen it before?" Then I noticed the conversational topics. I saw that he never once asked about me, where I was living, what I was doing. He talked only about himself. I could step back and observe Paul's insecurities as they played out in the interaction. I could untangle myself from past patterns and behaviors.

Previously, I had been so eager for affection and attention that I had totally focused on the other person's reaction to me. I was not observing or managing my reaction, nor was I observing the other person's true actions and unspoken messages, seeing that they perhaps signaled danger, manipulation, or insecurity.

Because of Pack Leader Psychology concepts, I can quickly identify those who might not be appropriate to allow into my life and have used this skill many times in my single life. For example, I had signed up for a dating service and got a call one day from a man named Rick who was matched with me. We started talking and I very quickly picked up on some clear signs he was a Dominator. Because I was able to remain calm and was not overeager to impress him, I was able to really hear his words. And they were all about how fabulous he was: He bragged about his big house, his pool, his boats and snowmobiles, how great his kids were, how much money he had, and how fit and good looking he was. He even bragged about how beautiful his wife had been. (She had died of a drowning accident, which he mentioned multiple times in the five-minute conversation, as if to make it clear he wasn't divorced – that he had not been rejected by someone.) He even bragged about how he had bought all his wife's clothes and even chose what she wore every day! Wow, now that's an extreme controller, I thought to myself. I realized in the past I would have thought this was a sign he really loved his wife, and I might have been impressed by his boasting.

Well, despite my clear knowledge Rick was not a match for me, I suggested that we meet for coffee. At the best, maybe I had been wrong about that first conversation; at the worst, maybe I would have a chance to observe some extreme Dominator behavior up close. After several phone calls to try to set up this date, I became concerned. Rick very threateningly talked about how he was trying to search for me on the Internet, tracking down my house address through my phone number.

I assertively told him his behavior was inappropriate and I no longer wanted to go out with him. I told him to never call me again or try to find me, and I reported him to the dating service. In a classic, predictable Dominator move, he called back dozens of times, leaving messages trying to convince me to date him. He clearly did not like being rejected.

Each time the phone rang and went to voicemail, I was very, very thankful for my new skills in observing and interpreting behavior.

....

Surround Yourself with Calm Pack Members

On "Dog Whisperer," Cesar Millan repeatedly proves that a dog's behavior is directly related to its owner's behavior. An anxious owner creates an anxious, misbehaving dog. It's that simple. It becomes obvious when Cesar removes a dog from its owner and the dog immediately calms down. Some owners even know the adopted or rescued dog was acting very friendly and sweet when it was adopted, yet the new owner can't understand why the dog is now acting aggressively. The dog's behavior changed because it is living with a nervous, fearful owner – a person who is not stepping up to become a calm, assertive pack leader.

In a healthy dog pack, this unbalanced behavior would be corrected by the pack. Cesar sometimes brings severely unbalanced dogs to his Dog Psychology Center for rehabilitation. Often these dogs are nervous, barking, and behaving in inappropriate ways – running up face-to-face to a new dog, jumping up and dominating other dogs, and generally creating bad energy in the pack. Cesar will discipline the dog, of course, to show he is the pack leader. But what is especially interesting is to watch how the other dogs deal with it. A more balanced dog will approach and hang out near the new, high-strung dog with an extra amount of calm energy. These pack members are communicating, "This is how we behave in our pack. We don't tolerate all this drama and hyperactivity."

At first, the new dog is acting so nervously it cannot even recognize what these calm dogs are attempting to do. But dogs have such strong communication skills using their energy and intention, helped by Cesar snapping the dog out of its most egregious behavior, the message quickly gets through.

In the dog world, the pack will work together to correct poor behavior. They do this because they want to be surrounded by balanced pack members. They know that one unbalanced, anxious pack member upsets the calm stability of the entire pack.

This type of negative energy is so powerful that one unbalanced dog walking down a street can cause other dogs to go on alert up and down the block. Fearful energy spreads.

As Reilly taught me with Piccadilly and many other dogs she's met: Avoid anxious dogs. Surround yourself with balanced pack members.

Surround Yourself with Calmness to Improve Your Own Emotional Health

New neurological research is showing that when we see someone expressing an emotion, our brain automatically sends signals to act. The research is now telling us that these emotional cues trigger immediate reactions in the primal processing centers of our brain. If we see someone expressing fear, the brain prepares us to snap into action, because like all animals we are genetically coded to respond when faced with stress or threats. This biological fact is, to me, quite clearly influencing our emotions and our behaviors in several ways that are explained by Pack Leader Psychology principles.

If you are surrounded by fearful, hyper-vigilant people, you will sense their emotional anxiety and see their physical signs of fear. Even if these signals are subtle and well hidden by bravado, I believe many of us instinctively pick up on this anxiety. Whether we realize it or not, it's as if our intuition is warning us about this unbalanced person and about the imaginary threats this person is sensing. We may then respond with our own hyper-vigilance, putting our own intuition on alert. If everyone around you is anxious and pinging with responses to imagined emotional threats, it is easy to see how this could devolve into an unhealthy, prolonged, or chronic state of fight-or-flight fear.

When someone near us is unbalanced, our intuition is warning us to be mindful of the external threats about which he is communicating. We also can't predict how he or she is going to react, so this adds another threat input, making us even feel more unsure.

Trust is a powerful concept that has ruled all animal social hierarchies for millennia. But trust demands predictable behavior. I wonder: What happens when so many of a society's citizens are fundamentally fearful and untrusting? What happens when nearly everyone is unbalanced, afraid of being taken advantage of by a Dominator? How can we feel part of a tribe when each of us is only and always out for herself? Won't this lack of trust cause anxiety levels to skyrocket? Who can live a balanced life feeling that no one can be trusted? I am concerned that the increasing number of unbalanced Dominators, Submissives, and Avoiders in society is, quite frankly, messing up the system. A healthy social hierarchy requires trust and predictable reciprocal behavior to succeed.

As you might conclude, our society may have created a cycle that is difficult to break. If we are insecure and fearful, we project fear, which makes our behavior unpredictable and untrustworthy. Those around us begin to fear our erratic, controlling behavior and become more anxious. This leads to more anxiety in our social groups and families, which overloads our intuition with fearful messages reflected back to us, which leads to more unbalanced behaviors. This uncertainly adds anxiety to our life, and when we are constantly anxious, we too easily perceive situations as threats, even if they are not. It is very likely that we will then react inappropriately with fight-or-flight behaviors, which makes others even more fearful.

I believe this is why we have so many children with emotional and behavioral problems: Their parents are loaded with fears and hypervigilance, which the children intuitively sense.

In addition, when you're in fear mode most of the time, your subtle physical and emotional signals project that you are insecure and frightened. You then attract unbalanced people who feed on your weak energy and bring more instability into your life. The weak social skills exhibited by frightened people also set up an additional cycle. People don't like them, so they don't have friends, so their social skills get weaker and they spend more time alone, over-thinking and over-worrying, becoming more and more anxious.

Low-grade anxiety not only causes overly emotional or inappropriate reactions, but also impairs the brain's cognitive efficiency. Research has proven that fear shuts down the ability to learn, think, and perform. For some people this chronic anxiety spirals into serious psychological conditions that the mental health profession has labeled as depression, panic disorder, obsessive-compulsive disorder, and anxiety disorders. I believe this cycle of fear has hijacked the emotions and intuition of a large number of people in modern society, leading to many of the behavioral issues seen in increasing numbers in the last several decades.

Pack Leaders Share Calmness

Sadly, unlike a balanced dog pack, most humans no longer exhibit calm pack leader behavior, so that many of us are often surrounded by anxious, unstable people. If you are a calm, self-assured pack leader, you can tell yourself to ignore and disengage from fearful energy. I've found that it isn't always easy, especially if the person is quite anxious. Previously, I picked up every emotional state of every person I was with, not by choice, put as a way of mirroring their behavior to make them comfortable, as a way to make the person like me. I hope that I've broken the anxiety cycle in my life and that my calmness is rippling out to others.

Pack Leader Wisdom:
Watch out for those who try to get you
to ignore your intuition. They know it is your
most powerful tool to spot an unbalanced person.
Be calm to let your intuition speak.
Observe yourself; observe others.
Surround yourself with calm pack members.

LESSON 6

Be Accountable

Many dog behaviors seem very similar to human behaviors, however that's often because we interpret them incorrectly. In case you haven't been paying attention, don't put your human paradigm on an animal's behavior. For example, to an uninformed person, a yawn signals that a dog is tired. To a knowledgeable, observant person, a yawn tells a completely different story. Dogs yawn as an emotional release when they are anxious. Reilly will yawn when I correct her for misbehaving. By yawning she is releasing some of her nervous energy after I regained control of the situation as a pack leader. Her yawn communicates that things were out of balance.

By submitting to my discipline, Reilly is also saying she knows what she was doing was wrong. She is recognizing she was overstepping her bounds and needs to get her behavior back in line with what the pack expects and demands.

Face Your Fears of Criticism

As I look back at my life, I realize one area that has undergone a major change is my ability to handle criticism. This was not a conscious decision, but an unexpected result of becoming more self-accepting.

Previously, my discomfort with criticism might not have been noticeable to others because I didn't lash out. I lashed in, as can be expected with my former Submissive personality. Yet I find it interesting to look back at my reaction to even very nonthreatening types of criticism.

I took a few golf lessons when I was learning the game in my mid-30s. I remember how I used to get very flustered and uncomfortable during lessons despite the fact that the pro was very pleasant and non-threatening. I now realize I perceived his instruction as criticism. Even though I didn't know how to grip the golf club or swing, I had such high expectations for myself I believed I should know these skills already – which made no sense, of course, because why would I take a golf lesson if I already knew everything?

I also recognize I used to well up with tears when I was critiqued or disciplined, even if it was by a boss or colleague. I hated this tendency, but I thought I just cried easily. Now I see it is because even neutral comments or helpful instructions about my performance were entering my brain as primal "threats." I had learned as a child to correlate discipline with disappointed expectations, to link having to learn something new with shame and then conclude it was an attack on my very value as a person. Perhaps this was because my parents didn't teach me how to behave, they shamed me into behaving properly. So even as an adult, learning a new skill felt as if I was shameful and less than perfect – and therefore an easy target for an emotional putdown or attack.

As a consequence, I lashed in at myself, driving myself to learn faster, to not show my ignorance. Of course, this inability to admit I was not perfect slowed my learning. Because I felt I should not ask for or accept instruction, I set myself up to constantly learn solely from my own mistakes, rather than from the mistakes and knowledge of others. I now see my reluctance to ask questions during something such as a golf lesson was a sign I somehow expected myself to "know it all" already. Admitting I didn't have a complete handle on something felt like I was vulnerable to shame-provoking criticism – a threat to my self-worth I did not feel capable of dealing with.

Dominators Rarely Accept Accountability

Because of their low sense of self-worth, unbalanced people feel that any criticism or imagined criticism is a threat to their need for acceptance and, perhaps, to their very being. In Dominators, one way they manage this fear is that they make excuses, rationalize, and blame others. They rarely admit mistakes, they find it difficult to accept responsibility for their actions, and many of them find it impossible to apologize.

As I watched a TV show on super-obese people, I was struck by the number of excuses they gave for their weight problems. One woman, weighing 890 pounds, said that gastric bypass surgery was her "only option." Really? At no point, during 20 years of gaining those 740 extra pounds did you not have an option to put down the cheeseburger, to back away from the burrito? She also stated that she would have surgery "for her children." Didn't your concern for your children and the fact that you are too obese to care for them enter into your brain at some point in the past two decades? I don't make these comments merely as judgment, but rather to highlight that the statements by this woman can seem very benign to most listeners: "Oh, she cares about her children. How nice." But take a step back and watch the pattern. You will see rationalizations and the desire to appear like a person who is sacrificing for others, rather than assuming true responsibility. If she really cared for her children or her health, she would never have gained that much weight. Dominators will go to great lengths emotionally to avoid taking accountability for their behaviors, often by rationalizing.

Because their natural tendency is to attack in some fashion, Dominators will also lash out at any perceived condemnation of their capabilities, reacting with an over-the-top response driven by fear, shame, and anger.

This attack mode is most noticeable when you get in an argument with a Dominator. She will question your facts, deny your opinion, refuse to take responsibility or apologize. It's almost always your fault.

Blaming others relieves anxiety and distances the Dominator from self-criticism, and this feels good. That positive sensation reinforces the behavior and it gets repeated in a cycle.

When arguing with a Dominator and she is clearly wrong and won't back down, it may be difficult to understand why she is so stubborn. The whole world may disagree with her, but she refuses to admit she made a mistake. This is because, to her, this criticism feels like a life-threatening attack, or at least a soul-destroying humiliation designed to expose all her inner flaws to the entire world. Just imagine how hard you would fight if you were fighting for your emotional "life."

And to Submissives, this is a very foreign way of thinking – completely different from their "give up and give in" attitude. It's not that we are from Mars and Venus, but that people are Dominators, Submissives, and Avoiders with very different reactions to threats.

Over the years I've seen many incidents where a person I'll call Linda displayed these classic behaviors of an aggressive person – combined with her tendency for acting out. One incident on a ski trip was the final straw.

A few years ago, I organized a ski trip to Colorado at Christmastime. A group of us were all sharing a rented condo and had a good time for about 48 hours. Then Linda, as often happened, seemed to feel as if not enough attention was being paid. She began testing the system to see if she could ratchet up the control, a pattern I had experienced many times before.

On Christmas Eve the entire group decided the next morning we would hike up to an ice waterfall. By 9 a.m. we were all up and ready to go, except Linda who was still in bed. (Sleeping late is a guarantee you can make an entrance.) By 10:30 a.m. she had finally gotten up and slowly eaten breakfast. By 11 a.m. the morning was nearly gone and we had been waiting for her for two hours. The rest of us were frustrated and began getting our boots and jackets on. What did she do instead? Still in her pajamas, she grabbed her laptop computer, opened it up, and announced she was going to read her 77 e-mails. Well, I saw this for what it was – a ploy to test how much control she had and how much attention she could garner. Could she make us sit and wait for her? Not if I was leading the pack. In one of my first pack leader moves I matter-of-factly said to her, "Well, if you're going to check your e-mail, we'll see you later." And I lead the rest of the group out the door.

Linda interpreted my action, which the rest of the group agreed was appropriate, as an attack on her. She spent the rest of the vacation pouting, stomping around the condo, hiding in her room, not talking to us, and even faking laryngitis. Her actions were so inappropriate that even teenagers in the group described her as behaving like a spoiled toddler. Years later, Linda has refused to take responsibility for or apologize for any of her behaviors. In fact, she has concocted elaborate stories of how I was to blame for her behavior. And this was just the final straw with me, after many years of similar misbehavior by her.

When I called Linda on the carpet about her controlling behavior I knew I was taking a risk, because she would very likely not admit her mistakes and that would cause a rift in the group. Sure enough, that's what she did. Despite all evidence to the contrary, she denied what she had done. When I pointed out there was a roomful of witnesses, she came up with rationalizations for her behavior. When I didn't buy her excuses, she moved on to yet another denial, then yet another rationalization. Her excuses shifted and realigned each time she backpedaled and tried to explain herself. It was clear her reality had nothing to do with the reality witnessed by the rest of the group. Apologize? Never a possibility. So when I said, "Either you apologize or we will no longer talk to you again," she chose, as Dominators often do, to walk away and cut all communication. It is easier to keep your fantasy world alive when there aren't people knocking on the door presenting reality to you on a platter.

Over the years I had wondered why it was impossible for Linda to say she was sorry or admit to a mistake. Based on Pack Leader Psychology ideas I realized it was because she saw such an admission as a threat. She relied on external affirmation to feel good, because her self-worth was so weak, so she felt that to admit she wasn't right meant others wouldn't approve of her. She overreacted by fighting back, refusing to admit a mistake, refusing to back down, attacking the facts presented to her.

To admit even a minor mistake may feel soul-destroying to many Dominators. The good news is that to the rest of us, we can use this as a clue to their personality type and a predictor of future behavior.

It Is Not a Weakness to Admit You Are Wrong

Dominators tend to define themselves as right and strong, and others as weak and wrong. Dominators have strong opinions on topics and often can't be swayed despite facts to the contrary. Trying hard to prove they are right all the time gives them a sense of both external and internal acceptance. It's almost as if being right sends them a positive message over-writing the many negative self-messages they are sending themselves and that they perceive others are sending as well.

I saw this play out many times in the behavior of Dominators. They give themselves affection the only way know how – by being correct. To admit they don't know something or are incorrect about a fact would cut the tenuous tie they have to their self-acceptance.

Not only do parents reinforce this behavior by teaching children to look outside themselves for approval, I also believe many children learn these behaviors because they gained affection from their parents for always having the correct answer.

I see this tendency in my family quite strongly, largely because my parents emphasized being smart and knowledgeable. Their emphasis on academic achievement was commendable, except that it led all of us children to rely on being right as a way to feed our self-approval. As a result, none of us lacks for opinions on just about any topic. I have tried to moderate my opinionated nature and back away from always having an answer.

In addition, insecure Dominators tend to see the world as black and white. This type of personality likes to settle on an opinion and then remain unwavering. Just as they don't like others to question their opinions, insecure people generally refuse to question their own ideas once they are formed. They don't like to make a change of opinion because they feel it would be an admission of weakness. (Certain politicians fit this description perfectly.)

I know one young woman who got into a raging fight and broke up with her live-in boyfriend because he drank straight out of the milk carton. Why would such a small thing cause such a major fight? Because she felt as if his drinking out of the milk carton was a criticism of her opinion. She felt it was his way of saying, "You are wrong." If someone has a different opinion, then she feels as if hers might be incorrect and this hits too close to the bone – she feels she is not just wrong about that fact but also completely unworthy as a person. "If you're right, I must be wrong. And if I'm wrong, and I feel unworthy to begin with, that's just way too scary for me to contemplate."

Ironically, Dominator behavior creates several unhealthy cycles that feed on each other. The more their intimidating behavior drives others away, the more Dominators must continue to construct a false sense of reality and self-acceptance – because they are not getting it from other places.

Traditional psychology uses the term "dissonance" to describe another cycle that reinforces the Dominator's behavior. Essentially, dissonance occurs when a person behaves in ways that are improper, yet he can't admit that to himself, so he performs self-justifying mental contortions to persuade himself that he isn't behaving poorly after all.

Say you're a Dominator who has abused his wife. You know intrinsically that this is morally wrong. Your wife may also tell you it's wrong or you may get arrested – a clear sign that it is inappropriate behavior. But an insecure person cannot bear to hear this negative information. So he engages in self-persuasion to convince himself he is justified in his actions. He reinforces his attitudes and behaviors by saying to himself, "It is OK for me to beat up my wife." The weaker his self-esteem, the more frequent and stronger these messages have to be to his brain. Each time he reinforces the message that his behavior is acceptable, the less likely he will change in the future.

This all goes back to the deep-seated cause of insecurity: fear of disapproval and rejection. For a Dominator to admit he made a mistake, it feels like criticism from without and from within. His fragile self-image can't handle what feels like self-betrayal, so he just doesn't go there.

Dominators generally don't like to be held accountable for their actions, whether it is their lack of ability to keep a job, manage their money, lose weight, do household chores, or be responsible with their personal affairs. They will make numerous excuses for their irresponsibility or misbehavior – a clear sign of a slippery Dominator. A Dominator may even blame his situation on bad luck or the fact that others somehow take advantage of him, but don't be fooled.

Ray rarely worked full time and never seemed to have any money, but he could never quite understand how this could be. Many overweight people blame their obesity on everything except the fact that they eat too much: I have food allergies, my thyroid is acting up, I can't exercise because I once twisted my ankle as a child, the weather isn't nice enough, and on it goes.

Certain types of Dominators feel they are "special" and so don't have to work as much or as hard as others. They always manage to be the ones sitting on the couch while you are vacuuming. Dominators also use this sense of entitlement to justify why others don't understand them or don't agree with them: "I moved here from France 20 years ago so that's why other people don't like me." Yeah, right.

Here is an example of an amazing and absurd attempt to blame others. I heard a story about a woman who had two miscarriages early in her marriage. In a horrific "red zone attack" she actually blamed her in-laws for these unfortunate events. She said to them, "Your son is genetically dysfunctional because he caused me to have two miscarriages." Wow! Now that shows a tremendous desire to blame others. Even in a situation with no one at fault, she had to find someone to lash out at – even if the victim was her husband, her in-laws and some imagined family genetic defect. She had to invent some way to feel better about herself, so she struck out at others. She and her husband went on to have three healthy children. I wonder how that fact was rationalized in her mind after her previous "genetic defect" comments.

This inability to admit to a mistake takes many forms from small to major. I heard an interview with one of Charles Manson's former followers who thinks the reason Manson went ahead with the murders of seven people was because he had been predicting a "helter-skelter" apocalyptic race war and when it didn't happen he couldn't admit his prediction was wrong. This famous mass killing may have come about merely because one extreme antisocial Dominator had the simple inability to admit to a mistake in front of a group of his followers. In watching TV interviews of Manson, I also saw small, but frequent, examples of his tendency to rationalize and excuse his behavior.

I've also found Dominators develop their own "moral codes" as a way to excuse their behavior. Ray consistently brought up a distinction that in his mind excused his violent behavior. When I would point out his abuse was wrong, he would say what he did was OK because he never "punched" me – which meant everything else was perfectly acceptable in his created world. Throwing me to the ground: OK. Grabbing my arms so hard they were bruised for a week: No problem. Shoving me into a door and bruising my cheek: Also acceptable. Screaming at me and verbally abusing me for hours at a time: Perfectly fine. Chasing me down the street? Getting arrested? Shooting at my dog? Ah, but he never "punched" me. Ray and other Dominators must manufacture this type of fine distinction as a way to be able to live with their behavior.

To me, this attempt at rationalization is evidence that they know what they do is wrong. The psychology and criminal justice professions debate whether criminals can tell the difference between right and wrong, but I think a large number of Dominators certainly do know. This is why I disagree with the "not guilty by reason of insanity" defense in most court cases. For example, John Jemelske of Syracuse, N.Y., over the course of 14 years kidnapped five women and girls and held them hostage in a dungeon – some for years. When interviewed in prison, he repeatedly said he "never hurt anyone." He had drawn some imaginary moral line in the sand that let his mind concoct the lie that kidnapping and rape were permissible. Jemelske actually told an interviewer he didn't know kidnapping and rape were illegal. He said he thought he would get probation for his crimes. But I want to ask Jemelske, "If you thought these weren't crimes, why did you keep them secret from everyone? Why not just tell the neighbors you had a 15-year-old chained in a dungeon in your backyard?" He also rationalized his actions by saying he needed to have sex every day and his wife was sick and couldn't have sex with him. He knew what he did was absolutely wrong, but the only way he could justify his actions to himself was to construct elaborate justifications.

This inability to accept criticism makes it very difficult for Dominators to recognize how their behaviors are affecting others and for them to change. To admit they might possibly be wrong would bring their whole fantasy world collapsing down, a concept too scary for most to contemplate. This is why psychologists claim those with conditions like Borderline Personality Disorder (one "diagnosis" for a Dominator type of person) are very difficult to treat. I've learned from personal experience Dominators also are often very reluctant to undergo marriage counseling or therapy. This is, of course, because they understand the process will force them to look honestly at themselves and admit they are wrong about something. It will force them to add critical messages from the outside world onto their internal messages of self-blame – a load they don't feel strong enough to bear.

Admitting weakness would disrupt the carefully constructed world Dominators have built that tells them they are powerful and in control. A fundamental inability to self-analyze and accept blame makes being successful in counseling, therapy, or any attempt at self-awareness very unlikely.

It's as if Dominators learned at some point early in their lives that to admit weakness means another person now has an opening to take advantage of you. Dominators may have been in a relationship in their family of origin that was overly critical and taught them to protect themselves at all costs. They learned never to admit to being weak in any way. And this sets up a psychological cycle: If you can never admit you made a mistake, you can never learn from that mistake.

I was thinking one day about the fact that so many of the dog owners who appear on Cesar Millan's TV show were very Submissive. I couldn't remember an episode with a Dominator personality. Then it hit me. Hypersensitive to criticism, a Dominator would never admit she couldn't control her dog. She would never contact Cesar and agree to go on TV to show the world she had made a mistake. Submissive types are much more willing to look for advice and are much more willing to consider change. I probably won't ever see a Dominator on Cesar's show for that reason.

It's unfortunate so much of the population has failed to learn that a balanced person can admit to a mistake and still be perceived as strong.

Submissives: It Is Not Always Your Fault

The topic of blame and responsibility are interesting to me, because I had been a classic accommodating type of person. If it were raining, I'd apologize. If someone didn't do the job correctly, I'd step up and fix it. If someone else made a mistake, I'd take responsibility. The words, "I'm sorry," flew out of my mouth like air. I'd even find myself saying things like, "I'm sorry, but could I purchase this please," as if my being a customer in a store was an inconvenience to a clerk. In my eagerness for acceptance, I cowered and slunk, hoping not to offend.

Quite the opposite of Dominators, Submissives often accept blame quickly and readily – even for things that are not their fault. Some go so far in taking blame on their shoulders they become depressed over their mistakes, even going into "all-or-nothing" mode that everything they do is wrong, which feeds a cycle of self-shame.

Behave with Humility and Integrity

Both being overly apologetic and being unable to apologize are warning signs of insecurity and an unbalanced personality. Both Submissives and Dominators have an inability to handle mistakes and criticism as a pack leader would – with calmness and aplomb.

Pack leaders should be self-accepting and strong enough to express humility. Being self-effacing at times does not make a person weak. A balanced person knows when to stand firm on an issue and communicate with intensity and integrity, and when to back down, admit a mistake, and learn from that mistake.

Pack Leader Wisdom:
Watch for people who cannot be criticized,
cannot apologize, cannot be accountable,
and cannot be wrong.
What holds most people back is not lack of ability,
but lack of courage.
Move forward from mistakes gracefully
and maturely.

LESSON 7

Honor the Pack

Reilly has many opportunities to run away, but she stays in the yard for hours without me watching her. When we get ready to go running and she is off the leash, she could certainly take off running down the road without me. But she chooses to stay near me, her pack, so we can "hunt" together. When we run or walk in the woods, she constantly checks where I am so she doesn't get too far away.

Certainly, I did train Reilly to stay near me, but it took only a small amount of effort. She clearly chooses to stay in her pack's territory and stay near her pack when we are out of our territory. This is evidence of the innate desire of the canine for the pack.

Wolves and dogs know that the pack offers food and safety, companionship and caring.

We All Need a Pack

This was one of the last lessons that Reilly taught me as I was writing this book. And the truth of it crept up slowly on me over the course of a year, then struck me hard one lonely Saturday night.

It had been about three years since I had divorced Ray and nearly four years since I had kicked him out. During that time I had dated one man for about a year, but it had been nearly a year since he had left. I hadn't had a date besides a few first dates in that entire year. As I stood crying in the bathroom that Saturday night I began mentally chastising myself.

But, as I can do now, I told myself: "Stop." I asked myself: "What would a pack leader do? A pack leader would stop being so self-critical. This is what got you in trouble in the past, Harper. If you are so judgmental of yourself, others will sense that energy and they won't respect you and, worse, may join in on that party."

223

Then I realized: I had chosen not to go out on second dates with the men that I had met for coffee. That was actually a good thing! A big improvement on my previous behavior, when I would have, without thought or selectivity, agreed to date men who were very inappropriate for me. So, sure, I was alone on a Saturday night, but it was largely my choice. I was not getting involved with some man who would, again, take advantage of me. I wasn't thoughtlessly grasping for a sense of acceptance from others. I wasn't behaving in an overly pleasing manner just to get a man to like me. Rather, I was compassionately providing my own self-acceptance.

I did not want to be like so many people who after a divorce get married in a rush to surround themselves with a companion and a pack. Often that partnership turns out to be unstable and unhealthy, because they have partnered up for unbalanced reasons – usually a search for external affection because both lack internal self-worth. Then these people become anxious, stressed, nervous, or depressed. I sure didn't want that again!

I might be feeling low at that moment, but I was feeling better about myself in the big picture. I was so much stronger, more self-confident, and less submissive than I had been ever before in my life. I knew these changes were a tremendous accomplishment.

That night I also forced myself to admit what I was feeling was to be expected. To feel lonely after all I had gone through in my life and all my time alone was perfectly and completely normal. It's not normal for a human to live alone for years. We need a pack. We need to feel we belong.

In fact, social isolation is such a powerful force that it can cause not just mental but physical health problems. Studies have shown that social isolation doubles a person's chances of sickness or death. Isolation is just as important in increasing mortality rates as smoking, high blood pressure, high cholesterol, obesity, and lack of physical exercise.

As I looked back over my life, I had to recognize I had been alone emotionally for large chunks of my life, in fact, perhaps most of my life.

My parents were emotionally distant and forced independence on me at an early age. I made major decisions about where to go to college and how to pay for it at age 16 all by myself. Paul was emotionally distant and then Ray never really saw me as a real person and had his own self-absorbed, manipulative agenda. So I never felt anyone "had my back," an essential attribute of a pack, tribe, or partner.

I had for much of my life kept a distance from friends and had not asked for advice or help. I now clearly recognize this wasn't healthy behavior. The positive result of my experience was that I was, indeed, very capable and independent. I managed my life very competently. But there comes a time when it is healthier to admit you need help, you need a partner, you need friends, you might even need an extra hand moving furniture or cleaning the gutters. You need someone to talk to about your feelings and concerns. Over the past several years I had made huge strides. I was now much more willing to call a friend and ask for advice or help. I reached out and connected socially and professionally more freely and comfortably.

Create Your Own Pack

The value of my friends has become very clear to me. It's true that romantic partnerships often come and go, but friends can be friends for a lifetime. It is unfortunate in modern society we have come to place far more value on our marriages than on our friends. We emphasize the importance of a spouse and de-emphasize the importance of an extended pack of friends and family. How many times have you seen it happen that a girlfriend gets a new boyfriend and ignores all her friends? Not only is this rude, but it is dangerous and unhealthy for her, sending a message of dependent submission to her new boyfriend. She also loses a valuable sounding board and reality check.

Much to my astonishment, I was also slowly learning to give compliments, something I had great difficulty with in the past. I had become much more comfortable telling friends that I love them or enjoy their company. These are basic social skills that I should have known, but I gave myself credit: I was learning. I was growing and changing.

So maybe my social life just needed to catch up to the stronger pack leader I was becoming. I also had to admit maybe there was a lack of pack leader men out there. And I was able to spot the overly submissive and overly dominant ones much sooner. But was I being too picky? In the past I would not have been so selective, but at least I would have had a date!

Ah, no, Harper, don't settle. Don't let someone into your life who isn't right for you, who isn't mentally strong.

About this time I had heard stories of people who couldn't be alone for even a night or a few hours. This was shocking to me, as I often spent days without talking to anyone, not by choice, but by circumstance. So I told myself: "Look how strong you are. You can go a week without talking to someone, you can spend time alone without fear. You don't need someone in your life just to fill it up and distract you. You are capable of being quiet and centered, of not having noise in your life just for the sake of noise."

This was a healthy behavior, much healthier than people who have to stay busy just to avoid being alone with their thoughts. However, I was feeling as if I had spent way too much time alone with my thoughts.

I also told myself that maybe I wasn't meeting a guy for a reason, maybe it was so that I could stay focused on writing, starting a new career, making life decisions, and becoming the most authentic person possible. I could be quiet, observant, and thoughtful without distractions. Harper, if it takes being alone on a Saturday night to discover yourself, then that's exactly what you'll do.

And for the first time, I truly felt and comprehended I really did not need a man in my life. That I was complete without someone to "complete" me. That I had a great life, a new career, friends, family, and a fantastic dog. If I met a man, fine. If not, also fine. Get up, dust yourself off and quit your whining. That's what a pack leader would do.

But I was left with the intrinsic understanding that we all do need a pack. Humans are social creatures.

We need others around to validate our lives and experiences, to bounce ideas off, to feel a part of a team. Because we are social, a primal need to feel secure never really leaves us. We instinctively want other people around us to feel safe, to comfort and be comforted, to celebrate successes, to support failures, to share emotions, to share work and resources. Sharing reinforces feelings of belonging and trust.

Of course, when I got done crying I went to pet Reilly and it hit me. I realized I already had a pack: Reilly. My relationship with her was unlike any I had experienced with a dog or human in my life. It was balanced and healthy. We were both behaving authentically and respectfully toward each other. We had a pack hierarchy based on mutual respect and kindness and we could acknowledge and accept our roles in the pack. We needed each other, but in a positive way. I was not dependent on her for affection, as I had been with Kiva (and the humans in my life previously.) Reilly was dependent on me for food and shelter, but she, too, could carry on without me in every other way. She didn't look anxiously to me for her personal affirmation. I felt responsible for Reilly's care, but in a fulfilling and satisfying way, not in a way that felt burdensome. I wasn't alone. I had Reilly and she had me.

• •

SUMMARY
What Would a Pack Leader Do?
Be Authentic
Be Assertive
Be Honest
Be Respectful
Be Intuitive
Be Accountable
Honor the Pack

• • • • • • • • • • • • • • •

Good luck on your journey toward becoming a Pack Leader!

• •

Thank you for reading Pack Leader Psychology. To contact Harper or follow her blog, go to http://www.packleaderpsychology.com

Harper West is a psychotherapist, author, speaker, consultant and pack leader – of course! She has a master's degree in clinical psychology, but, more important, an advanced degree of wisdom gained after unflinchingly examining her life and completely transforming her personality based on Pack Leader Psychology principles.

Lightning Source UK Ltd.
Milton Keynes UK
UKHW02f0726010318
318692UK00008B/123/P